Y0-BQD-814

"I DECIDE WHO IS A JEW!"
The Papers of Dr. Karl Lueger

Introduced, translated and edited by

Richard S. Geehr

UNIVERSITY
PRESS OF
AMERICA

943.61304
I 1
132 947
aug. 1985

Library of Congress Catalog Card Number: **81-43702**

TO EUGEN KALCHSCHMID

"I DECIDE WHO IS A JEW!"

THE PAPERS OF DR. KARL LUEGER

TABLE OF CONTENTS

Politisch war er von Anbeginn,
Halb Jungfrau, halb suendige Dirne.
So war er fuer Grosswien der richtige Mann,
Der Mann mit der eisernen Stirne.

Das Juengste Gericht
Berlin, 1908

vii

INTRODUCTION

BEGINNINGS AND CONTINUATIONS

Karl Lueger left a lasting imprint on twentieth-century social and political history. A pioneer environmentalist who transformed his native Vienna as mayor between 1897 and 1910, he created a form of socialism that permanently undermined the more radical Marxism of his rivals, and he actively contributed to the pernicious growth of anti-Semitism. His influence extended far and wide, and he inspired at least one important imitator.

Adolf Hitler enthusiastically admired Lueger and praised him on numerous occasions, both before and after the establishment of the nazi dictatorship. In _Mein Kampf_, Hitler refers to Lueger as "the greatest German mayor of all times . . . the last great German to be born in the ranks of the people . . . a statesman greater than all the so-called diplomats of the time."[1] But Lueger meant one thing to Hitler and the Christian Social movement Lueger helped to create meant quite another. The Fuehrer disliked Christian Socialism, finding its brand of anti-Semitism too half-hearted and religious, rather than racial, and Lueger himself lacking in enthusiasm for Germanism. In the autumn of 1925, when _Mein Kampf_ appeared, Hitler asserted that Lueger, even if he had lived beyond 1910, would have been powerless to halt the Balkan conflagration that led to World War I, the destruction of the Habsburg Empire, and with it the final overthrow of Germanism in Austria. Surely, the aspiring Fuehrer implied, he would succeed in saving Germanism where Lueger had failed. By mid-December of 1941, however, after reverses in Russia, Hitler seems to have realized the full magnitude of his self-imposed mission. His admiration for Lueger, the man and his achievements, grew accordingly. "It's certain that German policy would have followed another direction if Lueger hadn't died before the First World War," he said.[2] Once again he praised Lueger's greatness as a mayor, his personal and political style, his popularity among the people, and his effectiveness as a public speaker.

Hitler's comment about Lueger's powerlessness to alter the course of events that led to World War I suggests that the Fuehrer accurately perceived Lueger's political limitations. But what of the more important question of his position within a wider historical context as distinct from his sociopolitical impact? A full view of Lueger's career and its modern legacy must include an appraisal of his position in

3

middle-European affairs in relation to the social and ideological developments of the twentieth century. Such an analysis exceeds the scope of this introduction and the remarks introducing each chapter. My primary aim has been to facilitate the reading of Lueger's documents in order to place the man and his ideas in a working perspective as a basis for further study. An analysis of certain of these documents and an attempt to determine Lueger's wider historical significance belong in a biography I someday hope to write.

In any case, Lueger's historical importance was dismissed by most of his contemporaries, with the exception of party panegyrists, who were too secure in their pre-1914 world to think of Lueger as anything more than a passing phenomenon. At the time of Lueger's death in 1910, Karl Kraus likened the deceased mayor to a comet that had briefly blazed forth in the political firmament and had then vanished without a trace. But fifteen years earlier, Theodor Herzl had seen him in a different light, as the symbol of implacable lower-middle-class Austrian anti-Semitism, and perhaps had glimpsed something of Lueger's true significance. In 1895, when Lueger was campaigning for mayor, an indirect encounter between the two men occurred at a Viennese polling place. Herzl aptly pinpointed the source of Lueger's popularity:

> A man next to me said with tender warmth but in a quiet voice: 'That is our Fuehrer (leader)!' Actually, these words showed me more than all declamation and abuse how deeply anti-Semitism is rooted in the hearts of these people.[3]

Lueger's rise to power was aided by a number of circumstances he cleverly, and in the case of anti-Semitism ruthlessly, exploited. These will be treated later. What needs to be underscored as perhaps the single most important factor contributing to his early success was the widening of the franchise. In the 1880s, there was mounting agitation in Vienna for electoral reform. Although in the end the lower middle class benefited most by this, the initial advocates were largely well-to-do liberals or disenchanted ex-liberals, who had not intended to bring mass parties into existence.[4] The franchise was based on the curial system, in which twenty-four-year-old males who paid sufficient direct property taxes elected most municipal councilors, who in turn elected the mayor every six years. Before taking office, a mayor had to be approved by the emperor. The councilors and mayor together conducted most of the city's business. In 1885, suffrage was extended to those who paid as little as five gulden in taxes. The inclusion of the "Five Gulden Men" among the voters brought a new and volatile element into Viennese politics, for some of this expanded group of voters turned out to be radicals and activists. Specifically, they included small shopkeepers (the "Greisslerstand" in Viennese dialect), artisans, and the ubiquitous Hausmeister, who lent this city much of its varied and distinctive character. These new voters, however, resented the exclusion of their representatives from the overwhelmingly liberal Muncipal Council--one of the last bastions of upper-class privilege. By the early 1890s, Lueger had accurately appraised this situation and maneuvered himself into the position of their most prominent spokesman. With this leverage, he put an end to liberal hegemony in municipal government.

At the same time these political changes were taking place, the city itself was changing. The incorporation of several outlying suburbs in 1890 created a greater Vienna. Municipal services had to be expanded, and the city government further centralized. This expansion of the boundaries of Vienna was to be the last significant liberal achievement. Liberal strength had been eroded by the enfranchisement of the "Five Gulden Men," to whom "latter-day Voltairism," the liberal platform of progress through science, education and hard work, could never appeal.[5] As mayor, however, Lueger subsequently presented himself as the creator of this new greater Vienna, in spite of the fact that he had officially opposed its formation as a liberal measure in 1890. Nonetheless, the title of "The Creator of Greater Vienna" added luster to his already considerable fame, and from 1897 onward he went out of his way to assure the residents of the former suburbs that he had been their friend and ally all along, apparently convincing a large number that this was in fact the case. Even though his position was only a pragmatic one, he went so far as to take credit for the enlargement of the city in the presence of Franz Joseph, who must have known otherwise.[6] What those Christian Socials who had opposed incorporation must have thought when

5

Lueger posed as their champion as well has not been recorded.

The 1890s were probably the most crucial years for the empire since the Austro-Prussian War of 1866, and the compromise with Hungary the following year. These times saw the end of the comparative stability of the Taaffe Ministry, between 1879 and 1893, and a further extension of the franchise four years later, although universal male suffrage did not result until 1907. Most importantly, these years also witnessed the protracted crisis over nationalism, the worst that the Dual Monarchy sustained until its dissolution in 1918. This crisis was responsible for the fall of no less than five prime ministers between 1895 and 1900. Bismarck himself predicted the imminent collapse of the empire. Although nationalistic issues became less important during the enlightened absolutism of the Koerber Ministry, after 1900, a tendency toward disruptive and recursive violence had been established in parliamentary proceedings. Lueger was a member of parliament during these years, and used his position not only to participate in imperial politics, but also to advance his own career in his quest for the mayoralty, and to settle old scores. One prime minister who had advised the emperor not to approve Lueger's election, Count Casimir Badeni, earned Lueger's lifelong enmity. Later, as mayor, Lueger added his influential voice to the chorus demanding Badeni's resignation. Lueger neither forgave nor forgot.

The story of Lueger's struggle to win the mayoralty has been told a number of times and therefore need not be summarized here.[7] His two-year contest for that office, which attracted European attention, demonstrated his considerable skills as a coalition builder and as an architect of compromises. He sought and found support among such disparate groups and ostensibly implacable enemies as the Pan Germans on the one hand and the Czechs on the other. But if his apparent affinity for the Czechs was merely another pose, it was at least one that he maintained consistently.[8]

If there emerges one truly-consistent trait in Lueger's political personality, about which most historians could agree, it is his implacable antipathy toward the Hungarians, which his writings consistently bear out. With the compromise of 1867, Austria and Hungary had become partners, and the Habsburg

domination of that eastern portion of the empire was
permanently weakened. Other subject nationalities
were quick to note the implications of this compromise, and began to clamor for their own independence.
Like so many other nationalistic German Austrians,
Lueger deeply resented the diminishing power of the
Austrian half of the empire, and he lost no opportunity to make his feelings known.[9] During his
mayoralty, only Austrian wine was dispensed in the
Rathaus restaurant. In 1903, during a visit by Czar
Nicholas II, who had decorated Lueger, Vienna's First
Citizen could not restrain himself from reminding his
audience that it was the Russians who had come to the
aid of the empire during the aftermath of the 1848
revolution and crushed the Hungarians.

Such tactlessness was typical of Lueger, and
became a favorite target for Social Democratic satir-
ists. Another target was his anti-intellectualism.
Toward most of that fin de siècle group who gave
Vienna so much of its unique cultural position--
toward Schnitzler and Hofmannsthal, Mahler and Klimt,
Freud and his followers, toward the economists,
doctors, and scientists who made Vienna into "the
social matrix in which so much of twentieth-century
subjectivism took form"[10]--Lueger seems to have
evinced an especial indifference, if not outright
contempt. Political fact was the thing; ideas counted
for less. He seems to have detected among intellec-
tuals as a group a free-thinking, analytical spirit
he instinctively distrusted for its tendency to dif-
fuse the energies of concrete action. Thought
threatened his own dogmatic frame of mind, which
characterized his later politics. For as he grew old,
Lueger lost much of his earlier problematic flexibility, becoming more and more rigid and dictatorial.
Immediate, palpable impressions meant more to him than
the most convincing theories. The pragmatic politician crystalized into a style as elegant and brittle
as the jewelry and gems he came to wear in his later
years.

If, as some believe, Lueger "personified Vienna"
in the hour of its "gay apocalypse," it was in spite
of, not because of, contemporary circumstances. In
upbringing and preference, Lueger belonged to the less
complicated Biedermeier period. This contributed to
his rejection of cultural modernism in so many of its
manifestations. His outward appearance, "graceful,
attractive," and aesthetically pleasing as it was to

some observers,[11] his essentially simple tastes, his preferences for classical sculpture and architectural symmetry, extending as it did even to the mass political rallies he planned,[12] all suggest that he was by preference more of a traditionalist than a conscious innovator.

And yet his was a prophetic career. His most portentous skill, perhaps, was his ability to shape antagonistic elements within his own party into a harmonious and functioning whole. He charmed the hostile camps with the sound of his oratory. In multinational Vienna, where many inhabitants had only a scanty knowledge of German, the lower-class immigrant could at least respond to the spectacle and sounds of the mass rally and to the spoken word.[13] The visible respect Lueger exhibited for his constituents, especially when such regard came from a Doctor of Law and someone of great personal magnetism who had never repudiated his own lower-middle-class origins, must have been intrinsically flattering. Resentments and frustrations were articulated by this very rapport. For during Lueger's years of power, Vienna was the most important polyglot capital of Europe;[14] as long as the immigration continued, separateness and cultural diversity, along with their resulting frictions, persisted, even intensified--contemporary claims notwithstanding.[15] Lueger's ability to create a working political unity out of such diversity marks his career and its legacy.

He had an instinctive sensitivity to social frictions and to the irrational needs that nourished them. His ability to turn both to his own advantage also mark him as a political demagogue of the twentieth century, rather than a conventional Realpolitik statesman of the nineteenth century, such as Bismarck, with whom Lueger's own followers often compared him. While the Prussian chancellor could often count on Emperor William I's support during the course of his career, Lueger could not hope for similar backing from his own sovereign, who mistrusted Lueger as an upstart. He had constantly to struggle to win and retain whatever support he had. It is not surprising, then, that at least initially his politics had but one purpose: to create the necessary following. He was obliged to make power his immediate goal. In contrast to his German contemporary, Lueger was a self-made man and remained so; he could never ignore public opinion in attaining his objectives. His realization of this

8

fact brought him great success, for he thus became one of the first new-style political manipulators, a party boss whose personal power was feared and whose dictates were obediently accepted by his followers.

Despite this originality, however, Lueger had been to some extent anticipated. He had at least one important predecessor, and may have learned from one of his own contemporaries as well. Lueger's followers might better have compared him to Louis Napoleon, and his municipal administration in particular to Joseph Chamberlain's. Some, to be sure, might have been reluctant to see similarities in either case, because Napoleon's career ended ignominiously and the pro-Afrikaner Christian Socials blamed Chamberlain for starting the Boer War. Nonetheless, all three men shared imperial ambitions and expressed them in part through elaborate and costly building projects. They were also aware of the political importance of urban environments in achieving community.

In the space of a few short years, Napoleon transformed Paris in the 1850s. Wide boulevards replaced narrow medieval streets, crowded tenements were supplanted by more spacious and healthy living quarters, and new gardens were planted, so that Paris became the most beautiful city in the world. Far from being merely an attempt to prevent another 1848, this improvement was "the matter which he took most to heart--for it belonged to the essence of the Napoleonic idea, and affected the capital of the empire and prestige of the country."[16] A generation later, Lueger recognized the political significance of the economics and appearance of the imperial Habsburg capital beyond its bureaucratic centrality. Throughout his career, but especially during his mayorality, he tried to improve Vienna--a scheme actually begun by his liberal predecessors in imitation of Napoleon--[17] through physical and social embellishments. He built parks and monuments and brought international exhibitions and prominent visitors to his capital. His task, however, was rendered considerably more difficult than Napoleon's by two circumstances: Paris had no rivals as the French imperial center, but Vienna had Budapest; Napoleon had the money to build with, Lueger did not.

With the compromise of 1867, Budapest had grown steadily into an industrially vital and progressive metropolis. The Hungarian capital had begun an

electric streetcar system in 1889, while Vienna's cars
were still horse-drawn. Budapest also introduced
Europe's first subway in 1896, the year before Lueger
became mayor.[18] Lueger had also to contend with a
lack of financial backing. While Napoleon lavished
money on Paris and faithfully supported his master
builder Georges Haussmann against his many enemies,
for nearly twenty years, Lueger was confronted in his
attempts to raise money by the formidable hostility of
the court, the Magyars, and the Jewish banks. He had
to enlist foreign backing and make good on some of his
campaign promises in order to improve the city appre-
ciably within two years of his becoming mayor--or
be discredited.

     Louis Napoleon's example, however, stood for more
than mere city planning; it extended the political use
of the city. "'Nowadays (he had written) the day of
class-rule is over, the day of mass-rule has begun.
The masses must be organized so that they can formulate their will, and disciplined so that they can be
instructed and enlightened as to their own
interests.'"[19] Such ideological belief suggests that
Napoleon, essentially a man of the rationalistic
currents of the eighteenth century, had in his own way
anticipated a new era of totalitarian democracy. But
with the experience of a political generation later
than Napoleon's, so did Lueger in his own awareness of
the needs and power of the masses. Yet Lueger would
most certainly have rejected any ideas like these if
they had implied that political leaders should defer
to the mass will. For while empirical in his approach
to politics,[20] Lueger himself was a born dictator. In
this, as well as in his advocacy of municipal socialization, and in his own middle-class origins, Lueger
resembled Chamberlain more than Napoleon.

     Joseph Chamberlain, like Lueger, belonged to a
post-Enlightenment generation. Although the foundations of politics were more democratic in Britain
than in Austria at this time--Chamberlain's broader
political base explains his greater fame, perhaps, and
power--the parallels between the careers of the two
men and the implications of their political styles are
informative. Chamberlain, the son of a shopkeeper,
became lord mayor of Birmingham in 1873, at the age of
thirty-seven. To achieve this first major political
goal, he used demagogic tactics and attracted a mass
following, much as Lueger did twenty years later.
Toward the end of the 1860s, moreover, Chamberlain

became avowedly republican, criticizing the royal
family for its extravagance. Lueger, too, voiced
republican sentiments in his youth, but without
Chamberlain's occasions, always avoided openly anti-
dynastic remarks. This reticence may have come from
his own deeply-rooted class consciousness or from a
residue of thoroughly traditional respect for his
monarch Franz Joseph.[21] In either case, Lueger's
basic antagonism toward the emperor, as well as his
own envy and egotism, overcame his inherited attitudes
toward power and emerged on a number of occasions. At
an informal social gathering in the town hall, a
somewhat bibulous Lueger gestured toward the Hofburg,
the emperor's winter palace: "He thinks he's the
master of Vienna, but I am." On another occasion,
when both Franz Joseph and Lueger appeared together in
public, but in separate coaches, Lueger maneuvered his
own vehicle so that it immediately followed the
emperor's, then doffed his hat ostentatiously so that
he would receive more applause than Franz Joseph.[22]

In later years, however, other psychological
likenesses between Chamberlain and Lueger appeared.
The two became the very symbols of pugnacious
imperialism.[23] Each man aspired to higher positions
and greater influence than he was able to achieve. Of
the two, however, Chamberlain played the more important role in national politics, attaining cabinet
rank. Lueger preferred to play the role of the gray
eminence. Posterity has treated both men rather
nostalgically, at least in their respective countries.
But according to one observer, Chamberlain "is the
last man to choose for an exercise in nostalgic
evocation;" he existed for change, not for
preservation: . . . to get rid of the past and to get
things done."[24] Although Lueger may well have
disagreed, if confronted by such a summary, the same
can still be said of him. Furthermore, both men were
politically modern "in (their) conception(s) of party
politics." Both Lueger and Chamberlain believed that
"party. . . was an engine of power, fuelled by popular
enthusiasm."[25]

The most obvious resemblances between Lueger's
and Chamberlain's politics lie in their dogmatic
styles and mutual advocacy of "'gas-and-water-
socialism'."[26] However, more significant correspon-
dences exist between their preferences for central and
dictatorial control over their ostensibly democratic
machines, and between the varieties of religious force
informing their political ideas. Here lay the seeds

11

of totalitarianism, watered with psychological, if secular, compulsion. Egalitarian politics and what G. Kitson Clark called "the secularization of spirit . . . spread over life and politics in the early twentieth century."[27]   But by this time, both men had grown old. Chamberlain's ultimate defeat resulted from the diminishing popularity of his brand of imperialism and his abandonment of free trade.[28] His political career was ended by a stroke in 1906. The subsequent withering of imperialism in Britain and the evolution of democratic thinking toward socialism proceeded rapidly. Even after the upheaval of World War I, the conditions for a continental-style totalitarianism were not readily at hand, so solid were the broader social and political foundations. The situation in Austria was different.

At the time of Lueger's death, his impact appeared to have been largely regional. The arena of his politics was essentially urban; and his would-be protector, Archduke Franz Ferdinand, never acceded to the throne.[29] But Lueger's wider significance was yet to be felt and understood. In creating a mass party that looked to strong central leadership and never allowed political liberty nor required responsibility, he had brought a potentially destructive force into existence. After the sudden collapse of the empire in 1918, along with many of its religious and social bases, the Christian Socials had to face a choice between older values and newer ideologies. In German Austria, the fervid growth of totalitarian attitudes offered an available alternative.

The documents published here have been gathered from the partly-catalogued Lueger Nachlass in the Handschriftensammlung der staedtischen Bibliothek der Stadt Wien, the Handschriftensammlung der oesterreichischen Nationalbibliothek, from the Theologische Dekanat der Universitaet Wien, from photocopies of Lueger's letters in Marianne Beskiba's Aus meinen Erinnerungen an Dr. Karl Lueger, from portions of Gertrud Stoeger's 1941 Ph.D. dissertation, "Die politischen Anfaenge Luegers," and from two private collections, the owners of which have asked to remain anonymous. Materials have been selected primarily in order to illuminate previously untreated and obscure aspects of Lueger's career, such as his youthful theorizing and his political development, details of his friendship with Karl Freiherr von Vogelsang, as well as his personal, publicistic style. Related documents, however, shedding light on his non-political personality, have also been included.

Unfortunately, the selection presented here cannot be complete. In some cases, the draft of a document is all that survives of Lueger's scattered legacy. Letters written by him, which would have provided information on such matters as his relationship with other Christian Social leaders and his role in parliament, for example, appear to have been lost. Moreover, some of Lueger's speeches from the 1870s and 1880s, cited earlier in private collections, have disappeared. There are, in addition, only a few notes and memoranda surviving from the period during which Lueger was mayor, a fact that can probably be attributed to his failing eyesight and growing physical impairment. All told, Lueger's correspondence, regrettably, is not as well-preserved as one would like. What survives, however, remains forcefully, if subtly, symptomatic of that fatal blend of psychological projection and political pragmatism we have learned to live with.

My labor could never have been completed without the generous and untiring assistance of several dedicated archivists and historians. I especially wish to single out and thank Messrs. Johann Ziegler and Ernst Huebsch of the Staedtische Bibliothek der Stadt Wien, whose help in deciphering Lueger's handwriting, general encouragement, and unflagging enthusiasm have contributed so much to the accomplishment of the present task. Their many suggestions and criticisms have proved invaluable. Dr. Franz Gall of the Wiener Universitaets-Archiv contributed generously of his time in uncovering information about Lueger's university teachers. Professor Dr. Ernst Herlitzka of the Verein fuer Geschichte der Arbeiterbewegung provided facts about Lueger's early defense of Socialist workers. Dr. Heinz Schoeny of the Museum der Stadt Wien assisted on several occasions in locating obscure uncatalogued documents and other materials and, in addition, contributed Appendix I. Frau Dr. Isabella Ackerl was instrumental in shaping my work, read the manuscript with painstaking attention to detail, and weeded out many factual errors and inconsistencies. Dr. Ackerl also located obscure information about some of Lueger's early colleagues. Another highly knowledgeable reader, Herr Rudolf Oberhofer, contributed many helpful, substantive suggestions. Dr. Maren Seliger of the Archiv der Stadt Wien provided a

great deal of information about Lueger's early political activities as Municipal Councilor. She also read
portions of this manuscript and weeded out errors.
Professor Emeritus Robert Rie of the State University
of New York, Fredonia, corrected errors, added facts,
and provided encouragement. Frau Dr. Paul Schick made
a number of helpful suggestions pertaining to organization, furnished materials that I have incorporated
into the manuscript, and, through her constructive
criticism, caused me to re-evaluate certain documents.
The Messrs. Josef Brandenburg and Heinrich Matzinger
gave generously of their skills and time in
deciphering several documents written in part in
stenographic shorthand. Herr Klemens Hoeslinger of
the Haus, Hof und Staatsarchiv unearthed biographical
information about Lueger's friends and acquaintances
and helped make my tasks a pleasure. I owe a debt of
gratitude to the late Professor Harold J. Gordon, Jr.,
for solving a translation problem.

    I also wish to thank the staffs of the Austrian
Nationalbibliothek, Verwaltungsarchiv, Museum der
Stadt Wien, Dr. Andreas Weyringer and the staff of the
Theologisches Dekanat of the University of Vienna, the
University Library, the Kriegsarchiv, the Archiv der
Erzdioezese Wien, the Evangelisches Pfarramt, A. B.
Wien, Archiv der Stadt Wien and Archiv des
Maennergesangsvereins. Frau Dr. Gertrud Muckenhuber,
nee Stoeger, was kind enough to grant permission to
publish the documents bearing on the attempt to black-
mail Lueger during the Fogerty Affair. (See "The
Municipal Politician.")

    Special thanks go to Messrs. Heimo Fink and
Gerhard Schirmer of the Druckschriftensammlung der
Wiener Stadtbibliothek for making this a true
scholar's home. I also want to thank Hofrat Dr. Franz
Patzer and the staff of the Wiener Stadt Bibliothek
for facilitating my research. To the scholar who
stimulated my interest in Lueger's writings, in the
writings of other central figures of fin de siècle
Vienna, Senatsrat Dr. Karl Gladt, go my warmest
thanks. This project was really inspired by the many
conversations we have had, beginning in 1969.

    Professor Raymond P. Tripp, Jr., of the
University of Denver, a scholar's scholar, added more
to this manuscript, both substantively and stylisti-
cally, than I can repay. My thanks go to Dr. Susan
Tripp, as well, for commenting on stylistic aspects of

the introductions. Professor Alice McGinty, Mr. Leonard Krisak and two unknown readers made many helpful suggestions and corrections, for which I am extremely grateful. To Dr. Isaac Moore go my special thanks for his many insights, comments, and suggestions on the implications of Karl Lueger's career. For their translations and contributions too numerous to mention, my wife, Gerda, and Dr. Daniel Clayton of the University of Denver, deserve any praise this work receives. For any shortcomings and errors, I alone am responsible.

Finally, I wish to thank Bentley College for providing part of the necessary funds to defer various costs of preparing this work, and for the personnel to type the manuscript, the Austrian American Fulbright Association, Professor Dr. Anton Porhansl and his staff for supporting my researches.

15

NOTES FOR BEGINNINGS AND CONTINUATIONS

1. Adolf Hitler, Mein Kampf, Trans. Ralph Manheim, Boston, 1943, pp. 55, 69.

2. Hitler's Secret Conversations, Trans. Norman Cameron and R. H. Stevens, New York, 1972, p. 120. In the Third Reich, Lueger and Hitler's other Austrian mentor, Georg Ritter von Schoenerer, leader of the Pan German Nationalist Party, were heroes of a pointedly anti-Jewish film, "Wien 1910." In this film, Schoenerer was depicted as Lueger's successor in the fight against Vienna's Jews. Lueger was played by the popular Austrian actor Rudolf Foerster, Schoenerer by Heinrich George. Thus in certain artistic circles Lueger was seen as an important figure in the history and development of anti-Semitism and National Socialism.

3. The Complete Diaries of Theodor Herzl, Trans. Harry Zohn, Ed. Raphael Patei, 5 vols., New York and London, 1960, 1, p. 244.

4. See William A. Jenks, Austria Under the Iron Ring, 1879-1893. Charlottesville, 1965, pp. 104-121.

5. Carl E. Schorske has observed:

    Morally (Vienna's liberal haute bourgeoisie) was secure, righteous, and repressive; politically it was concerned for the rule of law, under which both individual rights and social order were subsumed. It was intellectually committed to the rule of the mind over the body and to a latter-day Voltairism: to social progress through science, education, and hard work.

    Carl E. Schorske, "Politics and the Psyche in Fin de Siècle Vienna: Schnitzler and Hofmannsthal," The American Historical Review, 66, (July, 1961), p. 933.

6. Erich Graf Kielmansegg, Kaiserhaus, Staatsmaenner und Politiker. Vienna and Munich, 1966, pp. 383, 384. Hereafter referred to as "Kielmansegg."

16

7. The most detailed though uncritical account is to
    be found in Rudolf Kuppe's Karl Lueger und seine
    Zeit. Vienna, 1933, pp. 331-383, hereafter
    referred to as "Kuppe." A good summary is con-
    tained in Arthur J. May's more readily accessible
    The Habsburg Monarchy, 1867-1914. New York,
    1968, pp. 309-311.

8. Lueger's choice of Anton Pumera, a one-time
    Bohemian cobbler, may instance his ties with the
    Czechs. In 1900, more Czechs lived in Vienna
    than in Prague. Friedrich Heer, Der Glaube des
    Adolf Hitler. Munich and Esslingen, 1968, p. 53.

9. No matter how much Franz Joseph may have appre-
    ciated Lueger's show of loyalty to the monarchy,
    the mayor's frequent and tactless anti-Magyar
    remarks must have been disturbing to one who
    tried to treat all of his subject peoples fairly.

10. Schorske, op. cit., 940. He did, however,
    express his condolences in an official letter to
    the widow of Johann Strauss in 1899.

11. Mark Twain, "Stirring Times in Austria," The
    Writings of Mark Twain. 25 vols., New York,
    1918, 24, p. 227.

12. His concern for such details as the proper place-
    ment of his political formations to achieve the
    maximum dramatic effect became vital parts of an
    emerging holistic concept of politics. Lueger's
    concerns parallel those of another famous
    Viennese contemporary, the architect Camillo
    Sitte, about proper monument placement. See his
    City Planning According to Artistic Principles,
    Trans. George R. Collins and Christiane
    Crasemann Collins. London, 1965, p. x.

13. After World War I, the response of a younger
    generation to popular demagogues had assumed a
    quasi-religious character. J. P. Stern has
    described this phenomenon as a "situation of
    total immanence, where nobody believes in
    anything. . . but all. . . believe in the image
    they have created." J.P. Stern, Hitler The
    Fuehrer and the People. Glasgow, 1975, p. 89.

14. This fact was recognized by the son of a larger
    and even more polyglot entity. In 1913, Lenin
    sent Stalin to Vienna to study the nationality
    question.

15. In his Wien im Zeitalter Kaiser Franz Josephs I.,
    first published in 1908, Reinhard E. Petermann
    remarked that although "the racial mixture in
    Vienna. . . had become even more varied and
    intensified. . . the vast majority of Viennese
    and older immigrants, already half Viennese, have
    time to overcome and assimilate the new
    elements," p. 148. According to C. E. Williams,
    however, "As late as 1934 there were still 50,000
    Czechs in Vienna (with their own primary
    schools)" and "the Czech community. . . retained
    a distinct subculture of their own. . . in
    defiance of and quite apart from the Viennese
    milieu." C. E. Williams, The Broken Eagle.
    London, 1974, p. 160.

16. J. M. Thompson, Louis Napoleon and the Second
    Empire. New York, 1967, p. 235.

17. Even the francophobe Hitler admitted this:
    "Every finished work is of value as an example.
    One takes the opportunity of learning, one sees
    the mistakes and seeks to do better. The Ring in
    Vienna would not exist without the Paris boule-
    vards. It's a copy of them." Hitler's Secret
    Conversations, p. 81.

18. William M. Johnston, The Austrian Mind.
    Berkeley, Los Angeles, and London, p. 343,
    hereafter referred to as "Johnston."

19. Thompson, Louis Napoleon, pp. 237, 238.

20. "'Please no programs, they only tie our hands,'
    he is reported to have said." Joseph Schwalber,
    "Vogelsang und die christlich-soziale Politik,"
    Ph.D. dissertation, University of Munich, 1927,
    pp. 37, 51, quoted in Alfred Diamant, Austrian
    Catholics and the First Republic. Democracy,
    Capitalism, and the Social Order, 1918-1934
    (Princeton, 1960), p. 141.

21. This same respect, which bordered on veneration
    in some instances, was wide-spread even among
    the subject nationalities, and lasted until the

emperor's death in 1916. In 1972, a former
imperial officer told me that during a visit he
made to Bohemia in 1914, a young Czech nationalist said to him that as long as "the old man"
lived the Czechs would make no movement toward
independence.

22. Kielmansegg, pp. 392, 393, 406.

23. Chamberlain was a favorite and well-known subject
of cartoonists. Although less well-known outside
of Vienna, Lueger, too, figured prominently in
political caricatures. Christian Social cartoonists portrayed him as a crusading knight in
shining armor who bravely defended Christian
Austria from its various enemies at home and
abroad.

24. John Vincent, Review of Joseph Chamberlain, by
Enoch Powell, The Times Literary Supplement,
March 24, 1978, p. 343.

25. Peter Clarke, Review of Joseph Chamberlain, by
Richard Jay, The Times Literary Supplement,
May 1, 1981, p. 493.

26. R. K. Webb, Modern England, New York and Toronto,
1968, p. 365.

27. G. Kitson Clark, The Making of Victorian England,
New York, 1974, p. 204.

28. Webb, Modern England, pp. 452, 453.

29. Lueger was to have become the new emperor's first
prime minister. William Jenks, Vienna and the
Young Hitler, New York, 1960, p. 40. The fact
that Lueger is primarily remembered as the
creator and boss of an efficient municipal
machine should not obscure the fact that he
intervened for the farmers of Lower Austria
and inspired the founding of Raiffeisenkassen,
agricultural warehouses, milk cooperatives, and
agricultural insurance companies. Adam
Wandruszka and Peter Urbanitsch, Eds., Die
Habsburgermonarchie. 9 vols., Vienna, 1973,
1, p. 458.

Stein, whose theories fill a number of Lueger's university notebooks and about whom his biographers are
silent to a man. When he was called to the university
in 1855 as a result of the special recommendation of
Finance Minister Karl Friedrich von Bruck, Stein was
already the author of a classic work on utopian
socialism, Der Socialismus und Communismus des
heutigen Frankreichs. First published in 1842, when
the author was but twenty-seven, Socialismus und
Communismus was subsequently expanded and reprinted a
number of times. This work in fact provided the basis
for Stein's reputation as well as his subsequent
theoretical development. It was Stein rather than
Karl Marx who introduced the concept of "class" into
academic discussion.[8] Marx, in fact, borrowed this
concept from Stein. Moreover, Stein differed from his
more famous contemporary by rejecting the possibility
of an ultimately classless society. Stein feared the
imminent widening of the already existing gulf between
the ruling capitalist class and the proletariat and
looked on the state as the source of reform.

Whether Lueger owed his mature theoretical
outlook more to Stein or Vogelsang, the influence of
Hegel through Stein is especially apparent in young
Karl's writings. Lueger's evident preoccupation with
the problem of personal fragmentation in a society in
which social divisions are widening appears in the
essay "Is State or Society the More Comprehensive
Concept and How So?" Like Hegel, as well as Stein,
Lueger believed that it was the responsibility of the
state to intervene to eliminate these divisions. The
larger problem of the general lack of social harmony
in the German speaking realm had in fact preoccupied
German thinkers since the last decades of the
eighteenth century. Goethe deplored the cultural
divisiveness in Germany that had led to a profound
complementary social dissention. The problem of the
lack of a vital common culture that could transcend
social and economic divisions became acute in the
Habsburg Empire after the revolution of 1848. As a
result of an inability to agree on a single language
in which to communicate official business, the long
standing problems among the competing social and eth-
nic groups were further exacerbated by growing
national antagonisms. What young Lueger and many
German philosophers of the early nineteenth century
argued for and more militant twentieth-century Germans
later sought to create by force, an all-embracing
Germanic community established along purely cultural

lines, would have been impossible without some countering fundamental economic integration like that of recent decades.

Toward the end of the nineteenth century, descendants of the utopian school of thought tried to realize their goals through a revived, "socially conscious" Christianity. Whereas Hegel had regarded Christianity as a private religion, one that led to further fragmentation through withdrawal and the development of self-seeking values, Lueger and his followers drew on the ideas of the Kathedersozialisten, who advocated a searching re-evaluation of the inner experience of religion and its relationship to politics. Where a purely cultural approach had failed to unify, a fresh Christian awareness of society would serve, they argued, as the means of unification.

But at the early stage in his development that these writings represent, Lueger would doubtless have agreed with the Hegelian analysis that:

> The need . . . for a comprehensive grasp of experience which, by enabling a man to have a very firm insight into the nature of the world confronting him, would change his view on that world so that it would no longer appear as a source of estrangement. This was to involve an understanding of modern political culture in an endeavor to show how the modern state did provide an adequate form of political environment for the modern man; an understanding of modern religious experience (which would, once grasped, remove its bifurcating effect on contemporary society) coupled with a comprehensive and total philosophical treatment of all the major modes of man's experience in modern society showing their deep interrelations, obscured at the level of conventional description-a treatment which would overcome the fragmentation of human personality.[9]

Yet some of the documents presented here, primarily from Lueger's university days, paint a rather different picture of the young Lueger. The serious scholar drawn by his most important biographer, Rudolf Kuppe, disappears, and something of a different personality emerges. For example, in two letters addressed to his friend, Friedrich Deutsch, no trace can be found of that extraordinary diligence lauded by Kuppe.[10] In September and October, 1866, shortly after the Battle of Koeniggraetz, Lueger was obviously bored. There was nothing to interest him: he missed the company of those friends who were serving in the army; and he was, at least for a time, thoroughly weary of his studies. There is also no mention made of the "pain and anger" which he was supposed to have felt after Austria's ignominious defeat.[11] All this points not to the the altruistic student, but to a self-centered complacent young man beyond even the general indifference to the nation's defeat. The second letter, written approximately three weeks before the death of his father, reveals very little of "the troubled atmosphere which burdened the family for weeks."[12] Young Karl seemed greatly but routinely interested in the fortunes of his university friends, and once again showed a like interest in his studies.

Two well-thought-out student essays from this period reveal Lueger's conception of the state as a living organism. In "Self-Administration Is Self-Taxation," he outlines a logical and well-designed administrative structure for the modern state. In another essay, "Is State or Society the More Comprehensive Concept and How So?" his aversion to capitalism becomes apparent, and he evidently held contemporary liberal economic policies that favored the affluent in low regard. For him, as he may have learned from Stein or indirectly from Hegel, the most important component of social organization was clearly the government, whose function was to protect society. Whenever the harmonious relationship between government and society broke down, bloody revolutions between the government and the people, he reasoned, were the consequence. Because political leaders very rarely admitted either their own personal shortcomings or those of the government, dissidents were as a result handled with brute force. On this point, too, episodes from Roman history very likely served Lueger as examples.

Of particular interest is his vision of the one true society, described in the same essay, probably written between 1865 and 1869. Here the man who later, as an experienced politician, would argue that Austrian nationalism was the bulwark of the Habsburg Monarchy, considered constitutional monarchy a

transitional phase in the evolution toward a peace-
loving and inclusive republic without national differences. "Liberae sunt nostrae cogitationes" (Cicero
in "Pro Milone") seems to fit the politician as a
young man. Lueger, though a sound and thorough student, does not appear to have beem primarily an
intellectual with solely academic concerns. His
interests in the classics and in philosophy were motivated by his own needs and integrated into the development of his own political ideas, which foreshadow
the course of his later career and the fate of the
city he came to administer.

FOOTNOTES FOR YOUTH

1. Kann, _History of the Habsburg Empire_, p. 372.

2. A description of the Theresianum at that time may be found in Eugen Guglia, _Das Theresianum in Wien, Vergangenheit und Gegenwart_. Vienna, 1912, pp. 133-149. Day students, or _Externisten_, were first admitted only in 1850. For information on the influence of this _Gymnasium_ on the young Lueger, see Carl E. Schorske, "Politics in a New Key: An Austrian Triptych," _The Journal of Modern History_, 39 (December, 1967), pp. 357, 358.

3. John Warrack, Carl Maria von Weber's biographer, could very well have added Lueger to the list of those "with overwhelming egos," for whom "Rienzi has always had a strong appeal. Napoleon is said to have carried a copy of Du Cerceau's biography with him in his carriage on the road back from Moscow; D'Annunzio's only historical effort was to interest himself in writing another biography; Mussolini modelled a good deal of his style on Rienzi, and like his hero was to end up hanged by his own countrymen upside down in a public square. Hitler once told a friend that the growth of Nazism as an idea in his mind could be dated from a performance he saw in Linz in 1906 or 1907 of Wagner's opera." John Warrack, Review of _Wagner's Rienzi_, by John Deathridge, _The Times Literary Supplement_, July 21, 1978, p. 813.

4. Kuppe, p. 14.

5. Lueger's school notebooks and the subjects he studied are listed in Appendix 2. For a summary of late Habsburg legal theories and their critics, see Johnston, pp. 88-98.

6. Werner Ziegenfuss, _Handbuch der Soziologie_ (Stuttgart, 1956), p. 16.

7. Stein influenced the economists and social reformers Adolph Wagner and Albert Shaeffle and also taught Eugen von Philippovich, Karl Renner's teacher, and Hans Kelsen, the famous legal theorist. Stein's ideas are summarized in Karl Theodor von Inama Sternegg, _Vertreter des modernen Verwaltungsstaats_.

Staatswissenschaftliche Abhandlungen. Leipzig, 1903, pp. 41-56. A more polemical treatment of Stein's career may be found in the Neue Freie Presse, September 24, 1890, p. 2. More up-to-date information about Stein and his impact may be found in Mathias Kamp, Die Theorie der Epochen der oeffentlichen Wirtschaft bei Lorenz von Stein (Bonn, 1950), Manfred Halm, Buergerlicher Optimismus in Niedergang (Munich, 1969), and Roman Schnur, Staat und Gesellschaft (Berlin, 1978).

8. Wandruszka, Die Habsburgermonarchie, p. 609.

9. Raymond Plant, Hegel, London, 1973, p. 75.

10. Kuppe, p. 16

11. Ibid., 17.

12. Franz Stauracz mentions this in Dr. Karl Lueger Zehn Jahre Buergermeister, Vienna, 1907, pp. 3, 4. Marianne Beskiba, on the other hand, suggests that Lueger was indifferent toward his father. Marianne Beskiba, Aus meinen Erinnerungen an Dr. Karl Lueger, Vienna, 1911, p. 14.

The missing portions of this letter, in parentheses, have been partly restored according to the sense of the letter. The condition and appearance of the letter indicate that Deutsch probably carried it around with him for some time.

IN 32292[+]   To: Friedrich Deutsch
                               Vienna, September 3, 1866

Dear Deutsch,

In a letter to Uhlik, you mentioned, among other things, that you hoped to hear something from me. I admit I (should) have written to you sooner since we were separated without (missing word). (You) can't imagine (how) boring it is here in (Vienna,) no colleagues with whom one can meet regularly. And in this state of boredom one either forgets, or rather can't comfort oneself by corresponding with a friend.

With regard to our colleagues, I see only Uhlik from time to time. Rothe has completely disappeared. Sande too. As regards our colleagues in the army, I regret that I can only report sad news, which I wish was false.

I understand poor Suppantschitsch had his foot amputated, as one of the Schweinburge is supposed to have learned from his brother.

Petrisch is apparently seriously wounded (and in) a Prussian prisoner-of-war camp. (missing name) is supposed to be dead. (missing name) was lucky enough to return in one piece, (but) contracted a disease in Pressburg from which he now suffers greatly. Beck has also finally returned to his home and thus everything is empty and desolate. As far as I'm concerned, I am quite well and only fervently wish that I were more diligent in order to get the third state exam out of the way as soon as possible. I passed the second (without trouble).

[+]Inventar Nummer. Documents with this designation are from the catalogued <u>Lueger Nachlass</u> in the Hand-schriftensammlung of the staedtische Bibliothek der Stadt Wien.

Well, I suppose you are doing well. I assume the Prussians have already left and neither will you be afraid of the Cholera. I don't have any other news since there is an absolute lack of it, and so, greeting you and wishing you better times than I am having, I sign,

                              Your (faithful friend),
                              Karl Lueger

IN 32293   To: Friedrich Deutsch
                            October 5, 1866

Dearest Colleague:

    You will have to forgive my long silence, but I have very good excuses: everyone is gone. I am all alone in Vienna. Even Uhlik is gone, or at least he must be, for I haven't seen him since September 1. Therefore, absolutely no news. Furthermore, I didn't receive your letter until September 15, hence thought you would be arriving soon, so the beginning of the school year and thereby the end of my state of loneliness has been delayed until October 15.

    I know nothing at all about our soldiers.

    But wait; a ray of light in the person of the Croatian stenographer has brightened my existence. He sends many greetings to you. He told me that Suppantschitsch did not have his foot amputated and he was a lieutenant. All this is just a rumor. But because it's good news, I gladly believe it.

    I also ran into Model once. He was in Krebitz and told me that Rothe would again be coming to Vienna next year. And even something good to report about the Reading Society:[+] three halls were made available

---

[+]Since 1863, Lueger belonged to the Committee of the "German Reading Society," which at that time held a leading position in political affairs. Lueger eventually withdrew because of the Pan German tendencies. Kuppe, 17, 18.

in the former academic high school building; therefore, after a long odyssey, it has finally found an
asylum. And I really believe it has a promising
future, unless the Slavs and Magyars gain complete
control, which is not unlikely.

Cholera is spreading here in Vienna as well,
although I haven't heard of any deaths among our
acquaintances, and I hope that this doesn't happen.

With respect to my exams, I had the following
examining committee:
Heyssler ./. Commercial and (Bank) Draft Law
Kagerbauer ./. Criminal Law and Process
Kramer ./. Civil Process and Non Litigious
Proceedings ./. and finally, an exceedingly nice
fellow whom I did not know and whose signature on the
examination reports I unfortunately could not
decipher.
I had the following questions:
Commercial Law: Commercial Business
Draft Law: Presentation of Draft and Domicile
Draft
Civil Law Code: Influence of Criminal Law on
Civil Business
Civil Process: No Appeal After Certain Date
Non Litigious Proceedings: Notations in the
Registry of Deeds
Criminal Law: Conflicts, Statute of Limitations.
Criminal Proceedings: Final Hearing.

Only one of them, Professor Heyssler, really
grilled me. The others are all praiseworthy and have
duly acknowledged the fact that the Prussians stood
before Vienna.

And now, farewell! Hoping to see you again soon,
I extend many greetings and

        sign,

           As your faithful,
           procrastinating friend,

               Karl Lueger.

Nachlass Karl Lueger[+]
St. Slg. Zl. 1257/12
Box 1

Foreign Aspects of Roman Law, Dvorzak, Notebook VIII
Karl Lueger

XLII

V. THE PEOPLE'S TRIBUNES

In the strictest sense of the term, the tribuni
were not actually magistratus because they didn't
possess a proper administration, but only the right to
veto and petition in the con. trib.[++] But since gradually their influence became very important, they
were designated as magistratus in the Roman language
and even received an imperium. lic adv. Nullum II.
5. Of particular importance was their right to intercessio, which consisted of their being allowed to protest the actions and decrees of other magistrates, the
effect of which was the suspension of execution until
further notice. The tendency of this veto in the
beginning was to protect the plebeians against the
patrician magistratus. The effectiveness of the veto
presupposed unity among the tribunes; this is not to
say that they all had to assemble and make a resolution, but that no tribune would veto a colleague's
veto, which would render the former's veto void.
Therein lay the danger of increasing the number of
tribuni. But later, when the differences between the
classes had disappeared, the right of intercessio assumed a different form. The significance of intercessio now was to limit the different magistratus.
lic. de leg. III 7. The tribuni also had the right
to convene the senate or, for instance, when the
senate was called together by a magistratus, to
appear there and to submit petitions. That the tribuni were sacrosancti has already been mentioned,[+++]
and for this reason their position became so powerful. Even though they were sacrosancti, they still

---

[+]Staedtische Sammlung Zahl. Materials with this
designation are also to be found in the Lueger
Nachlass in the Handschriftensammlung of the staedtische Bibliothek der Stadt Wien.

[++]underlined in the original.

[+++]This passage is an excerpt.

were accountable for execution of their power and could be brought before a court. It is of particular interest to note that Tiberius Gracchus petitioned the people to have a tribunus relieved of his position, i.e., when a tribune interceded against his colleagues.

As far as the limit of the territory within which the tribuni exercised their power, it did not extend beyond the city of Rome and the Bannmeile. And with regard to the election of tribuni, we know that this took place in the Com. Trib. Especially a lex from the year 305, lex Duilia, made the entire collegium of tribuni responsible, upon threat of a severe penalty, for insuring that the people always had tribuni for the next year. Liv. III 555. It could happen that in the comitia which were held on account of the election, that not all the elections took place. A different procedure took place at different times. In the beginning, those elected replenished themselves through cooptation, but this stopped after the passage of Lex Traebonia (306), instead, it was decided that the elections would have to be continued until the requisite number was elected. Liv III 54 or 56. We have already heard that the patricii could not be elected. Originally, no tribunus could be elected from the senate, either. This restriction was lifted by the Lex Alinia. (541) Gell. XIV 8. In fact a law in effect toward the end of this period and attributed by many to Sulla, stipulated the opposite, that tribuni should only be elected from the ranks of the senate. Appian de bell. civ. I 106.

From: "Theory of Administration II; Internal
Administration; from the lectures of Prof. Dr.
(Lorenz) Stein, second notebook-Karl Lueger"

THE INTELLECTUAL LIFE AS OBJECT OF ADMINISTRATION

The intellectual life is free. Freedom is self
determination. There is a contradiction, if one
thinks about the intellectual life as object of administration. How is it possible that that which in
itself is free can become the object of state activity
without becoming enslaved?

The life of the individual is a product of com-
posite life. Every intellectual development is the
result of reciprocal intellectual forces. The self-
determination of one may be part of the self
determination of another. In the intellectual world
my property can become the property of another without
my losing it. That is the tremendous dichotomy between the intellectual and the material world. The
possibility that the individual does not lose his
intellectual freedom when learning what others teach,
is based on this serious difference. This is the
basis of the intellectual life of the community.
Renewing the entire intellectual life in each individual existence is the task of the mind. This process
is called education and is as old as the world. It is
an absolute process. And its factors are: the community of people and the individual. Now, in so far
as the community is synonymous with the state, we
refer to education becoming the object of the state's
will. The state does not create education, but rather
the manner of education, or the rules by which the
community's task is to educate the individual. This
process is called the administration of education,
that is, education as a whole. Whenever there is a
state, it begins to regulate the entire field of education. Question: since the state's basic concepts
vary in its different epochs, it follows that education also undergoes significant changes. If we know
which principles make the state different, then we
will know which ideas dominate education. Ideas dominate education, i.e., the social movements. There are
states governed by sex, professions and citizens.
Each has its own form of education. The rules

36

promulgated by the state are reflected in the social order. Our present form of education is determined by the citizen's state, that is, by the free individual. These three forms of society are not mutually exclusive, but rather the civil society absorbs the two other forms. As a consequence, education rests on all three basic forms. The task of our constitution is only to try to provide the general principles of education.

Nachlass Karl Lueger
St. Slg. Zl. 1257/12
Box I

From: "Theory of Administration II; Internal Administration; from the Lectures of Prof. Dr. (Lorenz) Stein, second notebook-Karl Lueger"

ADMINISTRATION OF SOCIETY

Social administration is the administration of class relations, but not of occupational relations. The classes are: affluent, poor, rich. Categories result from the elements which unite mankind: 1. sexual 2. occupational 3. personal freedom. Therefore, sexual category, occupational category, civil category. They are called categories, because each unit has its leader.

The head of the sexual category is the father of the family, of the occupational category, the one who is most knowledgeable, and of the civil category, the one most influential. The element of property difference is powerful in each category, but in civil society it is all powerful. The main area of social administration is found in the consequences of property difference.

The state has no say in the sexual category.

In the occupational category, the fundamental concept of free occupation arises. That commenced with the Germanic race; it did not include nobility and wealth.

State administration first becomes influential when occupation is joined with possession. The occupation starts to say: I am indispensable for this world. Therefore, my existence must be made secure.

37

This I can achieve only through the possession of
property which is acquired. The distribution of
possession is now one of the state's tasks.

In the civil society, the intellectual category
does not concern the state. Here the state concerns
itself with the classes.

Part I

Family and domestic category ./. administrative
law of sexual category ./. II. Administration of
occupational category, which includes the agrarian
constitution. In the field of agriculture, the content and significance is not the law of land and soil,
but rather the emancipation from occupational
constraints. . . .

Nachlass Karl Lueger
St. Slg. Zl. 1257/12
Box I

From: "Part I, Execution Administration Theory; from
the Lectures of Prof. Dr. (Lorenz) Stein-Karl Lueger"

AUSTRIA'S COMMUNITY LEGISLATION SINCE 1848

In 1849, the people's standpoint was: we only
want a civil constitution and the result was the
constitution of governing communities of March 27,
1849. The mistake was: community law was supposed to
be general, but it was merely a municipal law.
Consequence: the law was valid without being imple-
mented. It could not be carried out because of the
large land owners. The large landowner said: I can't
be both elector and elected. Then came 1860 and 1861.
A new community law was supposed to be set up. It was
said: we want to make 2 laws. The conditions of
large landowners are different everywhere. Hence:
every crown land has to have a community law. We must
have a general community law, determined by the
Reichstag. Austria has a system of community laws.

Draft

SELF-ADMINISTRATION IS SELF-TAXATION

The state is the personification of the community of men, whose purpose is to represent the interests of the community.

Each personality's activity is divided into 2 parts: namely 1) the will to do this or that, and 2) the execution of the will (before: One might also call the will, the inner, and the execution thereof, the outer activity). Execution of the will is again divided into two elements. It is necessary first to determine the manner and way in which the conceived will is to be realized, and only after the person knows this, can he actually begin to carry out his will according to the plan.

These three elements, will, plan and the actual execution together comprise what one calls an action, an act.

Since (the state) is likewise a personality, it must also combine will, plan, and actual execution in order to speak of an action; that is, in a state these individual elements stand out much more clearly and, as a result, are more recognizable than with individual persons in which, often, all three elements, or at least mostly will and plan exist simultaneously.

Therefore, self administration is the law and execution carried out by individual members of the state, i.e., by the citizens themselves or by persons elected by them. And in this manner the basis is found on which subsequent conclusions can be supported.

According to the particular state form, the law is established by an individual, as in the absolute monarchy, or it is the right of an individual to make laws which are subject to the concurrence of a representation of the whole people or a part thereof, or such a representation has the exclusive right to legislate. So the question now arises: who should execute these laws? Or who should administer them?

39

Obviously, that can only be the one who has made the laws. In an absolutist state only the sovereign, or those officials selected by and responsible to him, can execute the laws; there is absolutely no provision for popular participation of the people, that is, for self-administration. The situation is different in states in which the people, or a part thereof, participate in legislation, in which, therefore, the law is also the will of the people or at least a portion of the will. Consequence: one could relinquish the entire administration to the people, or at least to those who participated in formulating the laws. This is nowhere the case, for 1) there will always be minorities who will not agree with the laws, who, therefore, will not execute the law and 2) there are tasks which only one person representing the totality can carry out. The consequence of this second consideration is that laws which permit local handling can <u>be an element of self-government only as local administration</u>.

If local administration is relinquished to the citizens of any particular village or community, it becomes then a question of avoiding the first eventuality, i.e., that the laws will not be executed if, by chance, the majority in the village in question does not agree with them.

Therefore, the society, i.e., the state, should appoint official bodies who will see to it that those laws which are inappropriate for local execution are carried out. This entire body is the bureaucratic apparatus.

Thus, there are two important bodies of state administration: the official bureaucracy and self-government.

Each act of administration, each execution of the law produces costs, and the question arises, who should determine and bear them? Obviously, the one who executes the law, for money is not necessary to make laws, nor to formulate the will. However, with regard to self-administration, the village or the district carrying out the law, bears the cost of bureaucratic administration.

Thus, the community, the chamber of commerce district, must bear the costs of self-administration. On the other hand, only the one responsible for

40

executing the laws can determine the costs and the resultant contribution, which the individual has to make and this right of determination is self-taxation. Therefore, self-administration without self-taxation, and vice-versa, is unthinkable.

The right to sanction taxes derives from self-government. Through this right and through the principle of ministerial responsibility, the people in its entirety participate in bureaucratic administration.

Nachlass Karl Lueger
St. Slg. Zl. 1257/12
Box 1

Draft
Probably written between 1865 and 1869

IS STATE OR SOCIETY THE MORE COMPREHENSIVE CONCEPT, AND HOW SO?

Introduction

Before dealing with the actual question, namely, definition of the concepts of state and society, allow me to explain the significance of the expression "more comprehensive concept."

Does this unquestionably mean that either state or society is part of the other, that is, either something else must be added to the concept of state for it to become the concept of society, or must a further quality be added to the concept of society in order to arrive at the concept of state? If so, I would merely have to decide which of the two concepts includes the other. It appears too narrowly defined, and I don't think it would be amiss if I formulated the question thus: how do the concepts of state and society relate to one another? I could also say: they are coordinated concepts.

In order to answer this question, it is first of all necessary to define the concepts of state and society.

Society

When a few persons come together to converse, or induce each other progressively to widen their horizons, or to undertake common business ventures, or to

41

support third persons in time of need, in short, to reach any common goal, such an association is called a society. If the word "society" were to be used in this sense, the state, which is also the association of several persons to achieve a common goal, would be a kind of society, and the issue raised above would be answered without difficulty.

But the word "society" includes yet another meaning: it is said, for instance, this coffeehouse is frequented by a decent group. What does "group" mean here? Certainly not an association of several persons to attain a common goal, for the guests of a coffeehouse do not have any. Rather, this expression means: each coffeehouse guest is respected by his fellow men. Thus, in this case, the individual member of his group, as opposed to the group, is being considered here.

While the term "society" as first defined does not consider the individual, but rather the people as a whole, without regard to the individual himself, the significance of the term "society" in the second definition is just the opposite: here, the individual in his relationship with others comes into question. The difference is more explicitly expressed thus: while "society" in the first sense is an entity consisting of individuals, in the second sense it is the attitude of several persons towards one, or a third person, or their standing resulting from the personal circumstances and qualities of the individual. By using the second definition of the word "society" for continuing this essay, we arrive at the following concepts: society is the superior and subordinate structuring of the community based on the personal relationships and characteristics of the individuals. Such personal relationships and characteristics include: 1) family relationships: ./. father, child, the marital relationship ./. 2) class: citizen, farmer, soldier, priest (before: workers) aristocracy ./. 3) religion ./. Christian, Jew ./. 4) the economic relations a) the division of labor: farmer, miner, craftsman, manufacturer, tradesman ./. b) differentiation in the distribution of goods ./. poor, rich ./. 5) the moral characteristics.

Depending on how the superior and subordinate structuring of a community is determined, mainly by the kind of personal relationships, the different forms of society develop, and so 3 main categories are

42

differentiated: 1.) the family or sexual category, 2.) occupational category, 3.) civil category, the present form of society, and it is therefore necessary to consider this more closely. It is based on the principle of the equality of all men, and is therefore supposed to remove the superiority/subordinate distinction. But economic conditions present an obstacle to attaining this goal, in particular, the differences in the distribution of capital, the struggle between private capital and public capital, or the struggle between worker and capitalist, and since the endeavor of the former is just, they will win. (before: for truly, why should the worker, since he is equal to the capitalist, not be able to eat and drink as much?) For as true as it is that the happiest condition is one in which personal and public capital harmoniously blend with one another, it is equally true that any endeavor to reach this goal is just, and cannot be brushed aside with the (before: plebeian) excuse that attainment of this goal is impossible. Many things were considered impossible which eventually became possible nevertheless.

The first step consists in modifying the presently existing inheritance law, since there is no good reason why the son of a millionaire should receive his father's millions, a situation which he, i.e., the son, had nothing personally to do with, while the one who is perhaps more hard-working, but the son of poor parents, lives in poverty. Well, you can say, most people save only for their children. Who, then, will be interested in acquiring a fortune? Even though there are frugal bachelors and therefore, the above statement may not quite hold true, the individual instead will simply save for his fellow men. He should bring up his children to be as industrious a manager as he was, and humanity will derive more than if, in their place, privileged and well-fed idlers exist, who make a mockery of the saying: he who doesn't work, shouldn't eat. This is certainly an additional powerful reason. But the effect will be even stronger if it is stipulated that, whenever the inheritance exceeds a certain amount, only a fraction of this will go to the descendants, and the remainder will go to the community. Moreover, the individual, in knowing that his descendants cannot live from their capital, will (here, Lueger breaks off).

State

The state, like the society, is a form of life of the human community. But while the concept "society" concerns itself with the position of the individual, with the relationships in which the individual interacts with other individuals, the state is a human community, again meant as a single entity. (Before: How does the state differ from other legal persons? Answer: through its purpose. The state has no other purpose than to protect the existing society.)

Hence, the state is the community of men personified which exists to protect human society.

In the human community, as I just demonstrated, individuals have a particular relationship with one another and, therefore, the individual does not have the option of changing or structuring his relationship without the other's approval. Therefore, as soon as one quarrels or disagrees, a third person is necessary to make a decision and avoid any misrepresentation of the true circumstances. But in order to perform this function this third person must be more than an individual; it can only be the community. To protect the individual in the social situation is obviously the responsibility of the human community, since the protection of the same is in everyone's interest. Only the human community in its entirety, i.e., the state, can guarantee this protection.

THE RELATION OF THE TWO CONCEPTS

Both state and society are expressions of the community, and whereas the state represents unity, society represents fragmentation.

Since the state is the means to protect society, it follows of necessity, that, as soon as society evolves, it will create a state in order to protect itself.

It follows further, that every state form corresponds to a social form and that society and state must conform to one another, so that the latter may protect the former. Consequently, as soon as the majority of people in a state are convinced that their social form corresponding to the dominant state form isn't right, i.e., as soon as another form of society appears, it will attack the state, in order to replace it with a new one. Revolutions develop, and in most cases, only after bloody struggles is the goal attained. For those people who dominate society also dominate the state, therefore, also have the power which the community has given them, and only very rarely are there reasonable people who understand that power can no longer be theirs as soon as the community removes it by virtue of the new social form.

However, even if the rulers, through the support of the standing army, are able to maintain themselves in power for a time against the will of the community and through its bloody suppression, in the final analysis they must yield, burdened with the curse of mankind.

Now, civil society corresponds to the republican form, and the constitutional monarchy can only be seen as transition, as a step toward the goal. Not only will the individual states assume this kind of state form, but the individual republics will also create among themselves a large republican confederation, which will eventually become one single large republic. And then the dreams of the apostles of peace will be fulfilled, dreams which now are so pitifully scorned.

More and more people realize that it is in the common interest of all mankind to have one all-inclusive society. This realization is evidenced by trade treaties, extradition treaties, international organizations for the care of war-wounded, the peace demands from all corners of the world, the increasingly urgent plea for the abolition of professional armies, which will immediately disappear when those persons in whose interest these armies are maintained are removed.

Nachlass Karl Lueger
St. Slg. Zl. 1257/12
Box 1

This draft for a student paper, probably written between 1868 and 1870, provides early evidence of Lueger's intense nationalism.

STATISTICS OF THE KINGDOM OF BOHEMIA

INTRODUCTION

The kingdom of Bohemia is a province of the Austro-Hungarian Monarchy, that is, that part of the empire which, after the division of the Austrian Empire resulting from the events of 1866 (before: or more correctly, through the shortsightedness of truly unbelievable provinciality) is usually called Cisleithania, but officially, the various kingdoms and states represented in the Reichsrat.

Therefore, it is first of all necessary to understand the position of the Kingdom of Bohemia as a province in its relationship to the empire.

Through the Pragmatic Sanction of April 19, 1713, the unity of all Austrian states was legally recognized for the first time, even though it had already existed in fact through a succession of Habsburg rulers. This represented the first state constitution of the Austro-Hungarian Monarchy, which was followed by the declaration of Emperor Franz II of August 6, 1806 relating to the acceptance of the title "Emperor of Austria."

The turbulence of 1848 demonstrated that, thanks to the wisdom of the government, there are all kinds of people in Austria: Magyars, Czechs, Poles, Ruthenes, Slovenes, Slovaks, Serbs, Croatians, and whatever else the noble nations are called, but not one Austrian was to be found.

The Magyars were able to effect the sanctioning of the so-called 1848 laws, while the other Austrian states occupied themselves with drafting a constitution. This work was interrupted by the victorious reaction, without a constitution having been established for these states.

The defeats of the year 1859 destroyed a system which, if blessed by the Josephinian spirit, might have succeeded in creating a new Austria, but which, based on the power of the sword, the cross, and the nobility, was destined to succumb.

The Imperial Diploma of October 20, 1860 was issued, the so-called October Diploma, and eventually the Imperial Patent of February 26, 1861, also

referred to as the February Patent, both of which were
accepted by all Cisleithanian lands and peoples and
became their true basis of constitutional law. The
Hungarians, on the other hand, held fast to the laws
of 1848 and refused to accept the October Diploma and
February Patent.

After the Sistirungsmaenner and the idea of the
special Reichsrat collapsed due to German opposition,
the Hungarians were finally able to realize their goal
of reactivating the 1848 laws. The Reichsrat of the
other lands of Austria revised the February constitution through the laws of December 21, 1867, in accordance with the new political situation.

In order to maintain the unity of all Austrian
lands recognized by the Pragmatic Sanction, the tragi-
comical delegations were created, tragic for the
Cisleithanians, comical for the Magyars.

IN 32294

Lueger's only known poem, probably written about 1866,
is strongly reminiscent of graveyard verse, with its
picturesque language, and must surely have reflected
the feelings of many Austrian soldiers returning home
after the war with Prussia.

> When is there a happier time
> Than when summer begins?
> Roses bloom in the garden
> And soldiers march to battle.
>
> And when I arrived on foreign soil,
> I thought of home again.
> Oh, if I had only stayed at home
> And had kept my word.
>
> And as I came home,
> There stood my girl at the door.
> Hello, my dear one, my precious,
> I love you from the bottom of my heart.
>
> I don't need to love you,
> I already have a man,
> Handsome, brave and rich,
> One who can take care of me.

What did he withdraw from his pocket?
A bottle filled with sweet wine.
Let's both drink from it,
It shall be our good-bye.

What did he withdraw from his pocket?
A knife with a sharp point.
He thrust it into the maiden's heart,
And the red blood spurted on him.

Oh, my God and Father.
How bitter is death!
Oh, my God and beloved
What untrue love does.

The following two drafts provide Lueger's own documentation about his earliest professional activities.

> Nachlass Karl Lueger
> St. Slg. Zl. 1257/12
> Box 1
> Folder: Dokumente und
> Notizen die Advokatur-
> pruefung betreffend

K. K. Oberlandesgericht, Vienna I   Undated
Dr. Karl Lueger, Candidate for Attorney
Vienna III
Marokkanergasse 3
Office of Dr. Karl Kienboeck, I
Spiegelgasse 8

Concerning admission to the bar examination

Most Honorable K.K. Oberlandesgericht,

After having completed political law studies as per certificate A dated Vienna, July 30, 1866, and after having successfully passed the three theoretical state examinations as per state certificates B, dated Vienna, June 23, 1864, C, dated Vienna, July 7, 1866, and D, dated January 15, 1867, I began work on March 19, 1867 as legal assistant in the office of the royal and court attorney Dr. Hermann Kopp and remained there until January 1, 1868 as per certificate E, dated Vienna, November 12, 1873 and notification F of the Lower Austrian Bar Association, dated March 19, 1867, no. 610.

On this day, as per certificate G, dated Vienna, November 12, 1873 and Notification H of the Lower Austrian Bar Association, dated Vienna, January 2, 1868, no. 4, I left the office of Dr. Hermann Kopp and began practice in the office of Dr. Anton Edlen von Ruthner. I remained in this position until June 15, 1870, on which day I, as per Certificate I, dated Vienna, November 12, 1873, and dated March 19, 1874 and notification K of the lower Austrian Bar Association, dated Vienna, June 15, 1870, began work in the office of court appointed attorney Dr. Karl Kienboeck, a position which I retain to the present time.

Meanwhile, after having passed the prescribed strict examinations at the kk University of Vienna, I was awarded the Degree of Dr. of Law as per the enclosed true copy of diploma L dated Vienna, January 21, 1870. I have therefore fulfilled all requirements prescribed by law for admittance to the bar.

I therefore respectfully request:
The kk Oberlandesgericht kindly permits me to take the bar examination and to set a date for the written examinations.

Dr. Karl Lueger

Draft

Nachlass Karl Lueger
St. Slg. Zl. 1257/12
Box 1
Folder: Dokumente und
Notizen die Advokatur-
pruefung betreffend

K. K. Oberlandesgericht
Vienna
Dr. Karl Lueger
Candidate for Attorney
Vienna III
Marokkanergasse 3:
Office of Dr. Kienboeck
Vienna I
Spiegelgasse 8

Regarding permission to take the attorney's oath

Honorable K. K. Oberlandesgericht,

As per certificate M dated Vienna, January 13, 1874, no. 24885, I most successfully passed the bar examination on December 12 and 13, 1873 and on January 10, 1874 before the honorable kk Oberlandesgericht.

It follows from the above that on January 1, 1869, which was the day the law of July 6, 1868, no. 96 of the imperial law code took effect, I had already completed more than one year of law practice, and therefore, as per article 36a of the above cited law, I am exempt from certifying the prescribed court internship as per article 2 of the cited law.

Now that I, as of yesterday, have completed a seven year total practice, I most humbly request:

that the honorable kk Oberlandesgericht allows me to take the oath, as prescribed in article five of the attorney's regulation of July 6, 1868, no. 96 (imperial law code).

THE ADORATEUR

THE ADORATEUR

Lueger's relationships with women have attracted the attention and stimulated the imagination not only of his contemporaries, but also of present-day historians. Carl E. Schorske has suggested that Lueger all too easily succumbed to what he calls "extreme maternal authority," as evidenced by his promise to his mother never to marry,[1] and that further it follows that his attitude toward women was far from a normal one. On the other hand, John W. Boyer believes that "Lueger enjoyed a rich, normal sex life, having a string of mistresses, with some of whom he maintained close spiritual relations as well."[2] The life-long bachelor seems to have exploited his good looks and charm, not only in the form of a marketable political commodity, but also as a profitable private currency.[3] His female political supporters, organized through the Viennese Christian Women's League, stumped vigorously for their candidate on numerous occasions, even though they themselves were not enfranchised. Their emotional enthusiasm, however, undoubtedly earned him many a vote.[4]

The selection of letters presented here for the most part represents Lueger's private, extra-political connections. His verbal dexterity, his occasional joke, and his humor, all of which characterize his speeches to audiences of women, are here exhibited for whatever psychological import one may wish to attribute to them. As early as 1882, Lueger revealed a preference for professional, artistic women, which seems to have lasted to the very end of his life. At this time, he entered into a friendship with the actress Valerie Gréy, born Caroline Valerie Loewey (1845? - 1934).[5] Since she is one of at least two women with whom Lueger was evidently on intimate terms and who attained modest fame of her own, a brief description of her career is in order.

Miss Gréy, the daughter of the commanding officer at the fortress of Komorn, at the age of five made her stage debut in Budapest with the legendary Adolf von Sonnenthal. Even the growing opposition of her parents, which extended to interfering with her education and burning her cherished edition of Schiller,[6] did not deter her progress. She continued her career and became a well-known multilingual actress. She toured Europe and became the first dramatic female lead at the Imperial German Theater in

53

St. Petersburg.[7] Later, around 1880, she established
her own small theater in Vienna, the Gréy Theater,
which was located in the First District, Canovagasse
5. Because of her "systematic thefts" of other
directors' works,[8] she fell frequently into conflict
with the law; and Lueger himself at least once served
as her attorney.

While many of Lueger's letters survive, most of
them are addressed to one person, Valerie Gréy.
Regrettably, however, it appears that only one of her
letters to him has survived. It was written at the
time of the Fogerty Railway Affair,[9] which involved
the bribery of municipal officials, when Lueger
emerged as a significant Viennese politician. Brief
and ungrammatical, it alludes to her own role in this
notorious scandal:

March 16, 1882

Most esteemed Doctor,

As early as yesterday, I wanted to congratulate
you, was delayed, but today's letter from Gunesch made
me decide to tell you for sure how very glad I am –
today Vienna will hopefully know whom it has to thank
if we don't get an elevated train – am I a prophet?
Please accept the expression of my genuine esteem.

Valerie Gréy[10]

In addition to her career as actress and theater
director, Valerie Gréy was also a teacher of rhetoric.
Lueger is supposed to have been her one-time pupil.[11]
His effectiveness as a speaker, never in doubt even
among his opponents, could very well have been a
result of Gréy's instruction. In her teaching method,
she placed particular value on breathing exercises
performed in a reclining position. These were
believed to have led to a mastery of the art of proper
speaking: "The actor, the speaker," according to her,
"has to have his body pumped up with air, if he is to
sustain a long drawn-out cry or scream. Above all
else, therefore, the student has to learn to
breathe."[12] A portrait photograph, taken during the
time of her close friendship with Lueger, shows a
stout, resolute, self-confident woman. One can
readily imagine that such a woman would possess the
ability to cow temperamental actors, to thrive in the
rough-and-tumble world of Viennese theater in the late

nineteenth century,[13] and to lend confidence to a
rising young politician whose prospects were for a
time uncertain.[14]

After 1885, when Lueger began to climb to
national political prominence with his election to
parliament, and he became more certain about his
future, his friendship with Valerie Gréy seems to have
cooled. His last letter to her, written by a third
person, although signed by him, appears to have been a
mere formality. In 1888, Gréy married Lueger's former
legal colleague, Eduard Franz Stipek. She divorced
him in 1909. As the author in 1907 of the peasant
drama, Der Schlierach Lois, she became famous outside
of Vienna, and she remained active for many years in
Viennese theatrical circles. She was survived by two
daughters from an earlier marriage with a certain
Kletzer.[15]

Another woman in Lueger's life, on whom he rained
a shower of letters,[16] was the portrait painter,
Marianne Beskiba (1868-1934).[17] One cannot draw any
clear conclusions from Lueger's letters to Valerie
Gréy about the kind of relationship he and the actress
enjoyed; it seems to have been that of an ambitious,
yet not entirely confident young man too busy rising
in the world to be commited, though the warm tone of
his letters in the spring of 1885 suggests that he and
Gréy may have been more than friends. But the relationship between Lueger and Beskiba does not allow for
any ambiguity; the man has "arrived," and for several
years she was his mistress. Incapable of sublimating
her relationship in the form of a novel or a play,
like Gréy, Beskiba produced memoirs that show her to
have been an hysterical woman, who pursued her lover
with marital intentions until the end of his life. It
is not surprising, therefore, in view of her nature
and intentions, to find the critics, even if for
reasons of piety, publicly doubting her version of the
liaison with Lueger, which she discussed in her
memoirs.[18]

Her observations about his relations with his
family and his effect on female audiences nevertheless
remain valid and important. "Julianne, his mother,"
Marianne wrote, "he loved quite extraordinarily and
revered her memory."[19] Lueger, however, was by her
report less fervently attached to his sisters. She
writes:
Officially much has been invented about

> the devoted love between Lueger,
> Hildegard and Rosa. A certain family
> feeling did unquestionably exist among
> the three of them, but a devoted kind of
> tenderness was not present. For Rosa,
> the younger sister, Lueger had a certain
> partiality; he didn't love Hildegard, only
> feared her strong character.[20]

He had nothing to fear, however, from the members of
the Viennese Christian Women's League, or "Lueger's
Amazons," as they were popularly called. Before one
of Lueger's speeches, Marianne writes, "every tiny
seat was fought over, no distance was too far for his
enthusiastic supporters, no weather too bad. Long before the doors to the hall opened, the masses lined
up."[21] Publicly, at least, his relationship with
women was good.

Yet judging from the overall tone and content of
his letters to Marianne Beskiba, Lueger was probably
not in love with her in any significant way. He seems
not to have been romantically devoted. The documents
presented here do not provide an adequate basis for
any definitive conclusion about Lueger's emotional
life, but in large, they seem to show that the energy
with which he pursued his political career would
naturally get in the way of deep emotional commitment
to any woman. This seems to be his meaning in his
reply to an unidentified friend when he wrote ". . .
If I someday tire of politics and could have time for
marriage, I'm afraid it would be too late." (See IN
151.956 pp. 299, 300). Marianne herself disappointedly
confesses that he maintained a truly "deeper affection
for one single (unnamed) woman" only.[22] His relationships with Marianne and other women were, according to
nineteenth-century mores, kept from public view.[23]
Discouraged by her own failure as an artist and by
worsening poverty, Marianne attempted suicide the same
year her memoirs appeared, a year after Lueger's death
in 1910. She never married and passed her remaining
years in obscurity and isolation, deeper even than
that she experienced during her affair with Lueger.
Her death came in 1934, and she was buried in a
pauper's grave.

Lueger's entire known correspondence to Gréy--
to show its characteristic drift--is included in this
section, as well as the surviving letters to Beskiba,
his mother and sisters. It seems probable from her

name, Caroline Valerie Loewy, that Lueger's actress
friend was of Jewish descent. If so, it is indeed
ironic that she taught rhetoric to one of the chief
spokesmen for and organizers of European political
anti-Semitism.

FOOTNOTES FOR
THE ADORATEUR

1. Schorske, "Politics in a New Key," pp. 356, 357.

2. John W. Boyer, "Church, Economy and Society in
    Fin de Siècle Austria - The Origins of the
    Christian Social Movement, 1875-1897." Ph.D.
    dissertation, University of Chicago, 1975,
    p. 606n.

3. The rising young politician Lueger once men-
    tioned to a friend that because of his substan-
    tial public responsibilities he would never make
    a good husband and added: "I have never been in
    love in my whole life and I have never ventured
    to write a love poem." Kuppe, p. 557. It was
    brought to my attention that "Hitler also re-
    garded his single status as a political asset."

4. Kurt Skalnik, Dr. Karl Lueger der Mann Zwischen
    den Zeiten. Vienna and Munich, 1954, p. 52.
    At a woman's meeting, one of Lueger's euphoric
    admirers reacted as follows: "You just can't
    believe how such a meeting affects your heart and
    mind. Lueger and the Prince (Alois Lichtenstein),
    and all the other gentlemen; they're tremendously
    intelligent and well-read. My heart simply
    flutters when I hear all the intelligent things
    they talk about." Marie Goetz, Die Frauen und
    der Antisemitismus. Vienna, n.d., p. 13.
    Die Oesterreichische Frauenzeitung and Christliche
    Wiener Frauen Zeitung were the semi-official
    organs of the Viennese Christian Women's League.
    For information about the League itself, see
    Beskiba, Erinnerungen, pp. 31-38; Antonie
    Schmolek, "Lueger und die christlichen Frauen,"
    Neuigkeits-Welt-Blatt, September 19, 1926,
    p. 23; Kielmansegg, pp. 386-388. Kasimierez
    Chledowski, Pamiętniki, 2 vols., Breslau, 1951,
    2, pp. 168, 169.

5. Viennese municipal records list Valerie Gréy's birthdate as February 10, 1842 and February 10, 1845, and her name is given as Charlotte Valerie, born Loewe, and Valerie Charlotte Loewy. In the Trauungsbuch des Evangelischen Pfarramtes A. B., Jahr 1888, Reihezahl 136 (Vienna), her name appears as Caroline Valerie, born Loewey, and her birthplace and birthdate as Pest, January 31, 1845. The last source would seem to be the more reliable, since the information was probably submitted by Gréy herself at the time of her second marriage (see below). The actress Hansi Niese was another of Lueger's friends and correspondents. Her letters thank him for flowers, photographs and a necklace. She also asked him to help obtain a building permit for the Theater in the Josefsstadt. On the last letter from Niese, Lueger dictated a few words for a response: "Thanks for writing - for the moment, make no promises." All these letters are part of the Lueger Nachlass in the Handschriften Sammlung in the town hall of the City of Vienna. For information about Lueger and Niese, see "Hansi Niese ueber Dr. Karl Lueger," Neuigkeits-Welt-Blatt, September 19, 1926, p. 5, and Hansi Niese, "Hansi Niese und Dr. Karl Lueger," Die Reichpost, September 19, 1926, p. 11; Beskiba, Erinnerungen, pp. 39-45, and Lueger's letter to Beskiba, IN 67559, in this chapter. For information about Niese see Wilhelm Kosch, Deutsches Theater Lexikon (Klagenfurt and Vienna, 1960) and the sources quoted therein; Maria Czelechowski, "Hansi Niese," Ph.D dissertation, University of Vienna, 1947.

6. Valerie Gréy, "Autobiographische Skizzen," IN 45778.

7. "Valerie Gréy gestorben," Neue Freie Presse, February 21, 1934, p. 3.

8. J. Nagl, J. Zeidler, E. Castle, Deutsch-Oesterreichische Literaturgeschichte, 4 vols., Vienna, 1937, 3, p. 826.

9. See the appropriate documents in "The Municipal Politician." Gréy's 1894 novel Paula and her 1903 play Helene contain quasi-autobiographical sections that may allude to her relationship with Lueger.

10. IN 203.120.

11. Leo Santifaller et al., <u>Oesterreichisches Biographisches Lexikon 1815-1950</u>. Projected in 6 vols., Vienna and Graz, 1959, 2, p. 59. Josef Kainz, Engelbert Pernerstorfer and Ferdinand Kronawetter were also students of Gréy. <u>Neue Freie Presse, loc. cit.</u>

12. <u>Ibid.</u> Lueger's oratorical effectiveness, which never seems to have been in doubt with either friends or foes, could very well have resulted from Gréy's instruction (see IN 124.771 in this chapter). On this point, the liberal novelist Felix Salten observed: "In parliament he fills the broad semicircle of the hall with the organ of his voice where other voices drowned. He swings his speech like a flag, then like a whip, then like a hammer. . . . A whole movement speaks when he begins to speak, a movement which never before spoke so loudly in the chamber." Kuppe, 273n.

13. Adam Mueller-Guttenbrunn offers a negative view of this world in his <u>Wien war eine Theaterstadt</u> (1887). See also Richard S. Geehr, <u>Adam Mueller-Guttenbrunn and the Aryan Theater of Vienna 1898-1903, the Approach of Cultural Fascism</u> (Goeppingen, 1974), Chapter 1, and the sources therein.

14. Rudolf Kuppe calls 1883 "the nadir of Dr. Lueger's political career," Kuppe, p. 82.

15. Lotte, married name Feldscharek, and Aurelie, married name Haumer, appear to have lived outside Vienna at the time of their mother's death. Both are mentioned in Franz Planer, Ed., <u>Das Jahrbuch der Wiener Gesellschaft</u>. Vienna, 1929, p. 204.

16. In addition to the letters to Beskiba in this chapter, there are in the Handschriftensammlung of the Vienna municipal library some 200 post-cards, visiting cards and, interestingly enough, empty letter envelopes. Beskiba burned the contents of these envelopes on the express wish of Lueger, who then extinguished the ashes with champagne. Lueger's correspondence to Beskiba lasted fifteen years, from 1894-1909.

17. Beskiba painted at least two portraits of Lueger. The more famous appeared in Richard Soukup's 1953 Lueger biography; the second is included in this book.

18. See "Erinnerungen an Dr. Karl Lueger," _Kleine Oesterreichische Volkszeitung_, May 31, 1911, p. 8, and "Erinnerungen an Dr. Lueger," _Neues Wiener Tagblatt_, May 30, 1911, p. 13.

19. Beskiba, _Erinnerungen_, p. 15.

20. _Ibid._, p. 13.

21. _Ibid._, p. 33.

22. _Ibid._, p. 23.

23. Kielmansegg stated that Lueger's love affairs remained unknown or concealed, and that Lueger was much admired in the female world of his party supporters. Kielmansegg, p. 386.

The following three letters are evidently all that survive from what must have been at one time a large correspondence to Lueger's mother and sisters. This collection is referred to in a special edition of the Reichspost of September 19, 1926, at the time of the dedication of the Lueger monument on the "Karl Lueger Platz," and in Richard Soukup's 1953 Lueger biography.[+] The owner of at least a portion of this collection at that time was a former Christian Social Municipal Councilor, Josef Mueller-Fembeck, incompletely identified as Josef Mueller. The letter collection was evidently scattered at the time of his death in 1961.

Although the contents of Lueger's letters to his mother and sisters are not exciting, they are noteworthy in that they reflect his lifelong addiction to travel, love of Vienna, and apparently somewhat formal relationship with his closest relatives.

From a private collection

Friday, July 24, 1874

Hotel St. Gotthard
Andermatt

Dearest Mother and Sisters:

Since my last letter, which you must have received by now, I have arrived here in Andermatt.

There was nothing but fog on the Rigi Mountain.

But during our trip across the Vierwaldstaetter Lake and over the St. Gotthard Pass, we had nice weather.

Here in Andermatt it is raining with a vengeance, and we may decide to wait another day before we move on.

We therefore will be in the Grimselhospiz tomorrow, the 25th, in Mayringe the 26th, in Grindelwald the 27th, etc.

[+]p. 260

Since I have not received a letter either from
you or from Dr. Vogler, I assume everything goes well,
for which I am delighted.

Except for the uncertainty of life, which is
somewhat unpleasant for me, I am fine.

Finally I greet and kiss you all many times,
greetings also to Dr. Vogler and Eppinger and ask them
to convey my greetings to my colleagues.

And so I bid farewell until I see you again soon.

Your loving son and brother,

Dr. Lueger

From a private collection

July 29, 1874

Dearest Mother and Sisters,

After a strenuous journey, I arrived yesterday in
Interlaken, the most charming village in all of
Switzerland. I did not find any letters from you or
Dr. Vogler, and I am therefore convinced that you are
all well, and that things in the office are going
routinely.

We traveled from Andermatt to Realp and went
from there to the Furka Pass in the middle of a
terrible snow storm.

The snow lay six inches deep and it was also
quite cold, so that I couldn't dress warmly enough.

The next day, in a snow storm again at first,
we went up to the Rhone Glacier. Later on, the
weather cleared up and we went the same day over the
Grimsel to Meiringen.

The next day I went from there up to the Little
Scheideck and from here to the Faulhorn, where we
stayed overnight. In the morning we had a very lovely
and clear view.

Yesterday we went to Interlaken.

We'll stay here <u>until tomorrow, Thursday</u>; we will be in Bern on Friday. Saturday in Vevey, Sunday and Monday in Geneva. Wednesday morning or evening I'll be home again with you, which I so look forward to.

In the meantime, many kisses and greetings; please give my regards to Dr. Vogler and Dr. Eppinger and ask them to say hello to my colleagues.

Once again farewell from

your loving son and brother,

Dr. Lueger

From a private collection

August 1, 1874

Dearest Mother and Sisters,

Today, I arrived in Geneva and will travel the day after tomorrow directly to Vienna, so that I'll be in Vienna Wednesday morning at the very latest.

I will be most pleased to see you all again, healthy and in good spirits, I hope. I look forward very much to Vienna again, a city that really has so many amenities and advantages that all the natural beauties are thus more than compensated.

And so, to a joyful and speedy reunion! Until then, greetings and kisses to you, dearest mother and sisters, and my greetings to Dr. Vogler and Dr. Eppinger.

Your loving

son and brother,

Dr. Lueger

IN 124.752
Dr. Karl Lueger
Vienna, 1st District, Renngasse No. 1

To: Valerie Grey
June 10, 1882

Dear Madam:

I knew that Bayer had become commissioner, and mentioned this, if I am not mistaken, during our wet excursion to the Vienna Woods. What can I say? It's nothing new. This is the usual course of events in Austria and especially with the police.

You'll find me tomorrow, Sunday morning, between 11-12 at the office, and I would take the liberty of visiting you, dear Madam, if I didn't have to be in the office. Monday, too, from 10 a.m. until 2 p.m. and from 3:30 p.m. until 4:30 p.m. I'll be in the office.

For tomorrow afternoon, I have already been invited to Vaugoin's, and therefore, regrettably, I will not be in the position to admire lovely Franz Josefsland.[1] I hope, nevertheless, that the opportunity will present itself again soon.

And while I kiss your hand, dear Madam, I remain most respectfully.

Your devoted servant,

Dr. Lueger

IN 124.751

To: Valerie Gréy

July 14, 1882

Dear Madam,

My colleague, Dr. Sigmund Wolf-Eppinger, informs me that you have come to an agreement with Berg.

You, dear Madam, know my viewpoint and will therefore understand my congratulating you.

---

[1]Franz Josefsland was a recreation area on the banks of the Danube Canal named after the explorers Peyer and Weyprecht, the discoverers of Franz Josefsland near the north pole. Several inns were built there, and this area soon developed into a little "Prater," which held great attraction for Sunday excursionists.

I can now say to you openly, that I never doubted that you would be acquitted. Nevertheless, the mere fact that you would have had to appear in court because of such a nasty pamphlet, would have severely damaged your reputation as a woman and you would also have suffered business losses.

It is therefore well that you didn't listen to certain people, who would have made fun of you, and obeyed the voice of reason.

Kissing your hand,

Dr. Lueger

IN 124.753
Dr. Karl Lueger
Vienna, 1st District, Renngasse No. 1

To: Valerie Gréy

December 19, 1883

Dear Madam,

On Monday, the 17th of this month at 8:15 p.m., after the meeting of the finance section, I went to the house in the Wollzeile on the corner of the Riemerstrasse, accompanied by a colleague, in order to keep my promise, in spite of very unpleasant rain.

I vigorously rang the bell next to the name "Valerie Gréy" and impatiently awaited the outcome. But nobody came, neither Mrs. Valerie Gréy, nor her little daughter, nor anyone else.

After having waited a while, I thought that you, dear Madam, and your daughters, had already left for Franz Josefsland and I went home.

This is how it happened and can be confirmed by witnesses under oath.

Whether I am liable for prosecution after this presentation of the facts, I will gladly leave to your well-developed legal judgment, honed by so many court cases.

It goes without saying that I deeply regret that

you, dear Madam, seem to have waited two hours with
hat, fur, and anticipation because of an organic bell
failure. Of course it would have been more enjoyable
for me to have undertaken the planned journey in your
company than to have gone home with the uncertainty
of "why" and to read briefs.

On Tuesday, December 25, 1883 at 6 o'clock in
the evening, I will arrive at your house, dear Madam,
and personally render my due thanks for your merciful
penalty. However, I ask only one favor. Please take
into consideration, dear Madam, that, on the evening
of the 24th of this month, I must fill my stomach
according to the venerable custom of our fathers,
that in this condition, I will depart on the 25th of
this month at 5 o'clock p.m. and that, therefore,
at 6 o'clock in the evening on the 25th of this month
I can eat only a minimum.

With all that said I hope to have satisfied your
curiosity which, incidentally, is quite justified, and
expect that you, dear Madam, are convinced of my
innocence and will blame the above circumstances
rather than me.

Kissing your hand, dear Madam, I most respectfully remain,

your devoted,

Dr. Lueger

In this letter, Lueger refers to an unflattering
comment about Gréy in one of Vienna's most influential
papers, the <u>Neues Wiener Tagblatt</u>.

IN 124.754
Dr. Karl Lueger
Vienna, 1st District, Renngasse No. 1

To: Valerie Gréy

February 6, 1884

Dear Madam,

If it is cowardly to insult and offend a person
from a safe hiding place, it is downright despicable
when a man does this to a defenseless woman.

What have you actually done, dear Madam, to the Czech German Schembera, to have so turned a heart once filled with love?

Or have you perhaps done _nothing_? What is it that has transformed this love sick Seladon[2] into a raging enemy?

It is odd at the fresh grave of one woman to summon the strange courage to insult another woman after having previously showered her with love letters and poems.[3] Yet, comfort yourself, dear Madam, with the knowledge that you wanted to pay tribute due a deceased artist[4] and let them growl away.

You have and will continue to have the esteem of everyone who knows you, while your opponent himself, sooner or later, will regret what he has done to you.

I was eager to send you these lines, dear Madam. May they be balm for the wound inflicted upon you.

Kissing your hand, I remain,

your most devoted,

Dr. Lueger

---

[2]Seladon is an ardent lover in Honoré d'Urfé's novel, _Astrée_ (1610).

[3]Schembera's commentary read: "The short time between the removal of the casket from the wagon and its arrival at the grave was used by the present proprietress of an obscure theater school and former directress of an obscure little theater to affix a sign with two lines of verse and broad borders next to the inscription on the grave stone. This publicity attempt at such a place, at such a time, was immediately aborted when the first mourners appeared with the coffin at the grave." _Neues Wiener Tagblatt_, February 6, 1884, pp. 3, 4.

[4]Josefine Gallmeyer.

IN 124.755
Dr. Karl Lueger
Vienna, 1st District, Renngasse No. 1

To an unknown friend

From the Gréy Collection

April 23, 1884

Dear Friend:

Yesterday evening at the Municipal Council meeting, I learned that there will be a special Municipal Council session <u>tomorrow</u> afternoon, Thursday, at 5 o'clock to resolve the question of the Northern Railway.[5] You will admit that I am regrettably forced to decline your friendly invitation under these circumstances. I have already notified Mrs. Gréy.

Today I have office hours from 4 to 6 p.m. and tomorrow from 10 a.m. until 12:30 p.m.

With best wishes,

Dr. Lueger

IN 124.756
Dr. Karl Lueger
Vienna, 1st District, Renngasse No. 1

To: Valerie Gréy

May 28, 1884

Dear Madam:

As promised, here is the answer to the question about a visit. As pleasant as it would be for me to greet you, dear Madam, and Dr. Stipek in your new home and to spend an enjoyable evening, I won't be able to do it this week, since either my official responsibilities or due consideration for my mother and sisters will keep me in Vienna. However, Wednesday of next

---

[5]See the relevant documents in "The Municipal Politician."

week, I will try to be available and appear in Hinter-
Bruehl in the evening.

I hope, dear Madam, you will be well by then,
something I sincerely wish. My courageous Gréy, whom
I and many others admire for her energy, will certainly survive the slight onset of melancholy; the
clouds will scatter and with that, the old confidence
and cheerfulness will return.

To be sure that I do not forget, it would be well
to send me a reminder, and I am sure you will forgive
the request to send me a few lines in time. To ease
the task, they may be as illegible as possible.

While kissing your hand, dear Madam, I extend at
the same time many cordial greetings to Stipek, wish
you the same appetite which my friend enjoys, and
remain most respectfully.

Your most devoted,

Dr. Lueger

P.S. The office just told me that you already
reminded me.

IN 124.757
Dr. Karl Lueger
Vienna, 1st District, Renngasse No. 1

To: Valerie Gréy

May 31, 1884

Dear Madam,

"For in the Hinterbruehl, the wind is so still."
Therefore, the storms in you will also subside, dear
Madam, and the peacefulness of the village will work
its healing powers on you. I presume it's only a turn
of phrase when you write that I have hurt you, and if
indeed it was supposed to have been meant seriously,
then I can only say it was not my intention.

Incidentally, I am truly delighted to have gathered from your welcome letter that your self-
confidence has returned again, and that is the most
important thing. You feel that I should be able to

69

spend a few days with you, dear Madam, in Hinterbruehl. Unfortunately, this is not possible. Early
Thursday I have to be in Vienna again. My business
and public profession necessitate this.

Since yesterday you have probably found
Dr. Stipek again and conveyed my greetings.

In conclusion, the following request: if you
are kind enough to write to me, please don't forget
to give me the exact address, so that I don't have to
ask around, but can steer directly to my goal.

While I kiss your hand, dear Madam, I send you
best wishes and remain most respectfully,

Your most devoted,

Dr. Lueger

IN 124.759
Dr. Karl Lueger
Attorney to the Royal and Legal Courts
Vienna
1., Trattnerhof
Goldschmiedgasse 9
Graben 29

To: Valerie Gréy

Vienna

December 4, 1884

Dear Madam,

How does one eat truffles? Pardon the question,
but everything has to be learned.

As Stipek tells me, Dr. Eisenschitz was already
here, but I was not. Well, he will come again.

You confront me with a puzzle, and it interests
you whether I can solve it. I think I have now
figured it out; still, in the interest of caution, I
request that you, Madam, tell me first, and then I
will tell you, whether I was right or not.

I kiss your hand and remain most respectfully,

Your most devoted,

(Lueger's name is cut out)[5]

IN 124.758
Dr. Karl Lueger
Attorney to the Royal and Legal Courts
Vienna
1., Trattnerhof
Goldschmiedgasse 9
Graben 29

To: Valerie Gréy

Vienna

December 5, 1884

Dear Madam,

Yesterday you wanted to recite to me, but I had to be impolite because I didn't have any time. But take comfort! Two holidays are coming up, and I now hope to have the pleasure, which I have missed for so long, namely, only to listen and not to talk myself.

The truffles are still on my desk, as if they belonged to the ensemble, and I look at them with timid admiration.

Dr. Eisenschitz hasn't been here yet.

Kissing your hand, and signing devotedly,

Dr. Lueger

IN 124.760
Dr. Karl Lueger
Attorney to the Royal and Legal Courts
Vienna
1., Trattnerhof
Goldschmiedgasse 9
Graben 29

---

[5]Lueger's signature was probably cut out by an autograph collector.

Dear Madam,

Since I sometimes have more to do than the average mortal, I must sometimes postpone the fulfillment of a duty. And so, in this case, I am the sinner. I received the letter, but then had no time to answer, and later, something always intervened when I thought of you, dear Madam. Kindly forgive me, therefore, and believe me that I am truly sorry to have caused you even one unpleasant moment.

Incidentally, Dr. Tugendhat didn't tell me that you wanted to visit me on Tuesday; in fact, I ask you not to speak with this gentleman at all.

Now, to something else. I have not as yet spoken with Dr. Eisenschitz, have, however, received a letter from him, from which I take it that he is now of the opinion that Miss Gréy is the offender. There could be a way to settle this matter; but you would have to agree to it. If you would have time this evening, we could talk this over, if you would be kind enough to visit me in the office.

At this opportunity, I could also listen to the humorous recital. We both need a bit more of this sort of thing, if we don't want to jump out of our skins, and it doesn't hurt to strengthen the unity between skin and man.

I will refrain from further questions about your and your daughters' health, etc., as I will learn about it all in person.

So, good-bye!

Kissing your hand, dear Madam, I remain most respectfully,

Your devoted,

Dr. Lueger

P.S. I hope they (or you?) are dry by now.

IN 124.761
Dr. Karl Lueger
Attorney to the Royal and Legal Courts
Vienna
1., Trattnerhof
Goldschmiedgasse 9
Graben 29

To: Valerie Gréy

Vienna

December 12, 1884

Dear Madam,

Since there is a legal meeting today, I don't know whether you will find me at the office between 1 and 2.

I ask you, therefore, not to come until 4 p.m., or better yet, to meet me tomorrow between 1 and 2 p.m.

Kissing your hand, I remain most respectfully,

Your devoted,

Dr. Lueger

IN 124.763
Dr. Karl Lueger
Attorney to the Royal and Legal Courts
Vienna
1., Trattnerhof
Goldschmiedgasse 9
Graben 29

To: Valerie Gréy

Vienna

January 29, 1885

Dear Madam,

Because of unavoidable office business, it will not be possible for me to go to Margarethen today, but rather I must sit and sweat in the office, and when I finish, it will be too late to make the long trip.

How did you rest, dear Madam? How are you? Should it perhaps be possible for us to see one another today, nevertheless, then you will please me.

Kissing your hand, I remain respectfully,

Dr. Lueger

IN 124.762
Dr. Karl Lueger
Attorney to the Royal and Legal Courts
Vienna
1., Trattnerhof
Goldschmiedgasse 9
Graben 29

To: Valerie Gréy

Vienna

February 6, 1885

Dear Madam,

For the moment, I do not have any time for longer discussions, so I will limit myself to the depressing news that I have meetings and conferences tonight, tomorrow night, Monday night, Tuesday night, etc.

I applaud your attending the masquerade ball; we'll talk later about the costumes.

Kissing your hand, dear Madam, and remaining respectfully devoted,

Dr. Lueger

IN 124.764
Dr. Karl Lueger
Trattnerhof Address

To: Valerie Gréy

Vienna

February 16, 1885

Dear Madam,

Enclosed is the ticket for tomorrow.

Today there is a supper in the office. If you
are in a good mood, you will make me and the somber
exam candidates happy. Anch'io sono pittore. I, too,
know what anxiety means. But the condition of my
office colleague can only be described with a German
word, which I will not write down for propriety's
sake. And this already 2 1/2 months before the exam.
How will this end?

Allow me to kiss your hand, dear Madam, and permit the expression of my highest respect, with which I
close,

Dr. Lueger

IN 124.781

To: Valerie Gréy

February 25, 1885

Dear Madam,

This evening 8 o'clock office supper.

Kissing your hand.

D. L.

IN 124.765
Dr. Karl Lueger
Trattnerhof Address

To: Valerie Gréy

Vienna

March 2, 1885

Dear Madam,

How much it hurt me that a meeting of the first

section[6] had to take place on the one day you appeared
in my office! It was even more painful, since there
won't be any more office suppers and I will therefore
have to forgo the pleasure of seeing you.

Wondrous is the race of Stipek. The "Gentleman
of Sandor" moves out and doesn't bid farewell. The
monster left yesterday morning without saying <u>where</u>
he was going, without leaving his regards, in <u>short</u>,
he's behaving toward me like a criminal toward the
police. Do you know perhaps, dear Madam, where he
has taken himself?

So here I am, abandoned, all alone.

For this reason, I have permitted myself to
bother you, dear Madam, with these lines.

Kissing your hand, and signing respectfully,

Dr. Lueger

IN 124.766
Dr. Karl Lueger
Trattnerhof Address

To: Valerie Gréy

Vienna

March 5, 1885

Dear Madam,

You could be a Municipal Councilor yourself;
that's how well you know the sessions. Or did I tell

---

[6]Sections were recruited from members of the Municipal
Council according to the municipal constitution.
These sections made recommendations and were responsible for supervising execution of Municipal Council
resolutions. Thus their function was to control and
to execute. In the subsequent constitutional development, the sections received the name "committees."
The responsibility of the first section was to handle
"general organizational and service affairs."
See <u>Bericht der Vom Wiener Gemeinderathe
eingesetzten Commission zur Revision des Gemeinde-
Statutes</u>, 1, Vienna, 1868, p. 82.

you this?

As curious as I would be to hear your reports about our mutual friend, and as much as I also want to laugh, nevertheless, I cannot accept your friendly invitation. First of all, dear Madam, you don't have any room, as I have already explained to you, because the particular verse must not apply to us, and second, I have a lengthy conference at 7:30 in the evening, whose end I cannot foresee.

I wanted to tell you all this today, dear Madam; but I and Anton von Padua[7] were alone in the office between the hours of 12-2 and I couldn't get rid of him.

But I have done one thing; I thought about and am now kissing your hand figuratively, dear Madam, and remain respectfully yours,

Dr. Lueger

IN 124.767
Dr. Karl Lueger
Trattnerhof Address

To: Valerie Gréy

Vienna

March 6, 1885

Dear Madam,

Regrettably, regrettably I cannot accept your friendly invitation; for today I have to attend a Municipal Council meeting and cannot, therefore, go to the theater. This morning, I dreamt that I would go to my office after the meeting and have the pleasure of meeting someone there and enjoying a cold supper. Yet dreams are only dreams. Valeria Valera!

Enjoy yourself, dear Madam, and when looking from the edge of your box into the yawning emptiness of the theater, then think to yourself: "So now yawns" But, I'm being altogether too naturalistic; therefore, let's forget this scene! Rather, I take your little hand,

---

[7]Nickname for the office factotum.

<u>unfortunately</u> only in my thoughts, and kiss it, your hand, that is, while I sign respectfully,

Dr. Lueger

IN 124.768
Dr. Karl Lueger
Trattnerhof Address

To: Valerie Gréy

Vienna

March 6, 1885

Dear Madam,

Well, flowers and perfume! Is this supposed to be the effect of love or fear?

Today Stipek appeared in Vienna again, wearing a loden jacket and maintaining that he is very satisfied with his studies. I am curious as to whether the examination commission will say so, too.

Allow me to kiss your hand, dear Madam, and if you want to tell me the word you were expecting, you can tell me today. I will be in the office until two o'clock.

Most respectfully yours,

Dr. Lueger

IN 124.769
Dr. Karl Lueger
Trattnerhof Address

To: Valerie Gréy

Vienna

March 8, 1885

Dear Madam:

With spring in the air, we all long for the out-of-doors. But if bitter destiny keeps us imprisoned, then we endure the sufferings of the caged little bird and its sorrowful song sounds as if it were seeking some sympathetic soul to relieve it from its sufferings.

Thus, I too am imprisoned in my office, and wait for my clients; wait, also, for Valeria. She doesn't come. And so my song sounds rather sadly out into the distance. But listen! There is a knock at the door. Perhaps it is she. O, hurry, hurry. But no, it is the janitor, seeking Anton von Padua in order to bring him the mail from Sandor Stipek, that two pillows which belong to him and which he needs are still supposed to be here.

This prosaic interpretation of human life feels like a cold shower. To the devil with poetry, I think, and sit at my desk in order to finish this letter quickly and to do some work. Tomorrow, Monday, you, dear Madam, may again find me here from 12-2.

Now permit me to kiss your hand and bid farewell. May sweet dreams envelope you and rock you to heavenly peace.

> Respectfully,
>
> Your most devoted,
>
> Dr. Lueger

IN 124.772
Dr. Karl Lueger
Trattnerhof Address

> To: Valerie Gréy
>
> Vienna
>
> March 21, 1885

Dear Madam,

Yesterday was the last election day.[8] Once again I can have human feelings, again be a human among humans. And then it occurs to me that a lady lives at 2 Fuehrichgasse who has a right to be angry with me and that it is my responsibility to appease her. And

---

[8]Lueger is referring here to the supplementary election to the Municipal Council.

so I approach, asking forgiveness, and counting on the good heartedness of the lady and on the plea in the Lord's Prayer: "Forgive us our debts as we forgive our debtors."

Gladly would I hear from the offended, that she has been appeased, and it would make me very happy if I could have the pleasure of seeing you, dear Madam, today, for an hour or so over a cold supper.

I ask, therefore, that you give Anton any cutting or impaling tools which we clumsy humans need if we want to eat. I will consider them a peace offering.

Kissing your hand, dear Madam, I sign with respectful devotion,

Dr. Lueger

IN 124.773
Dr. Karl Lueger
Trattnerhof Address

To: Valerie Gréy

Vienna

March 24, 1885

Dear Madam,

Enclosed is Karny's letter. Since I was not invited to go to Margarethen, I'll stay right at home. After the Municipal Council meeting, I'll go to the office and we can have supper there. At least, I take the liberty of inviting you most cordially, dear Madam, as well as your knives and forks, including napkins.

So the opportunity presents itself once again to kiss your hand, and I remain respectfully,

Your most devoted,

Dr. Lueger

IN 124.771
Dr. Lueger
Trattnerhof Address

To: Valerie Gréy

Vienna

March 31, 1885

Dear Madam,

Yesterday I was so incautious as to write to Frau von Schreckenstein to ask her to inquire about your health, etc., and kindly to report to me about it.

Well, I really got into something. As an answer I received a very rude letter from the old knight, in which he refers to his family as "old and proud," but then, in conclusion, offers me his regards as my companion and drinking chum.

I can do without such company. Well, that's what you get when you write to an old bag, and this sad experience has taught me that it is indeed much smarter to write directly to you, dear Madam. Well, I wouldn't be any worse off.

How are you, dear Madam? Well, I hope; for otherwise you would have come by, because you know that a compassionate heart is waiting for you.

Or, are you perhaps so busy that you don't have any time? I would welcome this only too gladly and also my colleague living in Dornbach would be pleasantly touched by it.

Do you know already that he is here in Vienna today? He looks quite well, is in great spirits, and thinks that he knows something already, which I, after a few questions, doubt.

Now to the actual purpose of this letter. Would you, dear Madam, perhaps have time tonight at 8:00 to give me some instruction over a cold supper? If yes, I ask you to give me the pleasure and supply Anton with the necessary tools. I dare not hope for an answer. By the way, you may bring the knight with you. I am burning with desire to repay his rudeness. Please don't tell him, though, otherwise he might be afraid.

Kissing your hand, dear Madam, I sign with respect and devotion,

Dr. Karl Lueger

IN 124.770
Dr. Karl Lueger
Trattnerhof Address

To: Valerie Gréy

Vienna

March 31, 1885

Dear Madam,

Before all else, I hope that you have returned safely from your trip. Incidentally, it was interesting for me to find out what excursions you are making and the means of transportation you are using.

It goes without saying that I thankfully accept your further offer to arrange a lenten supper. I am just not clear about the day. Is the supper supposed to be held today Wednesday or tomorrow Thursday? Either day would be fine for me, since I will be in the office both days.

With regard to Margarethen, the dice have been cast. The Rubicon has been crossed and the rest is God's will.[9]

While waiting to hear from you, I don't need to add that it is always a pleasure for me to see you, dear Madam, and chat for an evening with you.

So, till we meet again! Kissing your hand, dear Madam, I sign respectfully and devotedly,

Dr. Lueger

---

[9]On the same day, Lueger accepted the nomination for parliamentary candidate from the district of Margareten. This was a hard blow for his opponent Johann Heinrich Steudel, who had represented the district since 1873 in parliament and for over a quarter century in the Municipal Council. See also "The Publicist."

IN 124.774
Dr. Karl Lueger
Trattnerhof Address

To: Valerie Gréy

Vienna

April 4, 1885

Dear Madam,

Tomorrow is Easter Sunday and all of nature is celebrating the spring festival. People look to the future with more joy, and new hope enlivens even those whom fate has heavily burdened with all too many problems.

At such moments, we feel we must tell our fellow men what is on our mind and so I would very much like to have the pleasure to ask you, dear Madam, to have plain supper with me, after the lenten supper, and to chat away a few hours together.

But this is not possible; for Anton is leaving at 4 o'clock in the afternoon, driven to his wife by tender feelings and I am all alone.

Thus, I must wish you happy holidays in writing, dear Madam. May the clouds scatter and the sun of happiness finally shine for you.

Kissing your hand, dear Madam, I remain your respectfully devoted,

Dr. Lueger

IN 124.775
Dr. Karl Lueger
Trattnerhof Address

To: Valerie Gréy

Vienna

April 11, 1885

Dear Madam,

It is now a week since we have seen one another. From this, I gather that you have a lot to do, and if this is the case, I should be very glad.

In the meantime, there have been some changes. Anton was dismissed; everything is closed and the lovely evenings will return only if Stipek were allowed to live here in Vienna.

Perhaps you may have time to visit me now, dear Madam, and to chat a half an hour. Or, if this isn't possible, at least give me the opportunity to decipher the hieroglyphics of your hand-writing.

Kissing your hand, I sign most respectfully, your most devoted,

Dr. Lueger

IN 124.776
Dr. Karl Lueger
Trattnerhof Address

To: Valerie Gréy

Vienna

April 14, 1885

Dear Madam,

You must be very fed up with your business these days; for new ideas are crossing your mind. Your thoughts wander all over the place, on, above and below ground, and so you obviously thought of the town hall basement. I don't know what you are planning, but even so, I advise you to forget about it. The basement in question, I'm sure, will only become available through bidding. No other way is possible.

Now to something else. I am sure you will be very pleased again about the governor,[10] because he deals so categorically with the theater directors when it comes to going on tours. Perhaps, just perhaps, you will yet become a director. You may certainly believe that I wish that with all my heart.

Because of a serious tooth-ache and other

---

[10]Ludwig Freiherr Possinger von Choborski. Lueger was being facetious here.

unpleasant things, I am in a bad mood, and while the spring sun has an invigorating effect on nature, and while the beautiful gift on the table from my Valerie smells sweetly, I have autumnal feelings and, shivering, I force myself to think about unpleasant and cheerful memories.

And yet, this will soon pass and then I will use the first evening to keep a promise, if you, dear Madam, permit.

On this occasion, I have a request: On the 20th of this month, the benefit concert for the Christmas Tree Association, "The Bees," is supposed to take place. I don't know what speeches are going to be made, but I have one wish, that absolutely no allusions to politics are made, and particularly not to the parliamentary election. You will comply with my request, won't you?

Thanking you, dear Madam, for the violets, I kiss your hand and remain most respectfully,

Your most devoted,

Dr. Lueger

IN 124.777
Dr. Karl Lueger
Trattnerhof Address

To: Valerie Gréy

Vienna

April 17, 1885

Dear Madam,

St. . . .isn't coming; everything is therefore in vain. You will have to go to him in Dornbach and do it soon.

What is it now that distresses you again? What did you find out about Reli? Don't believe everything you are told.

Kissing your hand, I remain most respectfully,

Dr. Lueger

IN 124.778
Dr. Karl Lueger
Trattnerhof Address

To: Valerie Gréy

Vienna

April 17, 1885

Dear Madam,

Considerably better, but not well. That is how
I feel. On the other hand, you seem to be well,
which pleases me greatly. Good fresh air has many an
advantage. In particular, it is cheap and makes one
cheerful and healthy.

Our friend is not yet here. When he arrives and
I see him, I will comply with your request, even
though I feel it would be more practical if you came
to the office. He will know what's up, anyway, when
I tell him that he is supposed to visit you. He knows
enough that he will not receive any money. He won't
get a declaration of love either! He doesn't need
ladies' hats. He has umbrellas and perfumes already.
What is left is that he will have to sweat the thing
he loves the most: money. I am now of the opinion,
that the operation you have in mind must be performed
in such a way, that there is no other way out, and I
therefore repeat: the office is the best place.

Enclosed are 15 Gulden. You can keep whatever is
left over. You've really put me on the spot with the
perfume which you so lavishly spilled on my overcoat.
As I went home I met several friends and everyone
asked me about the surprising aroma. At home, as
well, there was a great deal of curiosity, and finally
the overcoat was banned to a vacant room to air out
overnight. This morning all windows were opened.

Well, adieu. Keep on dreaming and think about
your devoted servant who always kisses your hand in
writing only, and herewith signs most respectfully,

Dr. Lueger

IN 124.779
Dr. Karl Lueger
Trattnerhof Address

To: Valerie Gréy

Vienna

April 26, 1885

Dear Madam,

Had I known that really just one glance at the magistrate's order would have <u>sufficed</u>, I would have done it, though I hardly had any time. Therefore, please excuse me, in case I have unwittingly offended you.

With regard to the position taken by the "Allgemeine Zeitung," the reasons are unknown to me and I can only surmise that gossip caused this.[11] If you, dear Madam, would really be so kind as to talk to Hertzka, I would welcome this. It can't hurt. I only ask you to be careful of one thing: that you, dear Madam, not reveal with a syllable, not even with the slightest expression, that I have any idea of your action. If you, dear Madam, think you can do this, and further, if you are enough of a diplomat even to be able to listen calmly to the most unbelievable stories, then, dear Madam, I should be very obliged and most indebted to you if you undertook the proffered mission.

You think that I should spend 8-10 days in the country before the election. This would be nice, but impossible. I <u>must</u> hold out for these few weeks, even if the burdens placed on me sometimes get too heavy.

And yet, all of this is nothing compared to what you have to carry, dear Madam; I understand the tone

---

[11]Lueger was probably referring to the following comment in the "Wiener Allgemeine Zeitung": "The Democratic Party is . . .split; the fifth, eighth, and ninth districts have spoken out decisively against the involvement of the Democrats with guildsmen and anti-Semites and protest the misuse of democracy perpetrated by Dr. Lueger and Dr. Mandl." <u>Wiener Allgemeine Zeitung</u>, April 26, 1885, p. 2.

of your letter and admire your heroism. Perhaps a ray
of hope will break through the dark clouds earlier
than one supposes. How happy I would be if the train
of worries, which so often depresses you, would
disappear.

And now, farewell! Tomorrow evening at 8 when
you are finished with your day's work, think that
mine has only begun, since I must give my first
candidate's speech to the Margarethen Voters' Association.

> Kissing your hand, dear
> Madam, I remain in most
> respectful devotion,
> Dr. Lueger

IN 124.782
Dr. Karl Lueger
Trattnerhof Address

To: Valerie Gréy

Vienna

June 6, 1885

Dear Madam,

Your kind words proved to me that I did a very
foolish thing when I let you read the anonymous letter. If I were to heed your urgent plea and allow you
to borrow the above-mentioned letter, I would be making a mistake even greater than the first.

Why do you cry, dear Madam? Does this change
anything? No. Do you perhaps think that my
judgment, my viewpoint will be influenced? Surely
you don't believe this. So, kindly let the world
write and say what it will. You and I can't change
their opinions and we must bear this like an inevitable fate.

Console yourself, dear Madam! We are not the
first and won't be the last to whom things of that
kind happen.

When I eat the strawberries, with each one I
shall think about the donor; I even dare, dear Madam,
to kiss your hand and tell you that I am always glad
to see you.

Respectfully,
Your most devoted,

Dr. Lueger

IN 124.783
Dr. Karl Lueger
Trattnerhof Address

To: Valerie Gréy

Vienna

June 17, 1885

Dear Madam,

　　Today is the day that I had dedicated to you.
Now I receive an invitation from a Municipal Council-
or for today. Dare I ask you, dear Madam, to excuse
me, today? If yes, then I will make this up to you
next Wednesday. If not, I'll come today.

　　Kissing your hand, I sign your respectfully
devoted,

Dr. Lueger

P.S. Please say yes

IN 124.784
Dr. Karl Lueger
Trattnerhof Address

To: Valerie Gréy

Vienna

June 19, 1885

Dear Madam,

　　I was truly delighted that you were kind enough
to do me that favor and postpone our meeting for eight
days. For that, my warmest thanks and the promise,
all the more certain, to appear in Dornbach on
Wednesday in order to admire you in your new home.

Now a few words about that as well as the expedition. I have tentatively decided to leave the office on Wednesday at 6 in the evening, to take a tram at the Schottenring and by this route to arrive at my destination. Considering your business, can this plan be carried out?

How are you otherwise, dear Madam? I haven't seen you for some time and this explains the trivial question. I would sincerely be delighted if I didn't have to ask such a question, if for once my Valerie would find the peaceful haven where she could securely dock her life's ship, if she would finally find the reward for her unselfish friendship her good heart deserves instead of troubles. As sunshine follows rain, as quiet follows the storm, so will clear skies appear over my friend and the sun of happiness shine on her, and hopefully, in the not too distant future.

And now, farewell, dear Madam! Allow me to kiss your hand and remain most respectfully yours,

as your devoted,

Dr. Lueger

IN 124.785
Dr. Karl Lueger
Trattnerhof Address

To: Valerie Gréy

Vienna

July 18, 1885

Dear Madam,

You are right when you think that I am very busy, and you will therefore forgive me if I make use of only one stamp and save the second for better times.

After this introduction, I express my dutiful thanks for the present. Nowadays, every penny counts. I further thank you for your cordial interest in my health. I'm doing better, but to say that I am healthy would be self-deception. Mine is a life of continuous tumult and the consequences are gradual.

As you know, your daughter's appeal for a stay of execution has been denied. I have now read the report of the clerk on which the denial was based and can only say that you can thank God that the case was not transferred to the state's attorney. One doesn't want to wind up behind lock and key.

My visit to Dornbach will take place next week, provided you agree. By that time, I hope I will be in a better mood and can look at the matter more cheerfully.

E and D. Who is supposed to figure that out? One can't very well read through the register of nobility. Therefore, don't abbreviate, dear Madam, and remember that your lines are difficult enough to decipher without abbreviating.

Farewell, and allow your hand to be kissed by the respectfully devoted,

Dr. Lueger

IN 124.780

To: Valerie Gréy

Vienna

August 22, 1896

Dear Madam,

In reply to your letter of the eighth of the month, permit me to inform you that you can speak to me Wednesday of next week at 9 or 9:15 a.m. in the town hall.

Respectfully yours,

Dr. Lueger

(This letter, evidently the last to Valerie Gréy, was not written by Lueger; only the signature is his.)

Photocopy taken from Marianne Beskiba, Aus meinen Erinnerungen an Dr. Karl Lueger, published by the author, Vienna, 1911, p. 121, hereafter referred to as <u>Erinnerungen</u>

Seal of the Mayor of Vienna

To: Marianne Beskiba

October 7, 1900

Dear Miss,

My most heartfelt thanks for the small, but lovely picture.

You think that I am angry at you. That never entered my mind. But you will be angry, that I have taken so long to respond. But I have little time, and this is my excuse.

I hope, dear Miss, you are quite well in Hungary and then return strengthened and cheerful to your native land.

To a happy reunion! Best greetings and kissing your hand or your _____,

Your most devoted,

Dr. <u>Karl Lueger</u>

IN 66017

To: Marianne Beskiba

Slandered by the Viennese Christian Women's League because of her relationship with Lueger, Beskiba turned to the mayor for help and received this response:

Seal of the Mayor of Vienna   August 5, 1903

Mayor
Dr. Karl Lueger

Thanks most cordially for the letter and the picture postcards. Concerning the requested advice: just ignore the whole matter. A reasonable woman does not concern herself with gossipy women.

One lets such talk in one ear and out the other.

To a speedy reunion!

(without signature)

Photocopy from
Erinnerungen, p. 125

Seal of the Mayor of Vienna

To: Marianne Beskiba

December 27, 1904

Dear Miss,

I worked 3, literally three, days on the last letter I sent to you; interrupted again and again, I was glad to finish in time, in hopes that you would receive these lines on Christmas Eve. I don't know yet whether this was so.

How did you spend the holidays? Did you have an appropriate appetite? Are your nerves doing well?

Well, I shall soon find out. In a few days New Year's will be here and after a little while Epiphany, and then Miss Marianne will come to Vienna in order to continue work on the picture of the study. There I shall see her and immediately notice how Acsad[*] affected her. I survived the holidays quite well, and with a few lean days now, I plan to have every-thing back on the right track.

And now, farewell! Happy New Year! Joyful reunion!

Kissing your hand,

Your most devoted,

Dr. Lueger

---

[*]A village in Hungary.

Photocopy from <u>Erinnerungen</u>, p. 124
To: Marianne Beskiba

December 28, 1904

Mayor
Dr. Karl Lueger

thanks most sincerely for the portrait that he
will guard well and requests that on Epiphany, the
"room painting" will kindly be continued. No-one
will interrupt; not until 9 o'clock will a certain
Dr. Lueger arrive.

Happy New Year!

Dr. <u>Karl Lueger</u>

Photocopy from
<u>Erinnerungen</u>, p. 140

Seal of the Mayor of Vienna

To: Marianne Beskiba

(No date)

Dearest Miss,

You have given me really great joy with your
Christmas gift. Heartfelt thanks in my sisters'
name. How I can ever repay you, I don't know. Should
it ever be possible, then it will be done.

I hope you have had enjoyable holidays and will
successfully make the transition into the New Year.
In any event, I wish you a Happy New Year and greet
you most warmly and respectfully,

Dr. Lueger

IN 66018
Seal of the Mayor of Vienna

To: Miss Marianne Beskiba

                                    October 1, 1905

Dear Miss,

    I am doing considerably better. Please, I beg
you not to feel guilty. The sickness originated in
the stomach. I would be very glad to see you, dear
Miss, on Wednesday morning, at which time I hope to be
well and cheerful.

    I haven't written this much in a long time; you
can just imagine how delighted I am to comply with
your wish.

        Kissing your hand, dear Miss, and remaining,

                            Your esteemed,

                            (No signature)

IN 67559
                            To: Marianne Beskiba

                            (No date)

My dear, sweet darling,

    Writing has become difficult for me. My hand
shakes badly. When letter number two arrived, I
wanted to wait for the first analysis[12] before I
answered. It arrived very late and I couldn't write
any more. I had unbelievable diarrhea on Sunday and
Monday. Twice I drank - camomile tea. Then the third
letter arrived. My conscience didn't let me rest and
so I am writing with shaking hand. The second letter
moved me deeply. May you enjoy as much happiness in
the future as you have experienced unhappiness. The
grief because of Niese was absolutely unnecessary.

    Since when do you study the Odyssey? There
aren't any sirens or Circe here; there are only old
women and I can say with Napoleon: Millenia look down
on me.

    The analysis is good. The sugar has sunk to
1.45%. I think it will soon disappear. Walking goes

---

[12]Lueger suffered from worsening diabetes.

better as well, therefore, hope. Gastein is supposed to do what garlic can't.[13]

I look forward very much to seeing you again and if nothing else, we'll enjoy a few kisses. Your nerves will benefit from Gastein, and God willing, we will both return home fairly healthy and well.

Farewell, my adorable, sweet darling! May thousands and thousands of kisses cover your body and close your mouth. Always think lovingly and without jealousy of

> Your
>
> edes Krampussi

IN 67557

> To: Marianne Beskiba
>
> (No date)

My little angel,

The room is reserved for you from the 11th of the month. Beginning with the 7th you will send your luggage to:

> Franz Josef Mayer
> Director in Gastein
> Hotel Straubinger

who will receive it and carefully safeguard it. At noon on the 11th you will leave Vienna and arrive in Gastein at 9:33 in the evening, where we will await you at the train station and ceremoniously welcome you. So, are you satisfied now?

We already leave Karlsbad on the 7th of this month. Sunday is the last day on which letters can be mailed to here. The sugar has sunk to 0.2% and the albumin is almost gone as well. Therefore, chemically speaking, I am well; nevertheless my nerves torture me. Perhaps Gastein will cure this.

---

[13]Garlic is supposed to lower blood pressure.

Last night I had a rather unchaste dream about you. That's because of my exemplary life. You actually received those kisses I write to you about and you were so good, so wonderfully soft that I can only hope it will be like that in Gastein, too.

And so, to a happy <u>healthy</u> reunion! I'm so looking forward to seeing you after such a long separation.

My dear sweet darling! Quickly your little mouth which I kiss as long as possible. Farewell!

Your

édés Krampussi

IN 67540
Last letter <u>from Karlsbad</u>
this year

To: Marianne Beskiba

August 6, 1906

My dearest darling,

Tomorrow on to Gastein and only a few days separate us from our reunion. I look forward to this like a little child and even if we do not kiss each other, at least our eyes will speak. I hope you'll be healthy and well, and that will double the pleasure. No doubt we'll have time for kissing, perhaps for something else as well. For my part, I don't doubt it.

My dearest, sweetest darling! I have to go to the springs now - it is 7 a.m. - and must therefore close. When you read this letter, I will already be on my way and will think of you with sweet memories and anticipation. Kisses cover your face, your breasts, your entire sweet body.

Farewell, my little angel! To a happy reunion!

Your

édés Krampussi

THE APPRENTICE: LUEGER, CAJETAN VON FELDER,

AND IGNAZ MANDL

99

THE APPRENTICE: LUEGER, CAJETAN VON FELDER, AND IGNAZ MANDL

Lueger's interest in politics was evident in his student years. From the beginning, he seems to have been attracted to political figures. As his fellow student Hermann Mauthner once remarked, "The efforts of (liberal) Mayor (Andreas) Zelinka elicited admiration and inspired him."[1] Zelinka's achievements may well have inspired Lueger as Mauthner relates, but Lueger's first real experience of politics came through Dr. Cajetan von Felder, Zelinka's successor.

Felder was certainly a stimulating model for any young man. Orphaned at age twelve, his extraordinary talents and protean personality enabled him to overcome his family losses. He matured into an energetic and clever administrator, who earned for himself the appellation the "polyglot mayor," from his ability at the 1873 World's Fair in Vienna to converse with almost all the foreign guests of honor in their native tongues.[2] Such a feat foreshadowed the important role language came to play in Viennese politics and anticipated Lueger's own use of its power. He was also an enthusiastic student of Greece and Rome, possessed a "lively interest in the natural sciences (especially in entomology)," was a full member of the Academy of Science, and, like Lueger after him, commanded an autocratic personality and the resolve necessary to execute controversial projects in spite of opposition from all sides.[3] Again, like Lueger, Felder traveled extensively; few, if any, Viennese ever covered as much territory. By his own account, he toured three continents, besides Europe, and "took approximately thirty major ocean cruises."[4] Against this background, Felder understood the varied problems facing the Habsburg capital, much better than had his predecessors, and he sought actively to solve them:

> Under Mayor Cajetan Felder, almost all the
> major building projects of the municipality
> of Vienna which were started in conjunction
> with the expansion of the city entered their
> final phase; and most of them were finished
> during his ten-year tenure. Among them
> belong both those two projects which were
> initiated by his predecessors: the
> construction of the (first) mountain reservoir
> system and the regulation of the Danube.[5]

This energetic tradition of public projects was also something Lueger continued.

Although politically Felder attempted to bridge the gap between "the old feudal social order" and a more democratic approach towards solving Vienna's problems, still another line of development Lueger would later follow, he never fully succeeded in creating a democratic regime. Felder was an instinctive elitist and at least indifferent if not insensitive to the growing but potentially dangerous discontent that more democratic policies might have alleviated.[6] Here again, Lueger would later capitalize on this same dissatisfaction and direct it to his own advantage.

A collision between the two men seemed inevitable. Felder's authoritarian administrative style and Lueger's insatiable ambitions, as well as his increasing antagonism toward his liberal patrons, eventually precluded any broad cooperation between them. They were, perhaps, in some ways too much alike, particularly in their active improvement of the city and their autocratic personalities. Thus, when Lueger joined forces with Ignaz Mandl, who sought to depose Felder, the lines were drawn and cooperation permanently out of the question.

Mandl came from a wealthy Hungarian-Jewish family. He graduated in 1859 from the University of Vienna Medical School, but instead of practicing medicine turned to politics. In 1874, a year before Lueger, Mandl was elected to the Viennese Municipal Council. Following a course of obstructionist politics and contrived disclosures of ostensibly serious irregularities in the operation of the Municipal Council, Lueger and Mandl soon earned Felder's firm enmity. Nonetheless, their effort to unseat him finally succeeded.

Felder's autobiography records his reaction to this brand of politics. He had only contempt for the egalitarianism introduced into community life by Mandl, the "corruption monomaniac," and Lueger, "the corrupter, Goethe's liar":

With the Doctors Mandl and Lueger all of a sudden the incarnation of the evil principle appeared on the stage of the Municipal Council... Both have... immeasurably damaged the admin-

istration of Vienna. They have driven away...
most of the intelligensia from the council...
chambers and have so disorganized the administration by infiltrating a miserable
espionage and informer system, that the
entire community will suffer long after these
evil spirits have been banished.[7]

Felder's prediction contained an element of truth he
did not anticipate, insofar as it may be applied to
Lueger's legacy of mass politics.

But, initially, Lueger's and Mandl's intrigues
were unsuccessful. Felder was an experienced tacti-
cian and a man not easily dislodged. He countered
and forced Lueger to relinquish his mandate in
October 1876,[8] whereupon Lueger withdrew from politics for the next few months. Mandl, on the other
hand, continued to pursue his obstructionist tactics
with undiminished vigor. Soon, however, Lueger and
Mandl had joined forces once again and once more set
about agitating against the hegemony of the liberals,
all the while gaining in experience and mastering
more of the art of manipulating urban populations.
In March 1878, Lueger was again re-elected to the
Municipal Council. During the next three months, he
and Mandl intensified their pressure on Felder until,
sick and discouraged, the mayor finally capitulated
and relinquished his office on June 28th.

In this ousting of Felder, Lueger seemed at first
to embrace many of Mandl's ideas, on such issues as
the administration of community property, transportation, and public institutions. The younger politician, however, gradually outstripped the older. Their
collegiality and friendship could not weather all the
political turbulence. Disagreements swelled into
arguments and hardened into charges of betrayal and
recrimination, so that, reconciliations aside, the
final break came in February 1889, when such anti-
Semites as Karl von Zerboni and Cornelius Vetter
demanded Mandl's expulsion from Karl von Vogelsang's
United Christians, where there could be no room for a
Jew. This turn of events led Mandl to align himself
with the liberals and placed Lueger in an awkward
situation. He was compelled to choose between his
friend and associate and his own career.

Until the last, however, Lueger sought to avoid
this rupture with his former mentor and friend, either

for reasons of loyalty or expediency.[9] But when Lueger was confronted with "proof" of Mandl's "treason," during an anti-Semitic political assembly on February 18, which took the form of an invitation to speak as a candidate at a liberal meeting, he had to decide: either cultivate the support of anti-Semites or maintain his friendship with Mandl. He decided against Mandl. Mandl's bid for re-election to the Municipal Council in March was unsuccessful, and he also lost two years later as a liberal candidate for parliament. He then withdrew from politics. In reporting Mandl's death in 1907, the Neue Freie Presse stated that Lueger's rise would have been... impossible without Mandl and observed further a "bitter irony in the fact that the same people who harvested the fruits of Mandl's life-work condemned him and hurled him from the Tarpeian cliff of popularity."[10] The student had, indeed, left his master behind.

The two motions of urgency here presented were introduced by Lueger and discussed in the Municipal Council on September 5, 1876. The author of the article "Bubenstreich" ("Childish Pranks"), which appeared the following day in the Illustriertes Wiener Extrablatt, used these motions as a pretext to attack "the immoderate Mandl" and especially his "famous rowdy" Lueger "People... shunned like lepers." Of the thirteen paragraphs, only one was devoted to Felder's "strong and merciless," but justified response, whereas in the rest Lueger and his ilk were accused of "disgusting publicity stunts," and "childish insolence".

This was one of the first virulent liberal articles against Lueger. (See "The Politician and the Press.") He immediately responded to this publication with a legal complaint against the Extrablatt. At the very same time he also drafted a retraction whose publication he demanded. Lueger's reaction was typical, and marked the beginning of his protracted struggle with the liberal press.

FOOTNOTES FOR
THE APPRENTICE: LUEGER, CAJETAN VON FELDER,
AND IGNAZ MANDL

1. Kuppe, 18.

2. Felix Czeike, "Die Reisen des Wiener
    Buergermeisters Dr. Cajetan Felder," Jahrbuch
    des Vereines fuer Geschichte der Stadt Wien, 23-
    25, (1967/1969), p. 352. See also, by the same
    author, "Buergermeister Cajetan Felder und seine
    Zeit," Sonderdruck from Oesterreich in
    Geschichte und Literatur, and Irene Neuwirth,
    "Doktor Cajetan Felder Buergermeister von Wien,"
    Ph.D. dissertation, University of Vienna, 1942.

3. Both met with Kaiser Franz Joseph's opposition:
    Felder's plans to erect the new town hall on the
    area of the Josephstaedter glacis were at first
    rejected, and endorsement of Lueger's election
    to mayor was refused three times.

4. Czeike, "Reisen," p. 408.

5. Felix Czeike, Wien und seine Buergermeister.
    Sieben Jahrhunderte Wiener Stadtgeschichte.
    Vienna and Munich, 1974, p. 317. Lueger
    initiated construction of the second reservoir
    system, which was completed in December, 1910,
    nine months after his death.

6. Ibid., p. 316.

7. Cajetan Felder, Erinnerungen eines Wiener
    Buergermeisters. Vienna, Hannover, and Bern,
    1964, pp. 250, 216.

8. The events leading to Lueger's resignation are
    described in Kuppe, pp. 38-40.

9. Compare letters of January 21, 1889, and
    February 9, 1889, to Gessmann and Vogelsang,
    respectively, in "The Party Pragmatist," and
    Kuppe, p. 191.

10. "Dr. Ignaz Mandl," in Neue Freie Presse, May 5,
    1907, p. 11.

Draft

Nachlass Karl Lueger
St. Slg. Zl. 1257/12
Box V
Mappe: Gemeinde Propria

WHEREAS, the mayor permitted expressions such as,
"vile slander," "lies," "to censure" and the
like in violation of Article 33 of the Rules
of Procedure when they are used by his supporters against opposing members of the
Municipal Council;

WHEREAS, the mayor ruled members of the opposition
out of order for expressions such as "contrary to procedural rules," "compromise,"
and similar phrases;

WHEREAS, such interpretation of Article 33 of the
Rules of Procedure restricts freedom of
speech and members of the Municipal Council
are defenseless against such insults:

WHEREAS, the mayor often participated in debate without relinquishing the chair to a deputy;

NOW THEREFORE, we urgently move,
That the esteemed Municipal Council resolves
to request the Mayor of the City of Vienna,
Dr. Cajetan Felder, henceforth impartially
to administer his office as Chairman of the
Municipal Council meetings.

Draft

Nachlass Karl Lueger
St. Slg. Zl. 1257/12
Box V
Mappe: Gemeinde Propria

WHEREAS, according to the regulations of the provisional municipal constitution (of 1850) for
the City of Vienna, the Municipal Council of
the City of Vienna is responsible for the
strict supervision of magisterial management
and hence also for the activity of the incumbent mayor as the chairman of the magistrate;

WHEREAS, the position of a responsible chief of the
executive is irreconcilable with that of a
chairman of such corporation to which he is
responsible;

WHEREAS, when one person occupies both positions, he
can easily be induced to abuse the powers of
the office and suppress any and all criticism
of either of his official capacities and
any justified opposition;

NOW, THEREFORE, I move:

   That the Municipal Council of the City of
   Vienna declare the position of mayor as
   chairman of the magistrate irreconcilable
   with the position of Chairman of the
   Municipal Council and that it direct the
   Statute-Revision Committee to draft the
   necessary changes to the provisional municipal constitution of the City of Vienna to
   remove this drawback and to report on such
   to the Municipal Council.

Draft of a Letter   Nachlass Karl Lueger
                                 St. Slg. Zl. 1257/12
                                 Box V
                                 Mappe: Klage gegen das
                                 Extrablatt

Dr. Lueger
Extrablatt
k k. Landesgericht
for Criminal Matters
Vienna

Dr. Karl Lueger

Attorney to the Royal and Legal Courts in Vienna
petitions commencement of preliminary investigation of
Mr. Hermann Fuerst, editor-in-chief of the periodical
Illustriertes Wiener Extrablatt, domiciled at VII
Neubaugasse 31 and Mr. F. I. Singer, owner and
publisher of said periodical, domiciled at IX,
Berggasse 23, on grounds of slander in violation of
Articles 488 and 491 of the general criminal law and
aggravated slander according to Article 496 of the
general criminal law.

Most Esteemed K. K. Landesgericht,

A. In the morning edition A of the periodical pub-
    lished in Vienna under the title, "Illustriertes
    Wiener Extrablatt" which appeared on Wednesday,
    September 6, 1876, no. 246, fifth year, a slan-
    derous article entitled "Childish Pranks" appeared
    on page two which gives evidence of slander
    according to 496 of the General Criminal Law.
    Since the article is anonymous, I have no
    recourse but to proceed legally, according to
    Articles 239 and 7 of the General Criminal Code,
    against the editor-in-chief of said periodical,

107

known as Mr. Hermann Fuerst, and the publisher of same, Mr. F. I. Singer.

I herewith bring charge as private plaintiff against said persons, Mr. Hermann Fuerst and Mr. F. I. Singer, for having violated Articles 488 and 491 of the General Criminal Code (slander) and Article 496 of the General Criminal Code (aggravated slander) by publication of the article "Childish Pranks" in no. 246, 5th year of the periodical "Illustriertes Wiener Extrablatt," more specifically by its title "Childish Pranks" and its first, third, fourth, fifth, sixth, seventh, eleventh, twelfth and thirteenth paragraphs and by its dissemination.

As the said paragraphs of the incriminating article give proof of the punishable offenses, no further explanation is necessary and it will suffice to refer to their contents. Aside from the abusive language directed against me, the most dishonorable and immoral actions are being attributed to me, and I am suspected of the basest and dirtiest motives.

However, since I do not know whether and in what capacity slander and aggravated slander can be attributed to Hermann Fuerst and F. I. Singer, I propose the introduction of a preliminary investigation against Mr. Hermann Fuerst, editor-in-chief of the periodical, "Illustriertes Wiener Extrablatt," domiciled at Vienna VII, Neubaugasse 31, and Mr. F. I. Singer owner and publisher of said periodical, Municipal Councilor of the City of Vienna, domiciled at Vienna IX, Berggasse 23, because of the premeditated offenses.

I therefore request:
that the most esteemed k. k Landesgericht deign to grant my request and interrogate Mr. Hermann Fuerst and F. I. Singer as to the identity of the author of the incriminating article, whether they ordered or recommended the publication of the article, whether they were cognizant of the article before or during submission to press, and ultimately, whether they accept responsibility for its contents.

Draft of the retraction Lueger   Nachlass Karl Lueger
demanded of Fuerst and Singer   St. Slg. Zl. 1257/12
                                  Box V
                                  Mappe: Klage gegen
                                  das Extrablatt

Declaration

    We published an article entitled "Childish
Pranks" in no. 246 of our paper, dated September 6,
1876 in which a motion by the then Municipal Council-
or Dr. Karl Lueger was polemicized.

    Since the title, as well as the content of the
article regrettably infringed on the personal integrity
and honorable motives of Dr. Lueger, we consider it
our duty to retract unconditionally all the slanderous
insults and attacks against Dr. Karl Lueger contained
in the above mentioned article.

Draft   Nachlass Karl Lueger
                                  St. Slg. Zl. 1257/12
                                  Box V
                                  Mappe: Klage gegen das
                                  Extrablatt

KK.
Landesgericht
for Criminal Matters
Vienna
Dr. Karl Lueger
Attorney to the Royal and Legal Courts in Vienna
      v.

Mr. Hermann Fuerst
Editor-in-Chief of the periodical "Illustriertes
Wiener Extrablatt" and Mr. F. I. Singer, Owner and
Publisher of this periodical

                Requests the continuation on
                account of infringement
                of honor.

Most esteemed k. k. Landesgericht,

    In your letter of Nov. 6/7, 1876, no. Z40602, I
was informed that the preliminary investigation
against Hermann Fuerst and F. I. Singer for infringe-
ment was closed.

From the records of the proceedings I learned to my astonishment that according to Mr. Franz Ignaz Singer, he did not write the incriminating article, nor participate in its composition, and that Mr. Hermann Fuerst as well as F. I. Singer refused any explanation as to the identity of the author.

I proceeded on the assumption that he who has the courage to direct such insults against a person as were contained in the incriminating article also would have the courage to answer openly for them and not hide behind the editor-in-chief.

This has not happened and I am therefore compelled to request a continuation of the investigation, in order to determine whether F. I. Singer can be held responsible, within the purview of the criminal law, for the incriminating article on the basis of the evidence presented.

I call particular attention to the fact that F. I. Singer is a Viennese Municipal Councilor. (before: in this capacity he belonged for a year and a half or so to the club of the Middle Party and was considered an intimate of the present Mayor of the City of Vienna Dr. Cajetan Felder.) Thus it is understandable that Mr. F. I. Singer exercises the determining influence on the position taken in municipal affairs by his publication "Illustriertes Wiener Extrablatt," and it is downright improbable that an article in said journal dealing with an affair of the community of Vienna could appear without Mr. F. I. Singer's knowing about it, indeed without his express authorization.

During the Municipal Council session on September 5, 1876 the journalists covering the Municipal Council, as well as individual municipal officials who usually served as press liaisons, demonstrated great activity if this conclusion can be drawn from their scurrying around and the constant announcements transmitted to the reporters seated on the journalists' bench. Mr. F. I. Singer also participated in this activity and spoke with one of the men seated on the journalists' bench, probably the reporter of the "Illustriertes Wiener Extrablatt," and it may be concluded from his behavior that he gave this man instructions. (before: in the forenoon of September 6, 1876 Section I of the Municipal Council held a meeting. When I appeared, the meeting had not yet been convened and I went into the reading room where besides a few other Municipal Councilors, Mr. F. I. Singer was present, but he left the room soon after my arrival. The rest of the men stayed, but looked sheepish, as if they had just been caught doing something wrong. At the time I still did not know anything about the incriminating article, and the scene which at the same time appeared strange to me, first became clear when someone later pointed out the article in the "Extrablatt." I am not in the habit of reading this paper because of its tone, in particular because of its content. I therefore suggest:)

I now petition

To subpoena as witnesses Dr. Heinrich Penn, Editor of the "Extrablatt," III, Ungargasse 33, and Mr. Moritz Epstein, journalist, II, Hermin(en)gasse 7, to testify about the influence of Mr. F. I. Singer on the position of the "Illustriertes Wiener Extrablatt" in matters concerning Viennese municipal activities, and in particular on such related articles in said journal, further, to determine whether Mr. F. I. Singer gave instructions to the author of the incriminating article and approved same, and further to report on the events described above during the Municipal Council meeting of September 5, 1876. (before:
2.) Mr. Jacob Flucher, city architect and Municipal Councilor, IV, Theresianumgasse 8, Dr. Ignaz Mandl, Municipal Councilor, IV, Heugasse 58, about the events of September 5, 1876 during the Municipal Council session, particularly about the behavior of Mr. F. I. Singer.
3.) Mr. Karl Weiss, Archive Director, I, Wipplingerstrasse 8, about his contact on September 5, 1876 with reporters and particularly with F. I. Singer, and to what extent this contact concerned the proceedings of the Municipal Council meeting held on the same day, subsequently described in the issue of the "Illustriertes Wiener Extrablatt" which appeared on September 6, 1876.)

I therefore request

that the most esteemed kk Landesgericht deign to approve the continuation of the investigation which I have proposed.

The following two documents, probably written in the autumn of 1877, when Lueger was in the political wilderness, reveal the tactics he and Mandl used to maintain pressure on Felder. These documents also show that Lueger early grasped the potential advantage of playing off the Lower Austrian governorship against the Municipal Council and the mayor to weaken the collective municipal authority, a ploy he would reverse in 1882, when his aspirations for the mayoralty began to ripen. Lueger would brook no rivals to his own authority as mayor; twenty years before his accession, he began the policy of divide and rule.

Draft

Nachlass Karl Lueger
St. Slg. Zl. 1257/12
Box V
Mappe: Gemeinde Propria

Esteemed KK. Lower Austrian Governorship
Community Propria
Complaint of:
Anton Heller, Carpenter and House Owner, III,
Fasangasse 55
Heinrich Hess, Citizen and Merchant, III,
Hauptstrasse 9
Franz Hintermayer, Citizen, Merchant and Houseowner,
III, Kugelgasse 6
Wenzl Hruschka, Citizen, Painter and House Owner, III,
Fasangasse 6
Wilhelm Kruegermaier, Citizen and Watchmaker, III,
Loewengasse 13
A. Melzinschek, Secondhand Dealer and House Owner,
III, Leonhardgasse 19
Theodor Neuhaueser, Linen Manufacturer, III Rennweg 80
Benedict Puchwein, Citizen and Innkeeper, III,
Hauptstrasse 126
Moritz Riby, Citizen and House Owner, III,
Rasumofskygasse 2

    With regard to the decision reached by the
Municipal Council of the City of Vienna on September 5,
1876 and sent to and directed against the last named.
Esteemed KK Governorship,
    With letter A dated July 26, 1876 Municipal
Council Number 3231, we were summoned by the Mayor of
the City of Vienna, Dr. Cajetan Felder for the election of the district leader in the third municipal
district on Wednesday, August 9, 1876, 10:00 a.m.

On this day, we the nine undersigned members of the District Committee, Landstrasse, appeared for the election, while five members sent a letter to the election chairman, Municipal Councilor Franz Ritter von Khunn, declaring that they did not want to participate in the election. As a consequence, the election chairman refused to hold the election, referring to instructions he had received according to which the election of the leader would be held if twelve committee members were present.

We protested this illegal action.

The Municipal Council granted this petition according to the decision reached at its plenary session on September 5, 1876 because article 41 of the provisional municipal constitution for the City of Vienna, which deals with the election of the mayor, cannot at all be applied to the election of the district leader.

Strangely enough, the Municipal Council of the City of Vienna resolved at the same meeting that in order for the election of the district leader to be valid he had to receive 10 votes; i.e., the Municipal Council, immediately after it had declared the application of said article 41 to the election of the district leader illegal, applied the conclusion of paragraph 3 of said article and accepted this regulation as authoritative for the validity of the election of the district leader.

This resolution of the Municipal Council of the City of Vienna, of which we were informed by letter of September 6, 1876, Municipal Council no. 3678 from the Deputy Mayor of the City of Vienna, Mr. Eduard Uhl, was bound to astonish us all the more, since the Municipal Council must have known that District Committee member Chladek has been dead for half a year, Messrs. Matthaeus Mayer and Anton Oberzeller had resigned their seats some time ago, and Mr. Ludwig Lott, District Committee member, is on vacation in Philadelphia, and further since the Municipal Council failed to adhere to the rules of article 57 of the provisional municipal constitution for the City of Vienna and announce new elections.

Having said this, we will now prove the illegality of the decision reached by the Municipal Council on September 5, 1876.

According to article 54 of the provisional municipal constitution for the City of Vienna, the district committee members elect from their midst the district leader by absolute majority. The law does not mention anything about requiring a certain number present or a certain number of votes that have to be cast for one person in order for the election to be considered valid.

In order to appreciate the vital significance of the omission of such rules one must consider that the legislator must expressly stipulate in all those cases that both a certain number of people must be present and a certain number of votes are necessary in order for a resolution and an election to be valid. In order to affirm our statement, we refer to article 41 of the provisional municipal constitution which concerns the election of the mayor, and to articles 89, 90, 91 of same.

Since it is now a general principle of law that exceptional rules must not be applied analogously, since further there is no reason why the legislator if he had so intended, had not also expressly stipulated in article 54 of said municipal constitution as in article 41, etc., a special rule concerning the necessary number of votes for the election of the district leader to be valid, there is no doubt that the legislator did not want to include such restrictive rules for the election of a district leader, obviously because of the lesser significance of this office.

Therefore, the legal authority is not authorized to determine any restrictive rules not substantiated in the law and to make the validity of an election dependent on such rules.

The decision of the Municipal Council that the election of the leader can be considered valid only if he receives at least ten votes, is therefore not legally substantiated and is to be revoked.

Since the provisional municipal constitution of the City of Vienna has no stipulation whatsoever about the quorum of the district committee, the regulation concerning quorum requirements of the district committee as contained in article 15 of the governing statutes and instructions for the district leader and district committees apply to the district leader election; hence, the presence of nine district committee members renders the election of a district leader permissible.

The illegality of the appealed decision of the Municipal Council is immediately apparent when considering that according to article 60 of the provisional municipal constitution for the City of Vienna the number of committee members can be less that 18, and further that in District III there are presently only 14 active committee members; consequently a more than two-thirds majority for the election of a district leader was being required by the Municipal Council.

I cannot neglect to point out that the Municipal Council of the City of Vienna threatened to recall the district committee members if their arbitrarily made condition was not fulfilled, and did so subsequently and thus prematurely divested nine dutiful district committee members of their mandates.

The complaint herewith registered is of no personal benefit to us, since meanwhile, the new elections will have been called and held; nevertheless we consider it our responsibility to make this complaint, because we think that the law has been violated and consider it the responsibility of every citizen vigorously to contribute to the protection of the law; we consider it all the more our responsibility, since we had to appear before our voters even before the Municipal Council acted on our petition brought one year ago, which Mayor Dr. Cajetan Felder and the whole press made light of without cause, and offered us belated amends.

We therefore request:

That the esteemed KK. Lower Austrian Governorship deign to declare illegal the decision of the Municipal Council of the City of Vienna reached during its plenary session of September 5, 1876 that one person must receive at least 10 votes in order to have the election declared valid.

The following document is in Lueger's early agita-
tional style.

Draft

Nachlass Dr. Karl Lueger
St. Slg. Zl. 1257/12
Box V
Mappe: Korrespondenzen,
Notizen, Formblaetter
e.c., Wahlangelegenheiten
betreffend

Open letter of the nine recalled District Committee
members to the voters of the Third District.

Gentlemen,

The first general voter's assembly, which took
place last Monday, October 9th of this year, in
Dreher's Assembly Hall,[1] was prematurely brought to
a close by a scandal caused by the supporters of the
united German democratic and reactionary parties,
which made it impossible for us and our friends to
report our activities to our voters and to inform them
of events which are and were depicted in untrue or at
least one-sided, distorted fashion by almost the
entire press.

Thus, robbed of the opportunity to defend ourselves in front of our voters on the speaker's platform, unmercifully and unjustly mishandled by a
servile press, we had no choice but to respond in
writing.

As you know, gentlemen, we were elected for a
three year term in September 1874. On the sixth of
October 1874, the election of the district leader took
place, and from that day the beginning of our activity
can be dated.

Before we permit ourselves to elaborate further
on this matter, let us state that all the district
committee members elected in 1874 belonged to that
party of the district which can legitimately call
itself moderate liberal and therefore, considering
the impossibility of any political party disputes the

---

[1]Drehers Etablissement, Third District, Landstrasse
Hauptstrasse 97. See Richard Groner and Felix Czeike,
Wien Lexikon, Vienna, 1974, pp. 448, 449. Hereafter
referred to as "Czeike."

individual district committee members could attend to the specific tasks of their honorary offices, namely, supervision of the supply of goods and services for the Municipality of Vienna, of municipal property and assets, of intervention in tax and commercial affairs and supervision of sanitation and building codes.

When anyone assumes an office that he has not heretofore administered, he needs a little time to acquaint himself with all the rules he needs to observe, with the extent of his rights and responsibilities, with the method and style of the most appropriate execution and fulfillment of same, and it is all the more difficult for him to accomplish these things the less support and assistance he finds where he expects or can justifiably expect to find them, as we have unfortunately learned from the district leader and individual municipal officials.

Nevertheless, despite all these obstacles, we quickly gained insight into business affairs and thus also learned of the crass, deplorable state of affairs that have caused the municipality very significant material disadvantages which, however, as if sanctioned by custom, were considered secondary, even natural.

We believed we had served a useful purpose when we fought these bad conditions, and hoped that we were strongly supported in these endeavors by the district leader, by the esteemed magistrate of the City of Vienna, and in particular, by the mayor. This was all the more our hope since, according to the law, the district committee members have no authority to change norms or to release workers and civil servants, because the members are only auxiliary to the district leader and the entire power of the executive rests in the hands of the district leader, the magistrate and the mayor, respectively.

On November 21, 1874 Section II, whose responsibility was to address the problem of street conditions, was consulted with regard to a letter addressed to the district leader by the magistrate on November 10, 1874 in which the request was made to give information about the control of street sanitation in the district.

The inquiries already previously begun and dilligently continued by the members of Section II revealed: that one wagon averaged 7-9 trips per day, whereas formerly, as regularly as clock-work, twelve trips per wagon per day were charged and paid for; that the wagons furnished by the contractors do not have the contractually stipulated capacity; that workers paid by the community are being used for work of the contractors; that in the morning the drivers appear with chits; that on pay-day the amount due the workers never quite corresponded with that actually paid out, and the amount left over was set aside for so-called "pressure" men* and absent workers; that on the time sheets more working days were listed than the workers themselves indicated; that fictitious names appeared, etc., etc.

All these revelations were thoroughly discussed in the district committee meetings on November 28, December 3, and December 10, 1874 and it was decided that the district leader should make these deplorable conditions known to the magistrate. Not only did this not occur, but even the road superintendent who was most implicated was dismissed only after considerable pressure and reluctance in January, 1875.

The magistrate was informed of these conditions by Municipal Councilors Josef Huber and Dr. Mandl, and learned about them further from the minutes of said district committee meetings, and finally a report was submitted on February 4, 1875 written by the now deceased District Committee member, Engineer Chladek, in which the revelations of the irregularities were detailed and which was discussed at the district committee meeting of December 3, 1874.

However, the magistrate didn't do anything, did absolutely nothing, in order to determine the financial damages the municipality had suffered and to hold the guilty contractor responsible for these actions; it didn't do anything to prevent similar occurrences in other districts; in fact it didn't even do anything when it must have become clear that even worse conditions prevailed in other districts, and what is certainly the most striking is the fact that the magistrate has up to the present day done nothing to determine the damages incurred by the community and to collect them from the guilty contractor.

---

*These men operated water pumps and hoses to extinguish fires.

And when we were requested by the Municipal Council of the City of Vienna to evaluate the planned road inspectorate, we openly said, as is customary among independent men, that "even in cases in which an impartial party automatically assumes not just irregular but downright dishonest behavior, action from the responsible central agency could not be achieved."

Even though this evaluation was directed not to the mayor, but to the Municipal Council and thus was to be handled by the Council, the mayor felt justified to play the investigating attorney and ordered the district leader, by letter of July 16, 1875 to indicate within three days to which authorities the district leader or district committee had reported those cases and where subsequently no actions on the part of the responsible central agency had been taken.

Perhaps we would have a right to be somewhat indignant about the mayor's chosen method, but in the interest of the matter at hand we suppressed our feelings, and asked for an extension to ten days. But even this modest request was not granted and even more energetically, if that is possible, we were requested to answer immediately the letter of July 16, 1875.

In response, the committee decided to direct a second more comprehensive statement as proof of its evaluation not, however, to the mayor, but rather to the Municipal Council.

On August 4, 1875 the mayor's letter of August 2, 1875 addressed to the district leader in which we were depicted as flippant accusers appeared in most of Vienna's daily newspapers.

We passed over this insulting letter of the mayor when it was later officially transmitted to us, as a matter of routine and finally at the beginning of October 1875 submitted our much discussed petition to the Municipal Council of the City of Vienna.

We can flatter ourselves that this was drafted most objectively, that the irregularities in all branches of the administration were listed, and finally, corrective measures were proposed.

From the more than 100 cases discussed, the petition revealed that the opinions of the district committee members in tax and commercial matters were often ignored; that through the manipulation of purchase orders the existing regulations were not observed and, therefore, opportunity for embezzlement arose; that the supervision of goods and supplies was not undertaken with the required, even necessary precision; that sanitation and building codes are not uniformly followed; that serious sanitation defects were not removed while private persons were often importuned, that community goods and assets were not properly supervised thereby providing opportunity for theft or improper use; and such cases also occurred in which valid Municipal Council decisions were not obeyed in street matters, where in the process of street cleaning the municipality suffered at the hands of the contractor in the most sensitive manner, where embezzlement and fraud took place, etc.

The mayor designated us as flippant again on October 16, 1875 that is, at a time when the cases revealed by us could not be examined and were not examined, before the decision of the Municipal Council and repeated shortly thereafter, in a public Muncipal Council meeting, the insult directed toward us.

And what on the other hand did the Municipal Council of the City of Vienna do?

To be sure, during the course of the winter of 1875/76, a few of us were questioned by a commission of the Municipal Council. But since then we haven't heard anything from the Municipal Council. There were some notices in the newspapers from time to time, according to which everything that we had said was untrue, and sometimes articles written by a certain Dr. Berg appeared according to which we were also in the wrong. But we never learned whether and how the individual cases which were of the most serious nature were investigated, whether it was determined that the allegations were true, or, conversely why not, in spite of the fact that it had been more than a year since our allegations had first been submitted.

And when the District Leader, Matthaeus Mayer, relinquished his mandate, individual Municipal Councilors were able to persuade five district committee members first not to participate in the elections and then to relinquish their mandates. We don't want to discuss here the details of the illegal instructions given to the election chairmen, or the Municipal Council resolutions which in our opinion, violate the law. Suffice it to say, the Municipal

Council dissolved the district committee, thereby prematurely depriving men who were very conscious of their duties, of their mandates, without giving a plausible reason why this was done.

All of these events were accompanied by abusive articles about us in Vienna's press; we who only had the best interests of our fellow citizens in mind, who spared neither time nor effort in doing our duty, were depicted as disturbers of the peace, and all of this only because we didn't find everything as it should be, and because we dared to say this.

We want to focus on only one criticism, viz., that through our activities we endanger the autonomy.

In response to this, we can refer to the results of our activity. We were able to save in the District of Landstrasse alone, approximately 20,000 gulden in the transportation sector; our efforts were emulated in other districts, which also resulted in savings. For example, the District of Neubau needed 91,719 gulden 60 kronen for snow removal during the winter of 74-75, whereas during the winter of 75-76 approximately 50,000 gulden less were spent for the same period. According to the year end accounting report for 1875, around 95,395 gulden 55 kronen less than budgeted was used for the maintenance of the communication network.

Now we ask you, have we violated the autonomy? Yes, say our opponents, for you should not have said anything about the bad conditions. But to that we respond, what in fact is the essence of public life and why are citizens elected?

We are convinced that if a government authority perpetrated only a tenth of the sins of omission which we can legitimately ascribe to the magistrate, a storm of indignation in the public press directed against this authority would have burst forth and the taxpayers would have been called on to defend their rights and to protect their hard-earned tax money.

And why doesn't this happen to the magistrate and the mayor? Well, farmer, that's something quite different since it concerns the free community.

Oh, the fools! Those who complain about the oppression of the municipalities by the state and who so sorrowfully lament: "At the grave of the municipality stands the state as the first pallbearer," and those who do not suspect that through their own maladministration and silence, they are the grave diggers of the municipality.

In conclusion then, only one more observation:

From the beginning until the end of our activity, we were always guided by the thought that state and municipal property are to be considered just as sacrosanct as private property, and that the unfortunately widely held view: "It doesn't harm the municipality or the state," is reprehensible and leads to the destruction of society.

And as thanks we were relieved of our responsibilities.

We leave it to you, honorable voters, to render judgment on our activities with the peace of mind that the knowledge of faithful devotion to duty and honest effort bring.

Respectfully submitted,

Anton Heller   mp
Heinrich Hess mp
Franz Hintermayer mp
W. Hruschka mp
Wilhelm Kruegermayer mp
A. Melzinschek mp
Benedict Puchwein mp
Moritz Riby mp

Draft

Nachlass Karl Lueger
St. Slg. Zl. 1257/12
Box IV

Office of the Most Esteemed KK. Public Prosecutor,

On the 12th and 13th of this month the trial concerning the libel suit brought by the Municipality of Vienna against Messrs. Dr. Fuenckh and Liegelwanger took place at the kk. District Court in Hietzing.

In the course of same, Mr. Josef Rohatschek, Grave Stone Dealer in Simmering, was interrogated as expert witness and is said to have testified among other things, at least according to newspaper accounts about said trial, that the article which appeared in the October 8, 1876 issue of "Fortschritt" entitled "Mismanagement at the Central Cemetery," evolved as follows: that I had taken a deposition by him, Rohatschek, in my office in the presence of Dr. Mandl and Josef Huber, which he had been induced to sign through a promise of employment in the city government, allegedly made by me and Dr. Mandl, and that this statement was published in "Fortschritt" without his knowledge.

Since I consider it to be positively unbelievable that Mr. Josef Rohatschek offered such testimony, I asked Dr. Porzer about this who, however, confirmed the newspaper reports.

Under such circumstances I am compelled to inform the esteemed kk. Public Prosecutor's Office that should Mr. Josef Rohatschek truly have stated that I had anything at all to do with composing the article in question and that I had promised him employment in the municipal government, perjury has been committed.

I met Josef Rohatschek in 1876 through Dr. Mandl, whom Rohatschek had informed about fraudulent dealings at the Central Cemetery. In order to have his statements in writing, I took them down in my office in the presence of Dr. Ignaz Mandl and Josef Huber or just one of them. Mr. Rohatschek voluntarily signed the written document after careful examination of same. This document was transmitted certainly before October 8th, 1886 (sic) reference no. 12283 and since it is customary to hold pretrial investigations, the file is probably still located at the kk. Landesgericht in Strafsachen (Regional Court for Criminal Matters).

This information that I recorded is not at all connected with the article published in "Fortschritt," even though the dates of the article and recorded transcript are probably identical, since their source is the same after all. Just how the article in question evolved, I honestly do not know; but Mr. Josef Rohatschek himself has told about this in no uncertain terms. As a result of this article, slander charges according to articles 487, 488, 491 of the

123

Criminal Code were brought in the kk. Landesgericht
by Messrs. Jakob Fronz and Karl Braun against
Mr. Josef Rohatschek and Mr. Eduard Trexler von
Lindenau, and the jury decision A on this matter of
October 14, 1877, Reg. No. 5258-5317 has expired.

                    Z 52416

Rohatschek has recounted both during the pretrial
and trial proceedings how the article evolved, and
thereby showed that his present testimony is untrue.

I therefore humbly request:

that the Office of the Esteemed kk Public
Prosecutor deign in cognizance of the above to file
the appropriate petitions and especially to arrange
that Dr. Josef Porzer, Attorney to the Royal and
Legal Courts in Vienna, I, Schottenbastei 1,
Dr. Robert Pattai, Attorney to the Royal and Legal
Courts in Vienna, Mariahilferstrasse 170, Radislav
Merzick Ritter von Castel-Marino, kk. Court Assistant
at the District Court Hietzing, be called as witnesses
about the testimony of Mr. Josef Rohatschek before
the District Court, Hietzing, in the case of
Municipality of Vienna versus Messrs. Dr. Fuenckh
and Liegelwanger; as well as that I, Mr. Eduard
Trexler von Lindenau, Civil Servant in Simmering, Dr.
Ignaz Mandl, Municipal Councilor in Vienna, IV,
Heugasse 54, Josef Huber, Citizen and Distiller in
Vienna, III, Hauptstrasse 41, also be called as witnesses about the circumstances mentioned in the
deposition; and finally that the files concerning the
charges brought by me and Mr. Josef Huber and Dr.
Ignaz Mandl in 1876 ref. no. 12283, as well as the
documents relevant to Decision A that are found at
the Landesgericht in Strafsachen, be requisitioned.

Office of KK. Public Prosecutor, Vienna

Dr. Karl Lueger, Attorney to the Royal and Legal
Courts in Vienna, I. Kaerntnerstrasse 8
brings the enclosed charge against Mr. Josef
Rohatschek, Grave Stone Dealer at Simmering,
Hauptstrasse 146.

Draft   Nachlass Karl Lueger
                               St. Slg. Zl. 1257/12
                               Box IV

Re Criminal Case

Esteemed K.K. District Court,

    I learned from today's evening papers that Mr.
Josef Rohatschek testified as a witness during the
course of the trial of the Municipality of Vienna
vs. Messrs. Dr. Fuenckh and Liegelwanger and is
said to have stated the following:

1.) the article which appeared in the issue of
"Fortschritt" dated Simmering October 8, 1876 concerning mismanagement at the Central Cemetery was
drafted by me.
2.) I had made certain promises to him, Rohatschek.

    Since I cannot be indifferent to such statements
made about me, I request that the following be brought
to the court's attention during the course of the
trial.

    It is not true that I drafted the above-mentioned
article or contributed in any way to its publication.

    It is also not true that I made any promises to
Mr. Josef Rohatschek.

    As an explanation I inform you that on October 20,
1876 I relinquished my mandate as Municipal Councilor,
that I functioned as defense counsel for Mr. von
Trexler during the jury trial of October 13 and 14,
1877 and that it was not until March 1878 that I was
re-elected to the Municipal Council. During the
above-mentioned jury trial, Mr. von Trexler expressly
admitted having written the incriminating article.

    In conclusion, I state that I did not exercise
the slightest influence on Mr. Josef Rohatschek to
tell me or anyone else about his experiences with
regard to the mismanagement at the Central Cemetery;
Mr. Josef Rohatschek did this, at least as far as I
know, voluntarily and without having been influenced
in any way.

    I repeat my request to have this statement read.

                          125

                              Dr. Karl Lueger
                              Attorney to the Royal
                              and Legal Courts

K.K. District Court
Hietzing

Dr. Karl Lueger
Attorney to the Royal and Legal Courts
1. Kaerntnerstrasse 8

    Requests that this statement be read during the
libel case of the Municipality of Vienna vs. Messrs.
Fuenckh and Liegelwanger.

Letter copy   Nachlass Karl Lueger
                               St. Slg. Zl. 1275/12
                               Box II
                               Mappe: Redekonzepte

Fortschritt v. Fronz

October 20, '77

Dear Editor,

    A colleague brought to my attention a news item
about me in the supplement of the local edition of
the "Presse," no. 286, Wednesday, October 17, 1877.
In accordance with Article 19 of the Press Law[2] I
request the following correction.

---

[2]Article 19 read:
    Upon request of an authority or involved private
party a periodical publication must print in the
following or second following issue any requested
correction of facts printed earlier in exactly the
same way in which the article to be corrected was
printed, i.e., in so far as it refers to the place of
submission as well as the type of print. Official
corrections must always be printed free of charge;
those from private persons only in so far as the
correction is not more than twice as long as the original article to be corrected; otherwise the usual
fees have to be paid for any additional lines.
If so requested, a receipt must be given for any
requested and submitted correction.

It is untrue that during an alleged victory
celebration of Mr. Mandl and consorts on October 14,
1877 I was proclaimed delegate to the Provincial Diet
and Dr. Mandl delegate to parliament from the Third
District or that we were even nominated for these
positions.

Respectfully submitted,

Esteemed
Editorial Staff
of "The Presse"
Vienna

I N 74501

Dr. Karl Lueger
Vienna
1st District, Renngasse No. 1   August 2, 1883

Honorable
Dr. Cajetan Freiherr von <u>Felder</u>
Regional Marshal of Lower Austria, etc., etc.

Honorable Sir,

    Herr Kleebinder told me some time ago that you
collect portraits of all those persons with whom you
have come into contact during your long and varied
public career, and you therefore also desire my
photograph.[3] Since I have only just today received
one I could not oblige you earlier and I ask that you
not consider it a discourtesy that I am somewhat late
in granting your wish.

    Permit me, honorable sir, to express my highest
esteem.

Respectfully yours,
Dr. <u>Karl Lueger</u>

---

[3]According to Felix Czeike, "(Felder) possessed a
collection of over 50,000 portraits (which unfortunately were scattered to the winds in auctions after
his death)." <u>Wien und Seine Buergermeister</u>, p. 315.

(In Lueger's writing)   Nachlass Karl Lueger
Newspaper dated   St. Slg. Zl. 1257/12
October 21, 1883   Box III
                          Mappe: Saekularfeier 1883

Interpellation

of

Municipal Councilor

Dr. Karl Lueger

Some time ago, the copies of Mr. Karl Weiss's publication in celebration of the completion of the new town hall commissioned by the Municipal Council for this occasion, as sent to the Municipal Councilors, were retrieved in order to correct the list of members of the Town Hall Building Commission.

This is an indication that the author of this publication desired his work to justify the claim of historical truth.

In the issue of the "Wiener Buerger-Zeitung" of the 21st of this month, the assertion is made that the portrayal of the activity and achievements of former Mayor Dr. Felder in securing the parade grounds as described in the publication is based "on incorrect information" and that he was a much more effective mayor.

Even though I was an outspoken opponent of Mayor Dr. Felder, I consider it necessary, nonetheless, not to denigrate this man's great achievements for the Municipality of Vienna in a publication <u>commissioned by the Municipal Council</u>, and particularly because I was an opponent of this man, I consider it my duty to address the following question to the honorable mayor:[+]

Is the mayor inclined to make appropriate inquiries about the assertions made in the article "The Genesis of the New Town Hall" which appeared in the October 21, 1883 issue of the "Wiener Buerger-Zeitung" and, as a consequence thereof, to have the

---

[+]Edward Uhl

necessary corrections made in the aforementioned publication?

Dr. Lueger

Draft

I N 203.043
Dr. Karl Lueger
Vienna
Renngasse Address

March 14, 1884

Dear Editor,

On the basis of Article 19 of the Press Law, accept the following correction of the notice that appeared in your morning paper of today.

It is incorrect that I visited Dr. Cajetan von Felder a few days ago.

Even if I paid the baron a visit quite some time ago, the reason is not a subject for any public discussion and I can only emphatically declare that it had nothing whatsoever to do with the forthcoming Municipal Council elections. Moreover, I have never made a secret of my personal respect for Dr. Felder in spite of my political opposition and, therefore, I must strongly reject the attempt to make political capital out of private relationships.

Draft

Nachlass Karl Lueger
St. Slg. Zl. 1275/12
Box V
Mappe: Korrespondenzen,
Notizen, Formblaetter e.c.,
Wahlangelegenheiten betreffend

To the Honorable Businessmen of the 3rd (and) 5th Districts

Vienna, May, 1885

Dear Colleagues,

The general decline in business makes it more

than ever the duty of the businessmen to ensure that
men are sent to the representative bodies who fully
understand the present situation and who possess the
necessary independence and courage to propose and
carry through energetically those measures appropriate
to relieve our problems.

On June 1 of this year, we will be called on to
elect those men to parliament from whom we can confidently expect the determination to fulfill our
justifiable demands.

In the 3rd District
5th

Dr. Ignaz Mandl
Municipal Councilor, Heugasse 54
Dr. Karl Lueger
Municipal Councilor, Marokkanergasse 3

is campaigning in this election for the trust of his
fellow citizens.

Dr. Ignaz Mandl's
Dr. Karl Lueger's career of public service so far has
proved that he took up the struggle against every kind
of economic exploitation without regard to his own
person and courageously persevered in spite of all
attacks.

Dr. Ignaz Mandl
The diligent devotion with which Dr. Karl Lueger
has up till now represented the interests of his
fellow citizens leads one justifiably to expect that
if the voters place their trust in him, he will
fulfill his duties as a representative of the people
in the truest sense of the word with the same determination and energy. Because of these reasons we
highly recommend to you, dear colleagues, the election
of Dr. Ignaz Mandl
Dr. Karl Lueger and ask that you cast your votes for
him and recommend him for election to your friends and
colleagues.

Respectfully,

Although this draft is in Lueger's handwriting, the
name "Kopitschek" appears as signatory.

Nachlass Karl Lueger
St. Slg. Zl. 1257/12
Box V
Mappe: Korrespondenzen,
Notizen, Formblaetter, e.c.,
Wahlangelegenheiten betreffend

Open Letter to Dr. Ig. Mandl

Dear Doctor,

At the last meeting of our party committee, called for the purpose of announcing your withdrawal from the political Fortschrittsvereine Eintracht,[+] you declared on your honor the following:

"I am withdrawing from the Verein no matter what. However, it is my innermost desire that the Verein prosper and grow strong. I declare as my enemy anyone who for my sake quits the Verein; I implore all of you to remain loyal to the Verein, and even if I am no longer among you, I will never do anything against the interests of the Verein; rather, I will work quietly for the interests of the Verein; insofar as it is within my power. After so many battles, I simply want to withdraw from public service."

In spite of this declaration which you, Doctor, gave before honorable men you acted as follows:

1.) Immediately after your withdrawal from the Verein you gathered a clique of men around you who spread false and malicious rumors most detrimental to the Verein. This same clique attempted to persuade members of the Verein to withdraw and thereby dissolve it.

2.) You aimed to establish a new Verein that was meant further to render the Fortschrittsverein impossible.

3.) You had the audacity at the last official voters' meeting publicly to oppose the interests of the Verein, since you certainly know that Dr. Lueger was

---

[+]The "Eintracht" was founded by Mandl in 1872, and existed until 1900.

131

nominated by the Verein as our candidate.

I herewith declare as one of those trusted few in whose presence you gave the above-cited declaration that you, sir, <u>have played a dishonorable game with us, and that I consider you without character.</u>

J. Kopitschek
Plumber

This serves to bring the foregoing to the attention of those voters who perhaps are being misled by the designation: "German-Liberal Election Committee," behind which the clique devoted to Dr. Mandl hides so that they may judge for themselves how good Dr. Mandl's word of honor is.

J. Kopitschek
Plumber

This sketch for a polemic, probably dating from the late 1880s, reveals Lueger's implicitly anti-Semitic cultural and political values.

Nachlass Karl Lueger
St. Slg. Zl. 1257/12
Box II
Mappe: Duellfrage, politischer
Fortschrittsverein, Affaere Mandl

Political Fortschrittsverein Eintracht

Copy
<u>10 times</u>

A few days ago a notice appeared in local papers according to which a large number of members of the political Fortschrittsverein Eintracht allegedly announced their withdrawal from this Verein because of the attitude of Municipal Councilor Dr. Lueger. A few of Dr. Mandl's notorious agitators have now truly made every effort to undermine the Verein but the result was lamentable. It was revealed, for example, that a large number of those who declared their withdrawal were <u>never members</u> of the Verein, that a number of the signatures were <u>forged</u>, and that others were taken in by deceitful trickery.

However, in order to provide a purpose for the actions of Dr. Mandl and his cohorts, the executive committee of the Verein directed the following circular to its members: . . .

1.) against the Verein
Change in view

Not true, now as before committed to the democratic principles of the equality of all nations and confessions; we persecute and hate no one on grounds of religion and nationality, but as before committed to the relentless and tireless struggle against the corrupt and corrupting domination of capital, the struggle to defend the customs of our forefathers, for integrity in all areas of private and public life. No, not the Verein, but rather Dr. Mandl has changed his views. He has now become friend and supporter of and even collects notices from the "Deutsche Zeitung," "Neue Freie Presse," "Vorstadt Zeitung," papers which poison private and public life through their disgraceful activities, their assaults on Christian culture and customs, through their continuous instigation of the people.

THE PUBLICIST

THE PUBLICIST

Early in his political career, Lueger mastered the art of propaganda. Forceful, clear, and direct, his political messages were designed to be understood by the simplest of his constituents. In the documents presented here, Lueger appears as his own publicist. He composed broadsides and announcements--sometimes about himself in the third person--delivered speeches, on occasion, several in a single evening, organized political gatherings in minute detail, and contributed polemical editorials to newspapers.

He also became an expert fund raiser, both for general and campaign purposes, and he labored in innumerable ways to keep the party machinery running smoothly. The personal touch was always an essential element in his success. Much of this public relations and routine managerial work was later assumed by the party press personnel, and in particular by Albert Gessmann, his "chief of staff."[1] But Lueger never underestimated the importance of propaganda, particularly where his own image was involved. Until shortly before his death, he periodically resumed his earlier publicist role--and "threatened" to continue to do so. So powerful was his presence then that it might be argued that his spirit presided over the shaping of even his posthumous legend. He is supposed to have admonished Gessmann and Alfred Ebenhoch, "I'll look down from up there, so that you won't do anything foolish."[2]

The letters, broadsides, and drafts of speeches that follow were for the most part written before or shortly after the crucial parliamentary election of June, 1885. They reveal Lueger's development as a publicist and the direction this development took. Although the franchise had in fact been extended in 1882, 1885 was the first year in which those who paid property taxes of five gulden could vote in parliamentary elections. In this year, Lueger narrowly defeated the liberal Johann Heinrich Steudel in the district of Margarethen, and his life-long career in parliament began.[3]

His letters provide behind-the-scenes glimpses of his campaign tactics, while other documents demonstrate his efforts to create as broad an electoral base as possible. He was not yet at this time directing his propaganda toward a more exclusively

lower-middle-class constituency. Even a few
Socialists agitated for Lueger during this election.
Kurt Skalnik reports: "Never before and never since
was a politician the candidate of such a broad-based,
if patchwork 'People's Party,' as was Lueger in this
year."[4] Lueger's ideas about municipal socialization
are already at work, as are his nationalism and demagogic techniques, which were to prove so effective in
attracting his mass following. Lueger dwelled on a
classically <u>ad hominem</u> note: that he was an upright
man contending against a crew of scoundrels. He thus
subtly flattered himself as well as his prospective
supporters and implied that as honorable men, they
served the common interest in supporting him. The
tactic paid off. Lueger won the election with the
help of the newly-enfranchised Five Gulden Men:

> These (voters)...for the most part presented
> a very different picture. Hundreds poured
> from their small workshops in shirt sleeves,
> wearing aprons, waving their work caps in
> greeting to Dr. Lueger. As they came and
> went, most of them cheered their revered man
> of the people. These were the 'Five Gulden
> Men,'...eventually with these new
> battalions, he hoped to defeat the seemingly
> invincible liberals.[5]

Lueger had, in a new way, placed himself before a new
public.

FOOTNOTES FOR

THE PUBLICIST

1. Kielmansegg, p. 408.

2. Kuppe, p. 524n. Several years before Lueger's
    death, Adam Mueller-Guttenbrunn, bankrupt director
    of the Kaiserjubilaeums-Stadttheater, wondered at
    the mayor's power. Officials who had come to con-
    fiscate Mueller-Guttenbrunn's property refused to
    take Lueger's portrait, whereupon Mueller-
    Guttenbrunn embarrassed the officials with his
    rhetorical question: "Well, well, is Dr. Lueger
    so powerful?" Adam Mueller-Guttenbrunn, Der Roman
    meines Lebens. Leipzig, 1927, pp. 256-257.

3. Hans Arnold Schwer, an early Christian Social,
    provides a portrait of Lueger at this time. See
    "Persoenliche Erinnerungen an Dr. Lueger," Die
    Reichspost, September 4, 1926, p. 7.

4. Skalnik, Dr. Karl Lueger, p. 52.

5. Kuppe, pp. 128, 129.

I N   203.044
Dr. Karl Lueger
Attorney to the Royal and Legal Courts
Vienna
1, Trattnerhof, <u>Goldschmiedgasse 9</u>   Vienna, April 9,
                    Graben 29   1885

Dear Mr. Karny,

    While I thank you very much for your kind letter
of yesterday, I regret very much that I will be unable
to accept your invitation. An urgent, unavoidable
business forces me to remain in the office today and
finish the work.

    On this occasion, I would like to request that
complete unity be restored among the party members and
in the interest of the cause, to forget everything
that may have temporarily disturbed this.

    Once again, please excuse my absence today and
rest assured that I will soon appear among my friends.

                         Most respectfully yours,

                         Dr. Karl Lueger

I N   203.044
To an unknown friend
Dr. Karl Lueger
Attorney to the Royal and Legal Courts

Trattnerhof Address   Vienna, April 9, 1885

Dear Friend:

    Above all, many thanks for your efforts. That
the opponents are at work, I know and find understandable. Consequently, we should have complete
unity on our side.

    Now, Karny's withdrawal bothers me no end. For
instance, he invites me to a meeting of the executive
committee today in Zelinka's restaurant, 5th (District),
Wimmergasse 32.

If I go, I'll offend the voters' organization.
If I don't go, I'll offend Karny. I have now decided
how to get out of this mess and have excused my
absence because of work load, which is true by the
way. Perhaps you will be able to set things right.
I would very much appreciate it.

Most respectfully yours,

Dr. Karl Lueger

Draft of a letter

Nachlass Karl Lueger
St. Slg. Zl. 1275/12
Box V
Mappe: Korrespondenzen, Notizen,
Formblaetter e.c. Wahlangelegen-
heiten betreffend

Vienna, April 24, 1885

Honorable Sir,

The upcoming parliamentary elections also obligate
the Democratic Party in Vienna to enter these elections with a united front in order to help secure the
election of those men from whom we expect an energetic
defense of our ideas.

While the other parties stand ready and have
completed their preparations, our party has just
started to be active in a few districts; but no
attempt at gathering all our forces has yet been made.

Even though I waited long enough to see whether
someone competent would take the initiative, nothing
happened, and I, therefore, ask you to attribute it to
my good will to do something in the interest of the
whole party if I take the liberty of inviting you,
honorable sir, for tomorrow, Saturday the 25th of the
month at 5:00 p.m. to my office to discuss the
question whether perhaps a central election committee

of the Democratic Party in Vienna should be created.

Most respectfully yours,

	I.	F. A. Kment
	II.	Jacob Seitz
	III.	Josef Holzapfel
check		Dr. Ig. Mandl
	V.	Ludwig Dotzauer
	VI.	Karl Vaugoin
	VII.	Dr. A. Gessmann
		Kreuzig
	VIII.	Antensteiner
		Dr. Kronawetter
		Dr. Augustin Kupka
	IX.	Dr. Heinrich Glaser

Copy 12 times

This is one of the most important documents of
Lueger's early career because it neatly summarizes his
political goals and accomplishments between 1875 and
1885 and suggests the course of his future
development.

Draft

I N 41566

Fellow Citizens!
On June 1 of this year
Elect Dr. Karl Lueger
Municipal Councilor, Marokkanergasse 3
to Parliament

As Municipal Councilor, Dr. Lueger always represented
the interests of the middle class. He made efforts to
limit peddling to such extent that the business man
would no longer suffer damage. He opposed the
encroachment of foreign agents. He always opposed big
businessmen, such as Baron Schwarz, Frey, etc., and
supported direct placement of contracts to Viennese
businessmen for municipal work and deliveries.

Dr. Lueger struggled against corruption in workers' canteens, which harmed both worker and businessman alike, and he is one of the few who tried to remove franchise profiteering.

Our candidate fought the exploitation of the poor by the usurous practices of pawnshops.

Dr. Lueger has always supported the establishment of a municipal mortgage bank as well as the construction of municipal gas works. He has worked and continues to work energetically for the expansion of the street car system and at the same time works for the elimination of abusive practices in that system that are detrimental to the public and damage businesses through unhealthy competition and that burden as well those employed in public transportation, such as one-horse carriage operators, hackneys, and bus companies.

Among municipal officials Dr. Lueger enjoys the reputation of a man who is always solicitous and objective. He is a supporter of the school system, and it is he who made it possible for teachers to sit on Vienna's Municipal Council.

Dr. Lueger has proved himself to be an uncompromising defender of the rights of the municipality. He has always advocated economy where necessary and conscientious and honest management of community affairs. He and his colleagues succeeded <u>in preventing a new loan planned by the majority of the Municipal Council as well as the introduction of a new tax and an increase in existing taxes</u> (rent tax, etc.).

(before: Dr. Lueger has rejected all attempts to bribe him.)

Dr. Lueger supports the elimination of Vienna's tariff barriers and the tax on food consumption. He supports Vienna's central position in the empire.

Dr. Lueger remains loyal to his fatherland, Austria, and his native city of Vienna; he will always support the rights and safety of the German nationality without hating or oppressing other nationalities.

Dr. Lueger advocates the direct franchise, the protection of the middle class in the broadest sense of the meaning, and supports the nationalization of transportation and insurance, etc.

Dr. Lueger has proven to be immune to all bribery attempts.

Therefore, fellow citizens, elect our candidate Dr. Karl Lueger.

Vienna, May 1885

> The Parliamentary
> Election Committee
> of the Democratic
> Party of the Fifth
> District

Draft

> Nachlass Karl Lueger
> St. Slg. Zl. 1275/12
> Box II
> Mappe: Redekonzepte

> Vienna, May 7, 1885

Honorable Sir,

In order to please our friend, Mr. Franz Chmelarz, I suggest we all pay him a visit in his inn at <u>Ober-Doebling, Mariengasse 27, on Sunday, the 10th of this month.</u>

Aside from offering outstanding food and drink, the view from the restaurant is splendid and there's a piano, etc.--in short, everything to have a great time.

In extending to you, honorable sir, and your family, this most cordial invitation to participate in this outing, please note that we shall meet at the street car stop of the suburban street car line which is next to the Mariahilfer Line and that we'll leave from there punctually at 2:00 p.m.

> Most respectfully yours,
> Wilhelm Pfister
> (before: signed Dr. Lueger)

The following draft of a letter from 1885 is Lueger's
first known written request for political support from
the Catholic Church.

Nachlass Karl Lueger
St. Slg. Zl. 1257/12
Box V
Mappe: Korrespondenzen,
Notizen, Formblaetter, etc.,
Wahlangelegenheiten betreffend

Right Reverend Father,

As you may know, the Margarethen Voters'
Association has asked me to run as its candidate from
the 5th District in the approaching parliamentary
elections. I have accepted this great honor, have
presented my political program at the assembly held on
April 27th of this year, attended by more than 500
voters from the District, and as a consequence, was
unanimously nominated as the candidate.

I feel obliged to inform you of this, your Right
Reverence, and to ask you not only to cast your vote
for me but also to exert your great influence on
behalf of my candidacy.

In support of my request, I believe I can rely on
your knowledge of my character and my activities[+] and
with the expression of my highest esteem, I remain

Yours most respectfully,

Dr. Karl Lueger

[+](before: I might also point out that the Reverends
Rieder, now priest among the tawers, and Guenther,
now priest in Koenigsbrunn, as I understand, know me
as catechists in the former so-called
Taubenschule.[++])

[++]Lueger attended this school between 1850 and 1854.

Draft

Nachlass Karl Lueger
St. Slg. Zl. 1275/12
Box V
Mappe: Korrespondenzen,
Notizen, Formblaetter e.c.,
Wahlangelegenheiten betreffend

Vienna, May 15, 1885

Dear Fellow Citizens,

The great importance of the election of
parliamentary representatives implies that each of you
will endeavor to know precisely the views of the individual candidates in order to be able to judge to whom
to give your vote.

(before: The reports about meetings that appear
in individual papers do not suffice here either
because they are too short or partisan in nature.

The latter particularly applies to our candidate
Dr. Karl Lueger, who belongs to a party that does not
have a newspaper, and who can be counted among the
most hated men in Vienna.)

As much as it is to our candidate's, Dr. Lueger,
credit to be insulted and slandered by individual
journals (before: such as the "Wiener Allgemeine
Zeitung" and "Constitutionelle Vorstadt-Zeitung") and
as much as this proves that our candidate is a true
friend of the people, an opponent of lies, corruption,
and any kind of exploitation, and therefore deserves
the trust of the people, it is nevertheless necessary
to afford all voters the opportunity to be convinced
of the truth by listening to our candidate and to convince themselves that he is worthy of representing our
interests in parliament.

We have already held voters' meetings in various
parts of our district at which our candidate was
introduced and at which he was able to obtain unani-
mous approval.

We now call a meeting of all voters in our
district to be held on

146

Monday, May 18th of this year
8:00 in the evening
in the garden, poss. lounge of
G. Kerling's Inn "Zum wilden Mann"
Hundsthurmerstrasse 27.

We would like to add that all voters, in particular those who will be voting for the first time,
were sent written invitations to this meeting,
irrespective of their party affiliation.

On the agenda:

Talk by our Candidate
Dr. Karl Lueger
Municipal Councilor, Marokkanergasse 3

Dear fellow citizens,
Please heed our invitation in order to determine
for yourselves that Dr. Karl Lueger deserves your
trust.

Respectfully yours,

The Parliamentary
Election Committee
of the Democratic
Party of the 5th
District

L. Bermann   L. Dotzauer
Secretary   Chairman

Draft   Nachlass Karl Lueger
                          St. Slg. Zl. 1257/12
                          Box V
                          Mappe: Korrespondenzen,
                          Notizen, Formblaetter e.c.,
                          Wahlangelegenheiten betreffend

Resolution with regard to Attacks

The voters' meeting held today in the 5th
District hereby expresses its indignation over the

147

untrue attacks against its representative and the
Democratic Party in general, and declares that such
despicable maneuvers will not prejudice the judgment
of the people.

Draft of Circular

I N   41540

The political "Fortschrittsverein Eintracht" in
the Third District applauds the election victory of
the Democratic Party in three of Vienna's districts.
At the same time, it urges the leaders of the
Democratic Party energetically to organize the party
throughout Vienna, and to see to it that democratic
ideas are spread through constant indoctrination of
the people.

Lueger had his share of troubles with his own supporters, as the following two letters reveal.

I N   203.045

Dr. Karl Lueger
Attorney to the Royal and Legal Courts
Trattnerhof Address   Vienna, June 13, 1885

Most Esteemed Mr. Princeps,

The result of yesterday's meeting, to which I had
invited the executive committee members of the Third
and Fifth Districts, as well as Dr. Gessmann and Dr.
Kronawetter, is as follows:

We were particularly pleased about your
willingness, esteemed sir, to bear the costs of a
festivity for the entire Democratic Party. The
following requisites for the festivity were decided
on:

1. The title of the festivity is to be: "Evening Festivity of the Democratic Party on the occasion of the Parliamentary Election."

2. Public announcement of the festivity is not to be made. Rather, distribution of admission tickets to the festivity should be handled by the individual Democratic Party Clubs in Vienna.

3. Artistic presentations must not be offered on the evening of the festivity.

4. Conversely, the participation of male choirs and a military band is to be welcomed.

5. No admission fee whatsoever is to be charged because the festivity is to retain the character of a party festivity.

      Requesting your gracious response, I remain, with the expression of my highest esteem,

                        Dr. Karl Lueger

Louis Princep's ungrammatical response to Lueger's letter of June 13, 1885 indicates that the author was probably of foreign origin.

I N   204.316

Most Honorable Member
of Parliament,

      Your suggestions transmitted to me today do not in the slightest correspond with my intentions.

      My idea was that I sponsor the festivity for the entire Democratic Party, and that I invite the Party in my name, and it goes without saying that all my Democratic friends are completely free to accept or decline the invitation, as is always the case.

      As a loyal party member, I just wanted to have your brief personal recommendations, but never wanted to be subjected to a committee that, as honorable as it may be, doesn't know much about such things. And now permit me to respond in more detail to your letter.

Re 1. I have absolutely nothing against the name
selected for the festivity.

Re 2. A party that is not given publicity is no party
at all, but rather a private get-together. I
and those gentlemen with whom I have conferred
so far wanted the Democratic Party to appear
publicly for once, in order to show themselves
to all of Vienna as a strong, powerful party
and to convince Vienna of its existence.
Without publicity, this goal is not attainable;
therefore, I shall pursue my efforts, because I
have only had this purpose in mind.

Re 3. This point could probably be discussed further--
it need not be entirely rejected.

Re 4. The participation of the choirs from Josefstadt
Neubau, Margarethen, and Landstrasse is very
desirable; the participation of one military
band is too insignificant.

Re 5. I intend to give a decent, complete, true, and
great party and for that the entire establishment has to be closed off, and if this is so,
individual uninvited friends must be given the
opportunity to attend; therefore, I have decided
on the admission tickets and have set the price
at 1 gulden, although I don't care if the price
is set at 2 gulden. I am convinced that hardly
more than 50-100 tickets will be sold, but
necessary they are. And in order not to have
any trouble with the police because of this, I
have indicated on my poster that the entire proceeds go to charitable purposes.

Without appearing to be stubborn, I must
insist nonetheless that if I am supposed to give
the party in which case I alone am responsible,
we must adhere to my ideas for the party; since
your suggested gettogether would be so simple
and could be attended by anybody and wouldn't
cost anything anyway, I could not assume the
role of the sponsor, not even that of an
organizer.

Although time is precious, I am certainly
open to further discussion about the approval of
my program, and inform you that I can be reached
at home every day till 8:30 a.m., between 12:00

and 1:00, and between 4:00 and 5:00, and if so notified, could come to see you, honorable sir, at any time.

Please accept the assurances of my complete respect,

Your most obedient servant,

Louis Princeps

The following fragmentary speech is remarkable in its expression of Lueger's demagogic talents.

Nachlass Karl Lueger
St. Slg Zl. 1257/12
Box V
Mappe: Korrespondenzen,
Notizen, Formblaetter e.c.,
Wahlangelegenheiten betreffend

Question:

I. Who is Heinrich Steudel?

Answer:

He is a real estate owner, he is no businessman, he does not circulate among the people, and does not know their desires and needs.

Question:

Which offices does or did Heinrich Steudel hold?

Answer:

He is   1.) Municipal Councilor of the City of Vienna
        2.) Delegate to the Provincial Diet
He was 3.) Member of Parliament
He is   4.) Deputy Mayor of the City of Vienna
        5.) Chairman of the Finance Section
        6.) Member of fifteen commissions and chairman of four commissions.
        7.) Board member of the kk private Brandschaden Versicherungsgesellschaft (fire insurance company), etc., etc.

151

Question:

As Municipal Councilor, what has Steudel done for the people?

Answer:

Nothing

Question:

As Municipal Councilor, what has Steudel done for the District of Margarethen?

Answer:

Nothing

Question:

As Delegate to the Provincial Diet, what has Steudel done for the people?

Answer:

Nothing

Question:

As a Member of Parliament, what has Steudel done for the people?

Answer:

Nothing

Question:

Why is Steudel so lauded and praised by Vienna's corrupt daily press?

Answer:

Because Steudel has done nothing for the people.

Question:

Why was Steudel selected as Deputy Mayor by the

152

majority of the Municipal Council?

Answer:

As a reward for the fact that he goes along with the majority through thick and thin.

Question:

Has Steudel ever gathered all the voters in order to account to them?

Answer:

<u>No</u>

Question:

Has Steudel ever gathered all the voters in order to present himself as a candidate?

Answer:

<u>No</u>

Question:

Why hasn't Steudel done this?

Answer:

<u>Because he feared the interpellations of the voters.</u>

Question:

What does one call a party that seeks to win votes by paying for wine, beer, and cigars?

Answer:

<u>That kind of party</u> is called <u>corrupt</u>.

Question:

If, therefore, <u>Steudel's party</u> does this, what kind of a party is it?

Answer:

A <u>corrupt</u> party

Question:

If Steudel's party offers a businessman <u>500</u> gulden for breach of contract and desertion of the Democratic Party, what kind of a party is Steudel's party?

Answer:

A <u>corrupt</u> party.

Question:

If Steudel's party has induced a businessman to desert the Democratic Party by paying him 100 gulden, what kind of party is Steudel's party?

Answer:

A <u>corrupt</u> party

Question:

If Steudel's party seeks to influence hackney drivers, etc., who have been taken over by the opposing party by the payment of money and the promise of larger sums in the event of victory and agitates <u>against</u> Dr. Lueger, what kind of a party is Steudel's party?

Answer:

A <u>corrupt</u> party

Question:

What does a party deserve that employs such methods in election campaigns?

Answer:

The contempt of every honest thinking man.

Resoluteness, one of Lueger's salient characteristics, is here in strong evidence.

Draft

I N   203.046

Dr. Karl Lueger
Attorney to the Royal and Legal Courts
1, Kaernthnerstrasse no. 8
1, Seilergasse no. 5   Vienna, November 3, 1886

Honorable Mr. Adolf <u>Fenauer</u>
Chairman of the Association "Gewerbebund" (Trade Federation)

In response to your letter of the 1st of this month, I regret not to have the confidence of your association, (before: because it is much pleasanter not to have enemies) but on the other hand, it proves that I have faithfully fulfilled towards the honorable voters of the Fifth District the program developed on the occasion of my candidacy.

I request that you relay this to your association.

Dr. Karl Lueger

NB 122/8-1[+]

To Ferdinand Menčik   March 20, 1891

1, Brauenerstr. 5

Dear Sir,

It would certainly be useful if a uniform procedure of all anti-liberal groups were achieved for the next Municipal Council and district committee elections.

[+]Indicates Nationalbibliothek Handschriftensammlung

Therefore, allow me to inquire confidentially whether the Austrian Nationalities Club is inclined to support the anti-liberal candidates in the 3rd and 5th Districts, and to whom I should turn in this matter, respectively.

Anticipating your gracious response,
I remain yours most respectfully,

Dr. Karl Lueger

I N   33162

To Franz Stauracz

Dr. Karl Lueger
Attorney to the Royal and Legal Courts
Vienna
III District, Hauptstrasse no. 21

Vienna, January 5, 1895

Honorable Sir,

While I thank you warmly for the kind invitation, I very much regret not to be able to attend the celebration, because I have already accepted invitations to three places for the same evening.

I hope that the association continues to thrive and prosper and work actively in the interest of Christian people.

I send my most cordial greetings to you and all the participants at the celebration, and remain with the expression of my highest respect,

Yours faithfully,
Dr. Karl Lueger

These pictures of Lueger
and his friends were pro-
bably taken during his
university years between
1862 and 1870.

With kind permission of the
Museum of the City of Vienna

Leo Suppancic about 1863. (In Lueger's
writing): "Battle of Königgrätz, foot
lost."

Friedrich Deutsch- 1867.

With kind permission of the
Museum of the City of Vienna

Valerie Gréy

Playbill for the Gréy Theater

Beskiba's first known portrait
of Lueger (1895).

The Ring Theater fire of December 8, 1881. Nearly 400 lives were lost
in this disaster which revealed the inadequacy of theater safety regulations and municipal fire fighting procedure.

With kind permission of the
Municipal Library of the City
of Vienna

No Austrian politician before or since Lueger has been the
subject of so much popular music. The semi-official Christian
Social   Party composer was a municipal official Hermann
Quiquerez whose musical comedy "Prinz Anti und die weiße Nelke"
was performed at Christian Social   Women's League meetings.
The white carnation which adorned most of the cover sheets of
Lueger music was the official party flower.

The "Danube Steamship Company" of Vienna was one of the targets of
Lueger's anti-monopoly sallies.

The following pictures were all taken on May 21, 1908 at Schönbrunn Palace. The occasion was one of many homages paid to Emperor Franz Joseph in the sixtieth year of his reign. More than 82,000 school children participated in this particular ceremony which was stage managed by Lueger's party. It was an unseasonably hot day and the rival Social Democrats complained the next day about the possible ill effects of the weather and excitement on the children.

KINDERHULDIGUNG SCHÖNBRUNN 1908.
ORIGINAL-AUFNAHME VON ... ... CHNER, WIEN I. GRABEN 31.

The masses as ornament

Towards the end of his life, Lueger was increasingly attended by nuns.
This stimulated rumors about Lueger's salaciousness.

With kind permission of the
Museum of the City of Vienna

A tableau from Lueger's extensive collection of antisemitica. The
scene of departure Oświęcim is better known today as Auschwitz.

THE MUNICIPAL POLITICIAN

THE MUNICIPAL POLITICIAN

Biographies of Lueger have been consistently slanted in his favor. This positive bias has hampered an objective estimate of his administrative achievements. And though such a full revision would exceed the scope of this brief introduction, it must be recorded that much in Vienna changed as a result of his term in office. It was to Lueger's credit, for example, that in spite of powerful opposition from liberal circles, foreign ownership of utilities and transportation came to an end in the city. His incessant efforts to preserve Vienna's natural beauty and to add to the number of existing parks and public gardens make him something of a forerunner of today's environmentalist. And where he could not improve, he would, to be blunt, cover up. If he could not make the improvements he wished to, he would resort to palliatives at the very least, and conceal what he felt to be ugly, even if it were something itself new. Karl Kastner, a retired municipal official, recalled such an instance:

> When between 1903 and 1906, the embankments of the Wien River in the vicinity of the City Park were designed and constructed in the predominant 'Jugendstil' of that time, Dr. Lueger did not like the results, and he said so, at the grand opening of the park. He decided on the spot to cover up the convolutions and lofty linear ornamentation, and ordered the City Park Director, Wenzel Hybler, who stood beside him: 'Hybler, cover it up with greenery.' The order was obeyed, and even today a wild tangle of vines still obscures this grand project.[1]

Felix Czeike describes Lueger's reforms in another area:

> Under Lueger, who actually concentrated his efforts on economic matters, we can discern within the area of social legislation the beginning of municipal welfare and various investments in health care. For the first time the municipality assumed responsibilities that had hitherto been outside its activities (Kindergartens, hospitals, the Lainz Home for the Aged, convalescent homes, etc.) Considered revolutionary at the turn of the century, this development is more important

than many others, because for the first time a community showed interest in the welfare of the individual. In our overall evaluation, therefore, we should not let ourselves be overly influenced by some of the inadequacies as quite naturally and justifiably have been pointed out by the opposition.[2]

With the exceptions of his 1897 mayoralty address and a last draft of a speech of some ten years later, the remainder of the documents presented in this chapter date from the 1880s. These record Lueger's activities as opposition politician rather than his career as mayor. They do not, therefore, describe his actual achievements. It was, nonetheless, an eventful decade of a rich political life, and one in which the man and his later projects can be seen taking shape.

In the Municipal Council, the United Left, when Lueger was chairman, was gradually falling apart, and he steered more and more into populist anti-Semitic channels.[3] At the outset of 1882, the sensational Fogerty Affair revealed corruption within the munici- pal administration; considerable attention was thus focused on Lueger, who had refused to accept bribes. The English railway man had allied himself with Austrian industrialists, and wanted to build a Guertelbahn in Vienna. But Lueger's sustained struggle against foreign capital and its influence led him to oppose Fogerty and his methods. This stand grows more and more evident in his political speeches, and it won him the support of a large section of "Democrats," composed of small tradesmen to whom he owed his re-election as a Municipal Councilor in March, 1884.[4] A year later, he was elected to parliament, and remained a member to the end of his life twenty-five years later. His speeches in the Christian Social Association began to assume a greater clerical orientation from 1887 on. In 1888, he asso- ciated himself with Karl Freiherr von Vogelsang, who published the conservative Catholic paper Das Vaterland. In the 1890s, the Christian Social Party was formed.[5] Lueger's speeches even from the 1880s had shown that he was already an avowed anti-Semite. Clericalism, nationalism, anti-Semitism, glorification of the "little man," and municipal socialism all came together in his politics. Later, he devoted greater energy to attracting a mass following, as a leader of the Christian Socials.[6]

160

Lueger systematically courted, for example, the Vienna Tramway employees in particular, in order to win their support for his municipal socialization plans. The Vienna Tramway Company treated its employees in an utterly arbitrary way. In 1891, when Lueger's growing reputation had already spread outside the city and his law practice was flourishing, even as a member of parliament he defended a conductor who had been dismissed for criticizing the company's handling of pension funds. (See Lueger's defense of Salomon Meisl.) Later requests from still other employees for Lueger's legal assistance tell something of the story of his increasing popularity and his success in building a broad political base.[7]

Lueger's struggle for the mayoralty in the 1890s captured the interest not only of the imperial city, but also of all Europe.[8] The dramatist and journalist Robert Weil witnessed and described its prevailing mood, which overflowed into Lueger's handwritten acceptance speech:

> An agitation developed such as no metropolis in the world had yet seen. Demagogy, incitement, and slander celebrated veritable orgies. Sanguinary posters grinned from every streetcorner; every evening agitated meetings filled the halls, taverns and such, lasting until dawn; Dr. Lueger was often on hand, cheered by his followers, to harangue the masses, to shake the hand of the faltering, and to expose the enemy parties to ridicule and contempt.[9]

The elections of 1895 signalled the end of liberal power in Vienna's Municipal Council. A new era emerged marked by a shift toward socialization, when in 1897 Lueger's election was finally confirmed by the emperor.

1. Related to the author by Karl Kastner in 1977.

2. Felix Czeike, <u>Liberale, Christlichsoziale und
    Sozialdemokratische Kommunalpolitik (1861-1934).
    Dargestellt am Beispiel der Gemeinde Wien.</u>
    Vienna, 1962, pp. 81, 82.

3. The United Left, an association of "Leftists,"
    "Radical Leftists," and a few independent members
    of the Municipal Council, opposed the majority
    liberals. See Eduard Hausner, "Die Taetigkeit des
    Wiener Gemeinderates in den Jahren 1884-1888."
    Ph.D. dissertation, University of Vienna, 1974,
    pp. 77ff.

4. In the spring of 1882, Lueger received an admiring
    letter from Karl von Zerboni, publisher of the
    anti-Semitic <u>Der Oesterreichische Volksfreund</u>:
    "You have fought valiantly, honorable sir, and
    emerged gloriously. From such cloth is cut either
    a minister or a martyr. For both, the reward of
    posterity is certain." Letter of April 3, 1882.
    I N 45721. Zerboni's daughter Karoline married
    Lueger's law partner Josef Brzobohaty, and is
    alleged to have been Lueger's mistress.
    Kielmansegg, p. 386. She may indeed have been the
    only woman for whom Lueger felt deep affection.

    For details of the Fogerty Affair see <u>Ibid.</u>, 365,
    366, and Gertrud Stoeger, "Die politischen
    Anfaenge Luegers," Ph.D. dissertation, University
    of Vienna, 1941, pp. 65-79.

5. According to Vogelsang's biographer, Wiard Klopp,
    Vogelsang created the basic principles of the
    Christian Social movement. "Lueger and Gessmann
    joined the movement before it became publicly
    active, and in 1894, four years after Vogelsang's
    death, founded the Christian Social Party.
    Vogelsang had nothing to do with this party.
    Until his death (1890), all those who more or less
    followed his principles were called United
    Christians." Wiard Klopp, <u>Leben und Wirken des</u>

Sozialpolitikers Karl Freiherrn von Vogelsang. Vienna, 1930, p. 183. For a summary of the development of the Christian Social Party, see Adam Wandruszka, "Das Christlichsozial-konservative Lager," in Heinrich Benedikt, Ed., Geschichte der Republik Oesterreich. Vienna, 1954, pp. 301-358.

6. For a detailed account of Lueger's political activity in the 1880s, see Kuppe, pp. 50-220.

7. Some of these requests and pertinent information are to be found in the Nachlass Lueger, St. Slg. Zl. 1257/2, Box III, Mappe: Tramway Gesellschaft. Lueger later paternally referred to the tramway workers as "'his' street car workers." This was after the City of Vienna had bought out the privately-owned tramway system. Reinhold Knoll, Zur Tradition der Christlichsozialen Partei. Vienna, Graz, and Cologne, 1973, p. 184.

The life of a typical tramway conductor's family in the 1890s is described in Julius Deutsch, Ein Weiter Weg. Lebenserinnerungen. Zuerich, Leipzig, and Vienna, 1960, pp. 13-32.

8. For Lueger's election campaign, see Erwin Burger, "Die Frage der Bestaetigung der Wahl Dr. Karl Luegers zum Buergermeister von Wien," Ph.D. dissertation, University of Vienna, 1952, and Kielmansegg, pp. 62-65 and 367-381.

9. Robert Weil (Homunkulus), Rueck naeher, Bruder! Der Roman meines Lebens. Vienna and Berlin, 1920, pp. 46, 47. Further details of this campaign are also described in Rudolf Kuppe, Dr. Karl Lueger, Persoenlichkeit und Wirken. Vienna, 1947, pp. 82-89.

Lueger was possibly the first Austrian politician to stir widespread public controversy over a railway construction project that threatened some of Vienna's parks and gardens. To dramatize the issue, he and his lower-middle-class, property-owning followers constructed a mock-up of a viaduct resting on iron pillars on the Schwarzenberg Platz in the middle of Vienna to suggest that the proposed project would ruin the city's skyline and endanger property values. He thus pioneered in a political aesthetics and also tapped economic anxieties. The following document reveals Lueger's attempt to exploit political, aesthetic, and economic fears. In its concern for the preservation of Vienna's architecture, it also anticipates Camillo Sitte's classic City Planning According to Artistic Principles, which sold out the first edition within a few weeks in the spring of 1889. Through Lueger, politics had anticipated art.

From: "Protokolle ueber die Parteiversammlungen des Club Vereinigte Linke," volume II-I N 63518

Excerpt from Lueger's minutes of the club meeting of September 16, 1881.

Secretary: Dr. Lueger
Attendants: Lustig, Bachmayr, Baertl, Loquay, Schaeffer, Gugler, Pfister, Feucht, Matznetter, Scherer, Riss, Vaeth, Redl, Kreuzig, Kulisch. Guests: Simon, Mueller.

I. Dr. Lueger reports on the question of the Guertelbahn. After discussing the justification at some length, he moves that:

1. the Municipal Council declare that the transportation interests of the City of Vienna would be best served by means of a Guertelbahn connecting all Vienna's stations, combined with a Wien River line, as well as a line along the Danube Canal, and furthermore, the construction of a central train station at the site of the present chief customs office, perhaps by including the adjoining property and moving the chief customs office to the Danube metropolis. Because the proposed project is not a Guertelbahn, but rather, first, a Danube Canal line, second, a Vienna Valley line, and only in the third place, a Viennese

Guertelbahn, and further, because this line links only
two stations, provision should definitely be made to
complete the missing sections of the above train
system within a certain period, or at least to make
possible its realization by another party in such a
way as to allow for a coordinated system. It is to be
stressed that realization of this railroad project
does not in any way offer any particular advantages
for the City of Vienna within its present legal
arrangement; rather, in order for these rail lines to
be profitable for the City of Vienna, it is essential
that the tariff barriers and the present food consumption tax barrier[+] be abolished within city limits.

2. Concerning the proposed roadbed, it should be
noted that it cannot be approved because the park
areas would be extensively damaged, because aesthetic
considerations are insufficiently allowed for, and
finally, because it would endanger the safety of the
Wien River and preclude the regulation of the river
course. The City of Vienna could approve only the
kind of roadbed that would not entail too great a
sacrifice in accordance with the above-mentioned three
points and, therefore, must insist on a roadbed that
protects the parks for which so much was sacrificed,
allows for the bridging of the Ringstrasse and other
such outstanding and beautiful areas in a manner
corresponding to the demands of aesthetics, and
finally, a roadbed that is located outside the Wien
River and its present embankment, in such a way that
the long-desired regulation of the river is not rendered difficult or impossible. Lastly, the existing
means of transportation must be maintained and all
future means planned or actually executed must be considered, so that those businessmen concerned are
obligated at any time, at any place, and at their own
cost, to provide for the construction of such
buildings as are necessary for such a system.

3. The system must operate in such a way that the
occupants of adjoining buildings are not disturbed
either by noise or smoke, and that real estate is not
devalued.

[+]This was a tariff barrier within whose confines a
food consumption tax was levied. The effects of this
barrier on the population are described in Rudolf
Kuppe, Dr. Karl Lueger, Persoenlichkeit und Wirken.
Vienna, 1947.

The following acceptance speech was never given, because it was written for an election that Lueger lost. When Johann Schrank died on December 28, 1881, and his post of second deputy mayor became vacant, Lueger campaigned for the office but was defeated by Johann Prix, who would eventually become Vienna's last liberal mayor.

Nachlass Karl Lueger
St. Slg. Zl. 1257/12
Box III
Mappe: Wahlangelegen-
heiten

Gentlemen,

On the occasion of the election just concluded, I feel deeply obligated to thank all those colleagues who, by their votes, have today placed their confidence in me.

I am very well aware of the difficult task I am now assuming.

While I shall have to continue to fulfill my responsibilities as a member of the Municipal Council, I may, perhaps, be called on to represent the mayor as well.

First, I shall have to remain faithful to those political and economic principles that have guided me and my allies so far.

Nevertheless, I shall continue to work not only to preserve our free institutions, but also for their further development in the best interests of the people--particularly for the abolition of the curial system and for the extension of the franchise.

In economic questions, I will always advocate a conscientious and orderly administration, the protection of the rights of the community against anybody, irrespective of power and influence, and work towards the elimination of the present food consumption tax barrier. Now as before, I shall adhere to the principle whereby a happy solution of those great questions important to the positive development of the municipality that will shortly occupy the Municipal Council are possible only through complete unselfishness and consideration of public interest.

Second, I shall be obligated to forget being a party man, particularly if I am called to direct your negotiations and to observe the strictest objectivity, and I shall make every effort to live up to the great example set by my predecessor in this position, the unforgettable Deputy Mayor, Dr. Schrank.

I know I shall need your cooperation, dear colleagues, in my task, and I ask you all for the same.

In particular, however, I ask the mayor and his deputy to support me with your wealth of experience and I gladly assure you that I will always consider it my duty to preserve the unity in the Praesidium that appears to me to be necessary in the interest of the welfare of the community, and that I will gladly be prepared to subordinate my opinion to the judgment of your mature experience.

And so, with the help of God, I hope to fulfill the responsibilities you have given me today; and I have only one desire, only one ambition--namely, that I may succeed in convincing you, dear colleagues, that those who cast their votes for me today have not placed their trust in someone unworthy.

One of Vienna's greatest tragedies was the Ringtheater fire of December 8, 1881, in which approximately 400 people died. Shortly thereafter, Mayor Newald became involved in a bitter feud with the Lower Austrian governorship over the responsibility for the catastrophe. Lueger sided with Newald, who had become the target of liberal press attacks and at whom in any event much criticism had been directed by his own party members because of his indulgence toward the views of the "Vereinigte Linke." The spectrum of opinion about Lueger's willingness to assist Newald ranges from Felder to Kuppe. The latter wrote approvingly of Lueger's selfless defense of Mayor Newald. Felder, on the other hand, remarked somewhat cryptically that Lueger had "completely ruined" Newald.[1] Lueger's own contemporary writings suggest

---

[1]Cajetan Felder, Erinnerungen eines Wiener Buergermeisters, Vienna, Hannover, and Bern, 1964, p. 250.

that his main interest had been to uphold the power of
the mayor's office in relation to the governorship.
As mayor, Lueger would maintain the supremacy of the
office, at least symbolically. By 1882, the time had
passed when Lueger would appeal to the governorship
against the "illegal decisions" of the Municipal
Council, as in 1877, when he had been in the political
wilderness. An investigatory commission appointed by
the Municipal Council ultimately placed the blame for
the fire on the governorship and the police for
failing to implement and enforce adequate precau-
tionary measures. By that time, however, Newald had
already been forced to abdicate, and Lueger had
achieved further renown.[2]

Nachlass Karl Lueger
St. Slg. Zl. 1257/12
Box III
Mappe: Ringtheater

Note to File

    During my conversation with the mayor at the end
of July or beginning of August last year, he broached
the subject of fire precautions in theaters and the
magistrate's position on this subject. In order to
make this context understandable, I guess I must
briefly tell the first part of this conversation,
which has no connection with the law suit.

    The Municipal Council had passed a number of reso-
lutions in the spring of 1881 that concerned the elimination of abuses in peddling. When I visited the
mayor in his office at the end of July or the
beginning of August, he informed me, as Chairman of
the Peddlar's Trade Commission, that he had recently
found out that the magistrate had not carried out two
points of the Municipal Council resolutions. He
said, because there was no legal reason for non-
compliance, he reprimanded the magistrate and he
requested the director of the magistrate to assume
responsibility for prompt execution of Municipal
Council resolutions. The mayor complained about the

---

[2]For further details of the aftermath of the fire, see
Kuppe, pp. 59, 62, 63, 65.

unwieldiness and timidity of the magistrate, and went on to observe that these characteristics surfaced in an unpleasant way with regard to another matter. He then told me that, as a consequence of the theater fire in Nice, an investigatory commission had inspected all theaters and that the magistrate had submitted the relevant reports to the governorship to effect the issuance of a new regulation. But, he said, the governorship refused this, and stressed that the community was authorized to take care of all matters within its sphere. He then told the magistrate's assistant that he didn't need any regulation, but could simply order the theater directors to undertake everything prescribed by the commission. The assistant had thereupon expressed the fear that many complaints would result, whereupon he (the mayor) remarked that each theater director would follow these orders in his own interest. For if the public learned that a director refused to comply with the regulations ordered for the safety of theater-goers, they would simply not patronize that particular theater.

I did not speak further with the mayor about this subject, to which I ascribed no particular importance at that time, for quite some time after December 8th.

Only after the second interpellation had been submitted by Municipal Councilor Baron Somaruga was I asked by the mayor to assist him and Dr. Glossy, respectively, in this matter. At that time, the mayor's point of view in that matter had already been submitted in a report to the governorship, i.e., he unequivocally defended the management of the magistrate against the tendency of state authorities to place the entire blame for the tragedy on the community. Nevertheless, as I became more familiar with the file material, I considered it my duty to ask whether it would not be advisable to point out that the magistrate had not fully complied with the mayor's directives. This (the mayor) refused, explaining that he, as chief executive, was publicly obligated to represent and defend this branch. It would also create the worst impression if first the state authorities placed the blame on the community, and then, in turn, the mayor on the executive branch.

Draft   Nachlass Karl Lueger
                               St. Slg. Zl. 1257/12
                               Box III
                               Mappe: Ringtheater

The Municipal Council of the City of Vienna
refuses to approve the separation of monies from the
municipal administration that were appropriated by the
council and deposited with the praesidium for the support and care of those persons victimized by the fire
at the Ringtheater in Vienna on December 8, 1881, and
requests the mayor to change the proposed statute for
a trusteeship in such a way that the community's
authority over the administration of monies similarly
appropriated for like causes, as for example, welfare
fund, militia fund, hospital fund, is protected.

1. The monies received are municipal assets specified
for a certain purpose, and it was up to the mayor as
chief executive to distribute them.

2. The relief committee carries out the mandate of
the mayor, and not the Municipal Council, and has only
the rights of the mayor--Article 68.

3. The mayor has no right to draw on municipal assets
and to divert them to a special fund; therefore, the
executive committee has no right, either.

4. The Municipal Council must decide.

5. Disadvantages of a fund. Uncontrollable. . . .All
expenses of the community, but no rights.

6. Examples: <u>Mobilized Militia Fund</u>.
             <u>Emperor Franz</u> Joseph Foundation

7. Therefore (the authority should) remain with the
municipal administration.

Fragment   Nachlass Karl Lueger
                               St. Slg. Zl. 1257/12
                               Box III
                               Mappe: Ringtheater

WHEREAS, it has become obvious that an effort is being
         made to place the blame for the catastrophe
         of December 8, 1881 exclusively on the

shoulders of the municipality (before: and to divert the attention of the population from the truly guilty persons and groups);

WHEREAS, the mayor is responsible only to the Municipal Council for a response to an interpellation, and therefore the practices of the governor vis-a-vis the mayor represent a transgression on the autonomy of the municipality (before: aside from the rude, unjustified tone neither appropriate to the governor nor the municipality), this explains the insults inflicted on the mayor by the governor in their conflict and explains the Vereinigte Linke.

(Here Lueger breaks off)

Nachlass Karl Lueger
St. Slg. Zl. 1257/12
Box III
Mappe: Ringtheater

This printed motion of urgency, probably written by Lueger, contains his pencilled corrections, which are underlined.

Motion of Urgency

of the members of the Municipal Council

The corroborating reports about the terrible accident that befell our city on December 8, 1881 have convinced us that the cause of the accident was not so much the lack of regulations, but rather that the police neglected daily supervision of these regulations and contributed by their (before: irresponsible) fateful conduct to the magnitude of the disaster immediately after the outbreak of the fire.

We are further convinced that the leadership of the municipal fire department lacks the prudence and energy that can and must be demanded from it, and that therefore, despite the fire brigade's demonstrated

171

devotion to duty, the first and foremost responsibility of the fire department, namely to save lives, was only <u>partly</u> fulfilled and not enough <u>timely and extensive</u> efforts were made to check <u>the rooms inside the theater</u> to see whether the assertions made by the police, that all persons were saved, were true or not. And because the best and most useful laws and regulations are of no practical value if they exist only on paper and are not carried out, and because their purpose is not fulfilled as long as those responsible and those authorities supervising the execution of this responsibility are not devoted to strict performance of their duty, and because first and foremost we must awaken and sustain this devotion to duty, we propose the following

Resolution:

The Municipal Council of the City of Vienna expects that all irresponsible derelictions of duty, irrespective of the perpetrator, will be strictly and impartially punished by the competent authorities.

The following letter to Prime Minister Taaffe refers to Lueger's continuing efforts to uphold the power of the mayor over the governorship, and also refers to a previous personal appeal to the prime minister to intervene. On January 18, 1882, the <u>Fremdenblatt</u> commented on this second appeal:

> It has been reported to us from reliable sources, that in the last hours attempts have been made by the leader of the Vereinigte Linke to stop the decisive step of the governor. As someone assured us, Dr. Lueger is said to have gone to Prime Minister Taaffe in order to prevail on him. The outcome has proved how unsuccessful this was.[3]

Because this letter, together with the envelope addressed by Lueger remains among his legacy at the Vienna town hall, we can assume that it was never sent. Perhaps Lueger thought that it would have been

---

[3]<u>Das Fremdenblatt</u>, January 18, 1882, p. 2.

inappropriate to post it considering the delicate circumstances.

I N 203.065

January 18, 1882

Dr. Karl Lueger
Renngasse Address

His Excellency
KK. Prime Minister
Eduard Count Taaffe

Your Excellency:

I took the liberty of paying your Excellency a visit some time ago, because I considered it in the interest of the community that the conflict between the governor and the mayor not be prolonged until the bitter end. I could justifiably count on your Excellency's loyalty and presume that my actions would not be construed in any other way.

My efforts failed because your opinion was not shared by the other side to whom I related it.

Perhaps it should have been my duty to inform you of this, your Excellency, but, to be honest, I didn't have the courage.

In today's evening edition of the "Fremdenblatt," a pro-government paper that opposes my party, I suddenly read about my visit to your Excellency in a tone that is contrary to the honest intentions that guided me to take this step. This article probably will be only the prelude to attacks that will be continued in other papers.

I am fully convinced that this transpired without your knowledge and against your will, your Excellency, and I appeal not to the minister, but to the gentleman who will certainly know what to do to prevent other attacks.

With my highest esteem, I remain,

> Your Excellency's most devoted,
> Dr. Karl Lueger

The following two memoranda, the originals of which are now apparently lost, were located in a private collection of Lueger's documents in 1941. They were reproduced by Gertrud Stoeger in her 1941 Ph.D. dissertation, "Die politischen Anfaenge Luegers," and are presented here verbatim. These memoranda describe Lueger's involvement in the Fogerty Affair. He recounts the background of the events that ultimately led to a libel suit brought against him by two Municipal Councilors, Goldschmidt and Gunesch. The much-publicized trial that gained Lueger considerable notoriety took place in Vienna on March 1 and 2, 1882. Lueger was acquitted of the two charges involving a speech he had delivered, and his later letter to Mayor Uhl, in both of which he had exposed the two plaintiffs' irregularities, but was fined 100 gulden for his remarks made during the Municipal Council meeting of February 10, that all his assertions were true and could be proved through witnesses and documents.

Memorandum

Blackmail attempt in the matter of the proposed Guertelbahn project of J. Bunten and Fogerty.

On Monday, November 7, 1881, my solicitor named Richter called me from the meeting of the finance section and told me that Mr. Alois Theodor Buchwald had to speak to me today.[3] (Lueger describes how the conversation came about, which took place in the evening, on the way from Lueger's office to his apartment.)

He (Buchwald) told me that his business allows him to move among circles that are very interested in the realization of the Fogerty project. In particular, he mentioned Fajkmayer and pointed out that Rothschild,

---

[3]According to Lueger's notes for his own defense in the trial, which contain essentially the same information as these memoranda, Buchwald was a partner in the Richard Mauch Company, one of whose most important customers was Rothschild. "He (Buchwald) is an accredited businessman. We elected him deputy chairman of the . . . Unity, we nominated him as candidate for the chamber of commerce, and I myself have contributed much to Buchwald's election," Lueger wrote in these notes.

as an owner of large steel works and with whom allegedly 3,500,000 pounds sterling are deposited for
Fogerty, is interested.[4] He told me that the gentlemen believed the majority of the Municipal Council had
already been won over and that only I could perhaps be
an obstacle. Three Municipal Councilors, among them
Mr. Rudolf Ritter v. Gunesch and Mr. Ritter v.
Goldschmid, had been promised directorships,[5] and
additionally for R. v. Gunesch 1000 pounds sterling
had been deposited, which were to be given to him as
soon as the concession had definitely been granted.
In response to my question as to the identity of the
third Municipal Councilor, he replied that he did
not know him. In the above-mentioned circles, the
question had often been discussed whether it would be
possible to win me over and how this could be done.
He said they wanted to promise me a directorship as
well and create the position of legal adviser for me,
with a significant annual salary of about 20,000
Gulden. He (Buchwald) had declared that this could
not be accomplished, because Dr. Lueger would not
accept because of his career.

They then hit on the idea of sending me 1000
pounds sterling as well. Because his friendly
relations with me were known, he, Buchwald, had been
asked to talk to me about it, and as unpleasant as it
was for him, he could not back out of it because of
business reasons. He also remarked that it had even
been considered to assert house ownership rights,
because my office is located in a building that Baron
Rothschild owned.

To all of this I replied that he knew quite well
that accepting one or the other of the offers did not
correspond with my principles, and that I always act
according to my own and unprejudiced convictions.
Thereupon, Buchwald mentioned that he knew this and
had from the very beginning known that he would not
be successful with me. He then told me that Messrs.
Fogerty and consorts would do everything the

---

[4]The Wittkowitz Steel Works are specifically mentioned
in Lueger's notes.

[5]In his notes, Lueger states that Gunesch and
Goldschmidt should not have participated in meetings
and drafting resolutions because of a conflict of
interest.

municipality required; especially, they would develop
differently the stretch from the Aspern Bridge to the
Elizabeth Bridge,[6] that this project will soon be
submitted, that they feared I might prematurely commit myself to another project, and that only in this
connection did they want to be reassured . . . (Lueger
replies that he is not committed to anyone, and
replies to yet another apology of Buchwald's that he
understands his predicament and that he had spoken
only to Mandl about these matters, and thanks God that
he allowed him to pass the second trial--the first
concerned the tramway.

Dr. Karl Lueger

Vienna, November 1881

Memorandum

On January 26, 1882, my solicitor Richter told
me on the way home from a committee meeting of the
"Unity" at approximately 12:15 a.m.--Mandl was a
bit ahead, Buchwald had already said good-bye--"about
different cases of fraud and embezzlement that were
perpetrated against me by my legal intern, Dr.
Heinrich Loewy. . . . At the Heumarkt, Richter came
to the point. He told me that Dr. Loewy had for some
time been associating with Buchwald, a certain
Fajkmajer, and Fogerty; that Dr. Loewy had told him
that he and Fogerty had had breakfast in the Hotel
Wandl, for which Fogerty had paid 17 gulden, that
Loewy had been promised a large sum of which he would
let Richter have some; that this would all be decided
tomorrow, because Fogerty would come to Vienna on that
day. Loewy said that this would be his lucky day and
that he would thereupon finish his various tasks and
then leave me. He would become director of the new
railway and his future would be secure. He said Loewy

---

[6]The Aspern Bridge was built between 1863 and 1864,
destroyed during World War II, and was rebuilt in
1951, near the Urania, over the Donau Canal. See
Czeike, p. 377. In the early 1880s the Elizabeth
Bridge spanned "the Wien River between the
Kaerntnerstrasse and Wiednerhauptstrasse." The
Elizabeth Bridge was closed in 1897. Ibid.,
pp. 457, 458.

had been excited all day today (January 26th), and had prayed to God that nothing would happen within the next 24 hours. These revelations made a shocking impression on me. . . Because intervention was most urgently necessary, I ordered Richter to give me all letters received and sent by Loewy. I asked Dr. Mandl to request two friends as witnesses for the next day, in whose presence I would confront Dr. Loewy. . . .

January 27, 1882

Because Dr. Loewy had closed the cash and account books, I demanded from him the cash book that extended through December 1881. This seems to have struck him as unusual. . . (Lueger wanted to drive to Hietzing in the afternoon to take care of a deposit matter.) At that moment, Dr. Loewy ran up to the coach: "Sir, I admit that I have terribly abused your trust. I will confess everything. Please forgive me; I will again be your faithful servant." He began to cry and sat down next to me in the coach. I told him that I would forgive him his disloyalties if he repented everything, and especially if he revealed before witnesses his dealings with Buchwald and Fajkmayer concerning Fogerty. This he promised. I drove back to the Cafe John and asked the gentlemen present, Dr. Mandl, Vaeth, Ferd Mayer, and Gradt, to proceed immediately to my office, because Loewy wanted to confess. . .

In my office, I first asked Dr. Loewy to report orally his dealings, which he then did. After we had asked him a few questions, he wrote down his testimony, signed this document, which was then bound, sealed, and signed by the four witnesses. I now add to the statements in this document that Dr. Loewy declared that he had burned the letters from Buchwald, Falkmayer (sic) and Thursfield.

It was further decided to visit Fajkmaier the next day at 9:00 a.m. (Saturday, the 28th of January 1882) in order to ask for Dr. Loewy's two drafts. . .

Saturday, the 28th of January, 1882

Around 1:00 p.m. . . . . Mayer, Vaeth, Gradt, as well as I and Dr. Loewy went . . . to Fajkmajer. I told him that Dr. Loewy had confessed everything, that he had especially confessed to having given him two drafts about the representation to be signed over to

177

him and about the shares that are to be handed over
to him, and I added my deep regret that Fajkmajer had
played such a role in this affair. He remarked that
there was nothing wrong if a company used the services
of legal counsel; one always needs an attorney in
Austria--in fact several. I referred him to the more
detailed aspects of Dr. Loewy's statement that made
the matter appear not quite so harmless. Fajkmaier
said that he regretted that it had been interpreted in
this way, and requested that we not be misled by this
in our judgment of the Fogerty project, a request
which, in spite of the serious situation, elicited
some amusement. In response to my question who had
recommended him to my legal intern, he said he
couldn't say. Then I requested both of the drafts
composed by Dr. Loewy. Fajkmajer declared that he no
longer had them; they were with Fogerty, who had
returned today to Vienna from his trip. He,
Fajkmajer, would go to Fogerty today, even though
Fogerty was indisposed, in order to send both drafts
to Dr. Loewy. Only after I insisted that the drafts
be sent to me did he promise them for today. We then
left Fajkmajer.

On this day, however, the promised drafts <u>did
not arrive</u>.

Sunday, the 29th of January, 1882

The promised drafts did not arrive today either.

Monday, the 30th of January, 1882

When I arrived at the office in the morning, I
found a letter that, without any accompanying explanation, contained both drafts. . .

Then Mr. Alois Theodor Buchwald appeared in the
office. He had learned of the events concerning Dr.
Loewy and wanted to defend himself by saying that he
was guiltless and had not participated in the whole
affair. He asked what Dr. Loewy had said about him
and I told him in such a way that I read the relevant
sections of the confession written and signed by
Dr. Loewy. Buchwald then said that he would very
much like to have a conversation with Dr. Loewy in
my presence. I didn't have anything against this,
but felt that those witnesses should be present who
were present at the occasion of Loewy's confession.
Buchwald agreed . . .

Around 10:15 a.m., as a result of my invitation, Mr. Alois Theodor Buchwald, Ferd. Mayer, Vaeth, and Gradt appeared in my office. We went into my study and called in Dr. Loewy.

I told those present briefly about the purpose of this gettogether, and then Buchwald began to speak.

He first told us about his association with Dr. Loewy. When they went together to the District Court Landstrasse for a hearing in the case of Buchwald vs. Weinmann, he had talked with him about me, specifically about my rigid views concerning the impossibility of exploiting the mandate of the Municipal Council. Dr. Loewy said that Lueger's views were exaggerated, and that therefore the office would suffer, and he, Loewy, as well, because he shared in the profits. Dr. Loewy further said that Dr. Lueger had refused a sum of 30,000 gulden that had been offered to him in the tramway matter. Thereupon, Buchwald had told Loewy what he had discussed with me concerning Fogerty, especially that he had offered me either a directorship, or the position of a legal advisor, or 1000 pounds sterling, if I were for the Fogerty project.

Dr. Lueger had categorically refused all this and declared acceptance of one or the other as incompatible with his honor. After some time, Dr. Loewy had approached Buchwald to set up a meeting with Fajkmajer. He had fulfilled this wish and informed Loewy by letter when he could meet Mr. F. In the letter, he had only used the letter "F." Otherwise he, Buchwald, had had nothing to do with Dr. Loewy.

Now that we had finished with the actual heart of the matter, we conversed further, and it was Buchwald in particular, without being asked, who relentlessly revealed the corrupt machinations of Fogerty's enterprise. Apparently in order to justify himself before those present. . . he told . . . the details of the conversation between him and me of November 7th, but avoided, however, mentioning the name Rothschild, as he had done earlier. . . And now he spoke about the fact that all three Municipal Councilors had been promised directorships as well as 1000 pounds sterling and reluctantly named. . . the third Municipal Councilor. His further revelations documented how intimately he had been involved in

these matters and how carefully he had operated.
Before I repeat Buchwald's testimony as accurately as
possible, I emphasize that not one of us was requested
by Buchwald not to make use of his statements, and
that his story was so truthful that I had no reason to
correct him.

Buchwald related that one day Fajkmajer came to
him and gave him the assignment to speak to Dr. Lueger
and to win him over to the Fogerty project by offering
him a directorship or a position as legal adviser or
the sum of 1000 pounds sterling. He could not refuse
accepting this assignment because of his business
relations and especially because of a prominent
figure whom he did not want to name. Since his
(Buchwald's) clients wanted an answer by 9:00 a.m. on
the very next morning, he went to Lueger's office, did
not find him there, and was told by the solicitor
Richter that Dr. Lueger was in the Finance
Section. . . . In the evening, he had told Dr. Lueger
that he needed to talk to him in his capacity as
Municipal Councilor, and not as an attorney, that
Lueger should listen to him as a friend and not be
angry. He, Buchwald, moved in circles that were very
interested in the realization of the Fogerty project.
And the men in question believed that the majority of
the Municipal Council had already been won over and
that only Dr. Lueger could be a possible obstacle.

To three Municipal Councilors, among them
Mr. R. v. Gunesch and Mr. v. Goldschmid, directorships had been promised, in addition to 1000 pounds
sterling each. The third man, to whom the same had
been promised, was Stiassny, although he wasn't sure
of this. And now, either a directorship, or the
position of legal adviser, or 1000 pounds sterling
also should be offered to me. Fogerty's company would
also do everything that the municipality wanted, and
they would submit within a few days new plans for the
stretch--Aspern Bridge-Elizabeth Bridge. Dr. Lueger
had categorically refused everything, as he, Buchwald,
had expected.

During a conversation that related to these
revelations, Buchwald remarked that even if the
majority of the Municipal Council were against it,
the Fogerty project would be accomplished in any
event; it enjoyed a much too powerful patronage. In
response to a remark made by Gradt, that 1000 pounds
sterling appeared to be too little for Goldschmid,

180

Buchwald replied: "I beg your pardon, sir; he should have done it for nothing. After all, he is the brother of Rothschild's executive manager." In response to a question by Municipal Councilor Ferd. Mayer, whether the promises made to the Municipal Councilors were meant seriously, Buchwald vehemently asserted this. . . . Buchwald added: "You can be certain of it, Municipal Councilor Mayer! If the concession were granted today, Rothschild would pay out the money tomorrow." As the conversation turned to Municipal Councilor Rudolf v. Gunesch, Dr. Loewy remarked that Gunesch was always in the Fogerty offices, that Thursfield had complained about him because of his incompetence, and that they had indicated to him, Gunesch, that he need not come anymore. As I had to attend to something in my office, Buchwald, according to witnesses, said that it had been Baron Pino who had first brought it to the attention of the Fogerty company that it would be necessary to win over Dr. Lueger as well. In response to Municipal Councilor Vaeth, whether Pino had received money, Buchwald answered: "Not money, but drafts. . . ."

When the conference in my office was over, Messrs. Buchwald, Ferd. Mayer, Vaeth, and Gradt went downstairs to the restaurant to see Mandl and Kummer. . . . As my friends told me, Buchwald related the same story there as he had in my office. Only he appeared to have been even more open. For he said that it was Rothschild who, because of his steel works, was particularly interested and because of whom he had to make the bribery offer to me. Rothschild was their (Fogerty's) best customer, and therefore he had to do it. He also talked about Baron Pino and described in the following characteristic fashion the bribe he received, for Michael Kummer had wondered: "Well, does Pino also eat iron?" Whereupon Buchwald answered: "The one eats iron, the other drafts. . . ."

Wednesday, the 1st of February, 1882

When I arrived at the office in the afternoon, I had Dr. Loewy write down his confession of fraud, and I then told him that he was dismissed.

Sunday, the 5th of February, 1882

In the morning, the club held its meeting at

Dreher's. In the afternoon in my office, I wrote the letter to Deputy Mayor Uhl, which was actually composed by Dr. Mandl. I remark that he advised me to announce this to the Municipal Council, which I, however, categorically refused.

Monday, the 6th of February, 1882

As I sat in the Cafe John with Dr. Mandl, Gradt, Hugbensy, and Dr. Wengraf, Buchwald ran up to me extremely excited, demanding that I declare that he had not attempted to captivate me. First and foremost, I told him that the cafe was not a suitable place to discuss such things. If he wanted to talk to me he should visit me out at my office or suggest another private place where I would gladly talk to him. . . . Buchwald calmed down because the others had also intervened, and again related, in order to prove that he did not want to captivate me, the conversation we had on November 7, 1881, in the manner in which I had written it down. He mentioned that it was he who had pointed out to me that Municipal Councilors R. v. Gunesch and R. v. Goldschmid had been won over in the manner described. I remember still that Huybensy (sic) felt that one could not describe this other than with the word "captivate." I told Buchwald that in my letter to the deputy mayor the word "captivate" did not appear, but rather that I truthfully reported that he had been given the assignment to make me the offer and that at this opportunity he had revealed to me then, and later in front of three witnesses, the information with regard to Municipal Councilors Gunesch and Goldschmidt. He should go up with Wengraf and Dr. Mandl to the office of the former; I would get the draft of my letter and let him read it.

Buchwald did this; I went to my office, where I found the announcement of today's meeting of the Municipal Council, picked up the draft, hurried into the office of Dr. Wengraf, and let Buchwald read it. He wasn't quite satisfied with it, and whereas before in my office had himself revealed the matters in the way I had described them, now he felt, after I had refused to make a statement in his favor, that he certainly could present the matter in such a way as if I had been the first to mention the names Gunesch and Goldschmid.

As I arrived in my office in the afternoon,
Buchwald was waiting for me. He made a terrible
scene, threatened to go to Dr. Gruebl; he had to make
an explanation; his company had fired him, he was a
lost man. He cried like a baby, implored me to give
up my mandate. I was lost, he had to leave me and
testify against me. I was a bit excited myself,
particularly because Municipal Councilor Vaeth had
left the party and I felt sorry for Buchwald. I told
him that I would gladly help him if I could; I would
be prepared to explore every honorable way out. Yet
I could not relinquish my mandate, because that would
be viewed as an expression of guilt and I am, after
all, innocent. There was no stain on my honor.

In the evening, there was a meeting of the
chamber of commerce committee in the Hotel Elizabeth,
and there began Buchwald's deceitful defense. Since
that time, I have not spoken with him.[7]

Nachlass Karl Lueger
St. Slg. Zl. 1275/12
Box II
Mappe: Redekonzepte

At the meeting of the Municipal Council of
Vienna on January 30 of this year, a letter from the
kk. Minister of Commerce dated January 27 and addressed
to the mayor was read, in which in response to the
resoluutions passed by the Municipal Council on
December 29 of last year concerning the municipal
railway it was announced that "the requested concession for the construction and operation of the projected Viennese Guertelbahn, including branch lines,
was granted to the Civil Engineers James Clarke Bunten
and Josef Fogerty."

It was stated that "why the government had considered it its responsibility to solve the question of

---

[7]During the subsequent trial, Buchwald apparently
deviated from his statements to Lueger. Buchwald
seems to have wanted to serve Fogerty as well as
Goldschmidt and Gunesch.

the Viennese Stadtbahn system in this way without further delay," was because "the stipulations" in the concession instrument made it possible that execution of a Stadtbahn allegedly in the public transportation interest and the desires of the municipality of Vienna could be insured without using public funds "by private companies whose expertise and capability are beyond doubt, according to prior investigations."

The Viennese journals unanimously reported that the concessionnaires Bunten and Fogerty did not have the money to begin construction, let alone complete it.

These reports are in direct contrast to the above assurance of the minister, according to which "the capability of Messrs. Bunten and Fogerty is beyond doubt, according to investigations made," and it is therefore advisable to inquire of competent authorities about the invalidity of the newspaper articles.

Because Article 16 of the concession instrument requires "all authorities concerned strictly and carefully to supervise the concession and the conditions therein," I am thus convinced that the mayor has already conducted the necessary inquiries to be able to tell the Municipal Council about the true state of affairs.

Therefore, I take the liberty of addressing the following questions to the honorable mayor.

1. Has the mayor already made the necessary inquiries into the validity of the reports in the newspapers about the status of the Stadtbahn and is he inclined to report the results to the Municipal Council?

In the event that such inquiries have not been made,

2. Is the mayor willing to make the necessary inquiries of the kk. Ministry of Commerce particularly about the assertion that the concessionnaires Bunten and Fogerty cannot prove the necessary solvency to begin construction, that they want to change some of the conditions in the concession, and which ones, and whether the kk. Ministry of Commerce is willing in the event that these reports are true to employ those rights given the state in the concession instrument against the concessionnaires?

I N 41509
Draft of a letter
to an unknown editor
of the <u>Neue Freie Presse</u>   Vienna, February 23, 1882

Dear Editor,

        Pursuant to Article 19 of the Press Law, please
publish the following correction:

        In no. 6283, dated February 22, 1882, you re-
printed in the section "Community Journal," under the
title "Viennese Stadtbahn," an article allegedly from
the periodical "Times," in which it was asserted among
other things that I had been the one who had made
offers to the staff of the London Syndicate for the
Vienna Guertelbahn planned by Bunten and Fogerty.

        This assertion is not true. On the contrary, the
"offers" were made <u>to me by Mr. Alois Theodor Buchwald,</u>
who had been authorized to do this either directly or
through intermediaries by the Bunten and Fogerty
Company. As stated by Dr. Loewy, the negotiations
with him were begun by Mr. Fajkmaier and continued
by him and Mr. W. E. Thursfield, who was employed by
the above-named company.

        At the conclusion of the subject article, it was
asserted that the repeated requests for more time from
the Municipal Council of the City of Vienna for submission of the expertise had always been made by me or
some of my friends. This is also wrong, because, on
the contrary, it was I who repeatedly urged that the
expertise be made.

        Lueger probably delivered the following speech,
which here appears in a draft form, before a meeting
of his supporters in the Third District on March 6,
1882, shortly after the libel suit trial. He seems
to evince a need for the voters' trust and reassurance.
The tone of his remarks also suggests that he may
have feared that his popularity had been somewhat
undermined by his having been fined 100 gulden for the
failure to prove allegations against Goldschmidt and
Gunesch.

Nachlass Karl Lueger
St. Slg. Zl. 1275/12
Box II
Mappe: Redekonzepte

Draft

Gentlemen,

The party to which I have the honor to belong has always adhered to the principle that it is the responsibility of each elected person always to maintain contact with the electorate and to solicit its opinion before deciding any important question.

Observing this principle, I met with you on February 5th of this year, as you well know, to report to you about my activities, and prove that I have always represented the public interest and that I am not unworthy of your trust.

I ask you, gentlemen, to recall for a few moments that time.

The months of December, 1881 and January, 1882 will forever constitute an important, yet sad chapter in the history of Vienna. In these two months, the opposition party succeeded in disrupting the People's Party in the Municipal Council and breaking its hard-won power, not so much by its own strength, but through external circumstances and treason within our own ranks.

In these two months, the world witnessed the sad drama of a freely elected mayor's quarrel with the government, a mayor who lost many of his constituents and who had to yield to governmental pressure. (Lueger is evidently referring to the controversy over responsibility for the Ringtheater fire.--Ed.) We also saw how personal hatred and partisan passions can induce men who pretend to consider it a privilege ruthlessly to fight the present government actually to throw sand in the eyes of their constituents and ostentatiously become friends of the government.

Autonomy

On February 5, 1882, the struggle had already been decided and what followed was <u>to divide the spoils among the happy victors.</u>

186

Under such circumstances, it was my duty to report to you. I alone was attacked and all blame was laid at my door. I was obliged to tell my constituents how it all transpired, to give you a picture of the battle tactics of our opponents, and to show you the powers that opposed us.

This was the reason for my speech on February 5th. It was not the beginning of a new struggle, but rather the end of a struggle. (before: a confession of defeat) A passage of this speech and my letter to the deputy mayor, now mayor, and a declaration I made during the Municipal Council meeting on February 10, 1882, were used by 2 Municipal Councilors for 4 charges in a libel suit against me.

From reports, we learned about the results of the trial. You can therefore pass judgment on those points that arose during the trial. And you are also aware of the judgment against me.

As a consequence, I had to ask myself <u>whether it would be appropriate</u> to relinquish the mandate <u>that you have given me</u>.

I had to consider that my opponents--and I have many--could interpret my retention of the mandate in such a way that I would not dare to appeal to you, gentlemen, and to your judgment. Also, I had to tell myself that I had reached the limit of sacrifices that I could make. I had to ask myself further whether with the few friends I have left from happier times it would be possible to continue the struggle against those overwhelming odds opposed to our efforts. All of these considerations contributed to my decision to relinquish my mandate.

Then a delegation of my constituents met with me. Through their representative, my honorable friend Mr. Hintermayer, they implored me in a polite but firm manner to persevere and not to relinquish my mandate.

1.) Only responsible to electorate
2.) Important questions, especially on Stadtbahn make my promise contingent on decision of today.

So I request that you reach a decision. It will be easy for you. My life is like an open book. You can compare my weaknesses and my good points. If you believe I still deserve your trust, then I will persevere regardless of what may come, for I and my friends will struggle against these enemies not for ourselves, nor to advance our own interests, but for the people and against their enemies.

Lueger frequently drafted motions that other members of his party proposed. This was probably necessary because many of his supporters lacked the necessary legal knowledge.

Draft   Nachlass Karl Lueger
                                         St. Slg. Zl. 1257/12
                                         Box IV

Motion of Urgency of Municipal Councilor Ferdinand Loquai and Colleagues

For the meeting of the Municipal Council to be held on Friday, the 9th of this month, the election of 6 delegates from the Municipal Council to the board of the Kaiser Franz Josef Foundation for the support of Vienna's small enterprises has been scheduled.

According to point 2 of the foundation charter, the funds of this institution are to be used as follows: for loans at reasonable interest rates to existing and future commercial loan institutions that are chartered under partnership or limited liability statutes, cooperative, trade, and other associations in Vienna that are credit-worthy and exist for the purpose of supporting Vienna's small businesses.

WHEREAS, it is a commonly accepted principle of good management that those persons who are members of an audit committee may not have any financial interest either directly or indirectly in any trusts supervised by it;

WHEREAS, the Municipal Council of the City of Vienna, based on this principle, has always advocated strict interpretation of the regulation under Article 95 of the provisional municipal constitution of the City of Vienna, and that city contracts for labor and supplies should not be granted to Municipal Councilors;

WHEREAS, the Board of the Kaiser Franz Josef Foundation is authorized according to its charter and by-laws to examine the credit standing of those associations that are eligible for loans and to audit these associations, especially their administration of loan funds;

NOW, THEREFORE, we urgently move:

That the Municipal Council resolve to appoint to the Board of the Franz Josef Foundation only those Municipal Councilors who are not associated either as members of management or board of directors with any establishment eligible for loans from the foundation.

Draft for a motion of urgency presented at the Municipal Council session of July 6, 1883.

Nachlass Karl Lueger
St. Slg. Zl. 1257/12
Box III
Mappe: Tramway Gesell-
schaft

Motion of Urgency
of Municipal Councilor Dr. Karl Lueger and Colleagues

According to Article 28, section 8, of the Agreement between the City of Vienna and the Vienna Tramway Company on March 7, 1868, the street cars may not carry more passengers than seats are available.

Non-compliance with this contractual stipulation, i.e., overcrowding of cars, is in the sole interest of the tramway company, which thus reaps ever-increasing profits and expends as little as possible at the expense of comfort, security, and health of the people.

Since the onset of the mild weather, the overcrowding of cars has reached a point that is not only in violation of the agreement, but which, from the standpoint of the public interest, may no longer be tolerated.

During this hot weather, everybody calls for sanitation measures for fear of contagious diseases, but overlooks, however, the most obvious, and tolerates a condition that must be considered a <u>scandal</u>.

While existing regulations for transport of hogs and calves, etc., are strictly observed, it is quietly tolerated that a <u>profit-hungry</u> company ignores all considerations and transports people in a way contrary to all decency and to the standards of public safety and health.

Therefore, we feel obligated to submit the following

Motion of Urgency

That the Municipal Council resolve:

1. To order the magistrate strictly to supervise adherence by the Vienna Tramway Company to the transportation code approved by the Municipal Council and to demand that the Tramway Company cease and desist from overfilling cars, with the stipulation that in the event of non-compliance use would be made of the right to withdraw the security bond pursuant to Article 43 of the agreement.

In case of non-compliance, this demand is to be repeated within 3 days, and if it is not met again, the magistrate must immediately present its request to the Municipal Council for withdrawal of the security bond.

2. To request the kk. police administration <u>strictly</u> to enforce existing regulations to prevent over-crowding tramway cars.

Lueger's receptivity to technical innovations for the benefit of the community is evident in the following motion.

Nachlass Karl Lueger
St. Slg. Zl. 1257/12
Box III
Mappe: Saekularfeier
1883

Motion of Urgency
of Municipal Councilor Carl L. Lustig
and Colleagues

The international electric exhibition in Vienna
has more than exceeded all expectations. Its tremendous significance for science and technology was
unquestionably recognized both here and abroad, and
the stream of visitors from all over the world and the
praise of layman and expert alike are proof of the
brilliant achievement of this difficult task by the
commission responsible for this undertaking.

It is therefore the municipality's duty of honor
to convey its expression of thanks to those men who
tirelessly and ceaselessly contributed toward the
realization of this great undertaking.

Therefore we propose the following

Motion of Urgency:

That the Municipal Council resolve to invite the
executive board of the commission of the international
electric exhibition in Vienna to visit the historical
exhibition of the City of Vienna.

The committee for the historical exhibition will
determine the date and hour as well as all other for-
malities, and will be empowered to close the historic
exhibition to the general public for the duration of
the visit by the invited guests.

Draft

Nachlass Karl Lueger
St. Slg. Zl. 1257/12
Box V
Mappe: Stadtbahnbau

Motion of Urgency of Municipal Councilor
Dr. Karl Lueger and Allies

In the session of May 19, 1882, Municipal Councilor Eduard Suess and allies made a proposal.

This proposal was unanimously adopted, the commission elected, and it looked as though serious steps would be taken to solve these questions that could be considered <u>vital</u> for the City of Vienna.

In dealing with this question, however, the leadership of the commission demonstrated that more consideration was given to the interests of a political party than to the City of Vienna. With downright fearful anxiety, they focused on the suburbs, which are presently quite well off at the expense of the city, and therefore are opposed to anything that would change their situation for the worse.

Unfortunately, the City of Vienna itself gave the suburbs the best opportunity to delay the matter.

On February 25, 1884, it was decided to send a questionnaire to the suburbs in question. Months passed, and on June 17, 1884, it was reported that no answer had as yet been received. Indeed, this is still the situation <u>today</u>, and I only know from newspapers that there will be a noncommittal response from all suburbs.

All this suggests that nothing will be accomplished by negotiating with the suburbs, and that the Municipal Council of the City of Vienna has no other recourse but to turn to the only competent authorities, parliament and government.

The most important of the three questions is the <u>food consumption tax</u>. The consumption tax barrier prevents the prosperity of our city, devalues whole areas of property, makes life more expensive, and hinders construction development. Everything else is <u>secondary to this question</u> and it is the responsibility of the Municipal Council to demand constantly what all of Vienna desires:

<u>Elimination of the Food Consumption Tax Barrier</u>

The resolution reached at the last meeting of the Municipal Council could lead both parliament and the government to believe that, for the Municipal Council, other interests take priority, and it is therefore necessary to counteract this opinion. For this reason we propose the following

Motion of Urgency:

That the Municipal Council of the City of Vienna resolve:

A petition be directed to both houses of parliament and the government <u>request the elimination</u> of the food consumption tax barrier and reform of the tax itself.

The suburbs commission is to compose the petition and report on this within 4 weeks.

Draft

Nachlass Karl Lueger
St. Slg. Zl. 1257/12
Box III
Mappe: Vororteingemeindung

The Municipal Council hereby consents to the expansion of the municipal boundaries of Vienna by including the municipal areas and sub areas that fall within the expanded area of the food consumption tax barriers, <u>provided, however, there is no increase whatsoever in the present state tax rate and taxes in Vienna or the suburbs to be incorporated</u>, and no increase whatsoever in either the direct or indirect municipal taxes or municipal sur-taxes.

The Municipal Council requests the esteemed government to draft and submit the relevant bills to the Lower Austrian Provincial Diet as well as to both houses of parliament.

From a Private Collection

Dr. Karl Lueger
Attorney to the Royal and Legal Courts
Vienna
I, Brauenerstrasse no. 5   Vienna, November 26, '7
                                 (probably 1887)

To the Leadership
of the Democratic Club in the IXth
District

Because you have adequately documented your
defection from the Democratic Party by open cooperation with the liberal Wrabetz, I follow as well in the
footsteps of numerous honorable and dedicated men who
have left the club and I herewith withdraw from same.

Dr. Karl Lueger

The following document underlines Lueger's preoccupation with municipal socialization and anticipates one of the most important projects begun during
his mayoralty—the building of a second mountain
spring reservoir.

Draft probably written about 1892

Nachlass Karl Lueger
St. Slg. Zl. 1257/12
Box III
Mappe: Notizen zur Frage
der Hochquellenwasser-
leitung

1.) The motions of the City Council are to be
referred to a commission of 25 members elected from
the Municipal Council for discussion and submission.

This commission must be responsible for examining, both _financially and technically_, all projects
for the completion of Vienna's water supply and to
submit the results of these reviews in their report
in such a manner that the Municipal Council is in the
position to form an exact picture about the feasibil-
ity and costs of each project, as well as about the
quality and quantity of the water.

The commission must negotiate with individual
project directors for the solicitation of binding
offers.

194

The following principles are to be observed in resolving the question:

1.) The installation of a second water main system within the municipal area is to be avoided, and therefore consideration must be given for piping drinking water that is on a par with our present supply.

2.) Consideration must be given to the necessity that the City of Vienna be protected against the danger of interruption of the mountain reservoir supply through damage to the aqueduct or through other circumstances by the construction of a second pipe line to Vienna or other technical precautions, e.g., construction of reservoirs, and that if necessary good drinking water comparable to the present water is to be made available.

3.) The water supply of the municipal area is exclusively the province of the municipality and may not be placed in private hands. If a project is in private hands by a state-granted concession, every effort must be made to acquire such a concession. Even if the transport of water to Vienna is provided through private sources, the delivery of water to consumers may take place only through the municipality.

During the early 1890s, Lueger concentrated his efforts on winning over municipal workers employed by private companies. The following two documents tell us something about his persuasive techniques.

Draft

Nachlass Karl Lueger
St. Slg. Zl. 1257/12
Box III
Mappe: Tramwaygesell-
schaft

Honorable Administrative Council of the Vienna Tramway Company. <u>Appeal</u> by Salomon Meisl, Conductor of the Vienna Tramway Company through Dr. Karl <u>Lueger</u>, Attorney in Vienna I, Brauenerstrasse 5 against

the disciplinary decision of punitive
dismissal orally transmitted to him on
July 31st of this year.

Honorable Administrative Council,

On July 31st of this year, I was orally informed
that the disciplinary commission had decided to dis-
miss me as a punitive measure for allegedly having
said at a meeting of the tramway employees on July 18,
1891, that the Tramway Company is obligated to do
something for the pension fund and thereby for having
made inflammatory speeches against the interests of the
company. Pursuant to Article 45 of the staff regulations, I hereby appeal this _____ judgment _____ and
state:

First, I object to the fact that the disciplinary
decision was transmitted to me only orally, even
though Article 45 of the staff regulations refers to
a delivery of the judgment and therefore requires a
written execution.

Second, I object to the composition of the disciplinary commission. According to Article 42 of the
staff regulations, the directors, in naming the members of the disciplinary commission, must see to it
that each member represents a different employee class
if possible.

The disciplinary commission that passed judgment
on me, insofar as it concerned the members named by
the directors, was comprised of civil servants and
controllers only.

Considering that the director, i.e., that person
who brought charges against me, is simultaneously the
chairman of the disciplinary commission, and he cannot
be expected to consider his own charges as unfounded,
impartial judgment was effectively precluded from the
very beginning.

Third, I must emphatically protest the manner of
the proceedings, because this was contrary to Article
43 of the staff regulations. According to the pro-
visions of this Article, the disciplinary commission
has the responsibility to ascertain the facts in each
individual case through interrogations and official
inquiries. After hearing the charges against me, I

now affirm that I only spoke for, and with the authorization of, my colleagues. To this end, I presented a declaration in which the conductors confirmed my statement. The director simply rejected this declaration with the words: "That doesn't concern us. You have spoken and we'll get you."

I further requested that witnesses be called in order to prove that I only said: "the organization is morally obligated to do something for the pension fund because it requires everyone to join," and to authenticate the fact that my speech did not contain any hostile remarks against the organization nor any incitement against same. This request was also rejected with the director's remark: "Your kind?" to which I responded: "Yes, men of honor who will tell the truth."

Fourth, I object to the judgment because, even if the facts therefore were true, they do not constitute cause for disciplinary action, and therefore Article 46 of the staff regulations for punitive dismissal could not apply. But most of all, I was not on duty when I spoke at the meeting and am therefore liable only under the general civil laws for what I said. If the organization thinks that I have in some way harmed its reputation, then appropriate legal action is available, but it does not have the right to bring disciplinary action against me. Moreover, the government representative present at the meeting would surely have protested, if, as the disciplinary commission alleges, I had in any way "incited" when I spoke. This did not happen, and herein lies the best proof that the allegation of the disciplinary commission is false.

By the way, I told the commission, and I will say it again, that I never thought to incite my colleagues or other tramway employees against the company. Indeed, this is a suggestion that I indignantly reject. I intended nothing more than to express the wishes and complaints of my colleagues. No one is forbidden to have desires or complaints. And no one is forbidden to express such desires and complaints, nor to realize and correct them respectively, as long as this is done within the limits of the law. This is the decisive issue. How can one speak of incitement if I recommended following the legal course of action? Even if I had said that the organization were obligated to do something for the pension fund, this cannot be considered incitement, but rather a point of view that can be either correct or incorrect, but that no impartial person can possibly view as incitement.

That I have always been interested in drawing attention to the desires and complaints of my colleagues about the company and to improve the situation in cooperation with it, is demonstrated among other things by the enclosed copy of a petition, the original of which is in the possession of the chief dispatch clerk.

In conclusion, allow me to state in a few words that the facts accepted by the disciplinary commission, even if they were true, cannot be subsumed under Article 86 of the staff regulations. That they do not fall under points 1, 2, 3, 5, and 6 needs no further proof. Even under point 4, which is considerably vague, they cannot be included unless all basic principles of logic are violated. I certainly have not acted in any <u>dishonorable</u> way. <u>There is nothing dishonorable</u> in wanting to be secure in old age and such a desire is not only not "<u>completely incompatible</u>" with the interests of employment and the reputation of the company, but on the contrary, very compatible.

On the basis of the above, I believe I may justifiably hope for a favorable action on my humble request, which is:

That the honorable Administrative Council deign to void the disciplinary judgment of punitive dismissal orally pronounced against me on July 31st of this year on the basis that it was unfounded.

by_____
per Power of Attorney B

The following fragmentary draft of a speech, written
about the same time as the Meisl defense, suggests
some of Lueger's organizational techniques. He not
only barred meetings to potential trouble makers, but
also had bouncers available if his precautions proved
inadequate.

Nachlass Karl Lueger
St. Slg. Zl. 1257/12
Box III
Mappe: Tramway Gesell-
schaft

<u>Leitz</u>

Gentlemen,

First and foremost, many <u>thanks</u> for <u>your</u> <u>heavy</u>
<u>attendance</u>. I have seen to it that <u>only</u> <u>tramway</u>
<u>employees</u> have gained admission.

(Marginal comment: <u>(D)eutsches (V)olks B(latt)</u>
<u>Presse A(ll)g.(emeines) W(iener) T(a)gbl(att)</u> There
are a <u>few newspaper reporters reporting objectively</u>

    (have secret
    (informers
    (removed)

<u>Only tramway employees</u>, to prevent outsiders
from infiltrating, who are more interested in partisan
politics than in the welfare of the tramway employees.
I honestly believe that we don't have to make politics
here, that it is simply our task to achieve those
<u>rights</u> for the tramway employees that the law provides
to each worker, and to obtain guarantees to insure
that as a consequence of disability caused by old age,
sickness or other circumstances, a tramway employee
will not become disabled and a beggar, so that he
knows that his family will be cared for even when the
provider is dead.

Counting on <u>discipline</u>, I have <u>guaranteed a</u>
<u>peaceful and undisturbed meeting</u>. I am convinced that
your <u>model behavior</u> will <u>justify</u> my <u>confidence</u>.

Why did _I_ call this meeting?

" not the tramway employees?

I don't want to give the company the ammunition again
to set the notorious disciplinary commission into
action.

Thank God, they can't discipline me.

For this reason, I suggest that you elect me
chairman.

In the event that you agree to this proposal, I
promise you

1.) full freedom of speech. You can criticize
me, too. I'm used to criticism. Schmied Fischer Deputy Staff Chairman
Conducter Scherer Secretary

2.) I would three men
    driver
    conductor
    remaining tramway employees

3.) Secretary

Vote

Draft, ca. 1895   Nachlass Karl Lueger
                               St. Slg. Zl. 1257/12
                               Box III
                               Mappe: Tramwaygesell-
                               schaft

1.) The City Council declares that the overdue elimination of overcrowding on tramway coaches is under the
exclusive province of the esteemed governorship and
the subordinate police authorities, respectively, and
with only half-way good will, that could long ago have
been corrected by the enactment of appropriate regulations and by penalizing the tramway company.

The City Council calls attention to the fact that
the present situation is only in the financial interest

of the tramway company, and therefore the latter aims to insure its continuation.

2.) Proposal I of the speaker

3.) With regard to the new routes suggested by the tramway company, the City Council reserves judgment until it has had a chance to review the appropriate plans and method of operation and until it has been notified about those contributions the company is willing to make if removal of houses, etc., becomes necessary.

It is further noted that in case the tramway system is expanded, consideration must definitely be made to include the former suburban communities of Grinzing, Sievering, Gersthof, Poetzleinsdorf, Salmannsdorf, Neustift a. W., Neuwaldeck, Dornbach, Ottakring, Baumgarten, Penzing, Hacking, Hietzing, Unter-and-Ober St. Veit, Speising, Lainz, as well as the market community of Schwechat, if the City Council is to approach the Municipal Council for approval of the construction of the new routes.

In submitting its applications for construction of new routes, the tramway company has to realize that this is in their own financial interest, as was proved by the results of this year's fiscal report.

A change in operation/: Rejected modification to electric operation:/ the City Council will approve, and will endorse to the Municipal Council, respectively, if and insofar as this does not involve any change in the legal relationship between the municipality and the company.

4.) With regard to the car types, see proposal 7 of the speaker.

5.) With regard to the operating regulations, see proposal 8 of the speaker.

On this same case, see also letters I N 41529, 41528, 41530 and 41531, in "The Politician and the Press."

Draft of a letter

I N   41526

Honorable   Vienna, July 22, 1892
Mr. Johann Wittassek
Etui Manufacturer
Vienna, VI, Hirschengasse 5

Even though I do not know you personally I will,
for reasons of courtesy, answer the letter signed by
you of July __, 1892.

I have no intention of holding you responsible
for its contents, as I may justifiably assume that not
you, but someone else is the author.

Please inform the latter of the following:

1.) If he or others wants to hear me personally,
they may attend the meetings of our party any time unless otherwise expressly noted, where they will enjoy
freedom of speech. It is only requested that they
behave decently.

2.) If I apologize for not being able to accept
an invitation, the author of the letter has no reason
whatsoever to doubt the sincerity of this apology.

By the way, it is rather strange that your party
held those meetings, to which I was invited, on precisely those days on which, as was surely known, the
meetings of our own party take place. For example, on
the same Sunday your meeting is held, a meeting of the
Christian Social Club is held in Koenigstetten, where
I shall speak. Your party knows this because this
meeting was announced some time ago. The connection
and the intent that motivated your party's actions in
this matter are clear to every judicious person.

3.) I accepted your party's invitation to the
meeting on July 19th. Factual debate and complete
freedom of speech were intimated in your party paper.
The truth was, however, that your party leaders
invited guests only for the purpose of insulting and
even perhaps beating them in the most despicable manner. It may very well be that such actions perhaps

belong to the attributes of the <u>future state of free-dom</u> about which your party colleagues dream. Your party comrades will have to forgive my still being entangled in the bonds of the Dark Ages to such an extent that I consider your action silly and a breach of promise.

4.) As the author of the letter knows quite well, I had the repeated honor in past years to serve as the defense attorney for accused Socialists, as for example in the Bambusroehrel case, in the Merstallinger case,[8] etc. From the records, I know that many a brave worker has become a victim of unscrupulous informers. Nowadays, the informer business does not pay. Another certainly safer, and also less dangerous business appears to have taken its place--namely, the struggle against the Christian Socials, who do <u>not</u> belong to the capitalists, but rather who impartially oppose the influence and preponderance of big business. (before: The author of the letter will forgive me if I tar with the same brush the former police informers and the present attackers of our party.) Whether such actions are in the interests of the working classes, I confidently leave to the judgment of thinking men. (before: I am finished with the author of this letter. Now a few words directly to you.)

Because even before I received it you or the people behind you sent the letter addressed to me directly to all pro <u>big-business</u> papers <u>for publication that are apparently your allies</u>, you will forgive me if I also make public my response forthwith.

And now, farewell, and provided you are a Social Democrat whose struggle for the welfare of the people is well meant, allow me to express my esteem with which I sign,

Faithfully yours,
Dr. Karl Lueger
mp.

---

[8]The robbery committed against the cobbler Merstal-linger in July, 1882 had a political background. The charge was high treason, because the Socialist Party had presumably instigated the crime to get money. See Ludwig Bruegel, <u>Geschichte der oesterreichischen Sozialdemokratie.</u> 5 vols. Vienna, 1922, pp. 263ff., and <u>NFP</u> from March 8-21, 1883.

Some of the overheated political atmosphere of Vienna
during the spring of 1896 can be felt in the following
speech. Franz Joseph had already refused to sanction
Lueger's election to mayor three times, and a delighted Sigmund Freud wrote Wilhelm Fliess that he had broken his nicotene abstinence and smoked a cigar to
celebrate. After the fourth election, the emperor
agreed to allow one of Lueger's henchmen, Joseph
Strobach, to rule in Lueger's stead. The following
year, Lueger was again re-elected. This time Franz
Joseph had had enough of internal municipal strife.
Disregarding an earlier statement that he would never
sanction Lueger's election, the emperor approved this
fifth election and Lueger began his thirteen-year rule
as mayor.

I N   29926

Draft speech delivered on April 18, 1896

Gentlemen,

    For the fourth time in the course of a year, I
have the honor to be elected mayor of my native city.

    Twice has Vienna's entire electorate indicated,
unequivocally and very clearly, how and by whom they
want their affairs to be administered.

    In both elections, the Christian people of our
city demonstrated how a self-confident people defends
its rights. It didn't allow either insults and
threats to arouse it, or was it diverted by mere
promises from its proper course. It fought with the
legal weapon of the ballot and won.

    On behalf of my friends whose wish I gladly ful-
fill, I express our thanks to the Christian people on
this solemn occasion.

    It is now our duty to do justice to the legally
demonstrated will of the people.

    Indeed, we believe this will should also be
respected by the government, all the more because they
themselves were the ones who practically called on the
people to serve as judge, and whose judgment is not
just the result of sudden passion but rather the consequence of careful deliberation and the clear recognition of the situation of the Christian people.

When my honorable friends recently cast their ballots for me, for which I thank them warmly, they did so not to indulge in a personality cult, but to express the will of the people, and when I accept this mandate, I do it not to satisfy personal ambitions, but to fulfill a difficult duty.

It is no secret that I was gladly willing to offer my person as a sacrifice. If my friends did not accept this sacrifice, they realized that under the present circumstances, it was more than ever necessary to stand solidly behind me.

The mayoralty question in Vienna is not merely a local issue, but one that has far-reaching significance, both economically and politically.

The present ruling party in Hungary is attempting to expand its sphere of power even further and to assume an undue influence on Austrian affairs.

This must be opposed calmly but with determination; indulgence on any point would have incalculable consequences.

We need only read in the authoritative Hungarian newspapers the almost daily repeated diatribes against Vienna to appreciate immediately the magnitude of the mayoralty issue in Vienna.

This question is not a duel between Badeni and Lueger, as is frequently said. No, this would be a rather narrow point of view. Rather it is a part of the great struggle to free the Christian people, and the struggle for the independence and freedom of our fatherland Austria. To persevere in this struggle and not to budge an inch is the duty of a German Christian man, a good Viennese and a patriotic Austrian.

In consideration of these views, my friends have again voted for me, and with these same considerations in mind, I have accepted this mandate.

I have nothing either to add to or detract from, those words that I expressed to you on similar occasions in October and November of last year.

When we are permitted to take over the administration of the city according to the will of the

people, my friends and I will follow the path of justice, and we hope to be able to count on the support
of all those who take seriously the welfare of the
people.

I close with the wish:

May it please God that finally the people receive
what belongs to them.

The published version of Lueger's draft acceptance speech, which follows, appeared with few changes
in all the major Viennese newspapers after his fifth
election in April, 1897. On April 21, the Neue Freie
Presse reported that Lueger had taken the oath of
office while a mob of his followers outside the town
hall had chanted: "Der Dr. Lueger soll regieren und
die Juden sollen krepieren." There are some suggestions in this speech of the turbulence that had dis-
rupted Viennese political life for nearly two years
since Lueger's first election. The speech itself is a
remarkably self-contained unit, and was principally
intended as a statement of his plans. It was also a
summation of his theories, and evinced concern for
Vienna's environment, the abuses of capitalism, and
various municipal deficiencies. Lueger clearly had a
plan of action, and he wasted little time in imple-
menting his various projects.

Note preceding Lueger's speech draft in an unknown
script: "On the night of April 19th-20th, 1897, Dr.
Karl Lueger wrote this draft of his major acceptance
speech delivered to the governor on April 20th, 1897,
on the occasion of his inauguration as Mayor of the
City of Vienna."

(illegible signature)

Your Excellency,[+]

I begin my term as the elected, confirmed, and
inaugurated mayor of the Imperial and Residential City
of Vienna in fulfillment of a duty, as well as a
heartfelt desire, and express my gratitude, which I
owe to his Majesty, our Emperor and Master, for his
most gracious confirmation of my election.

I thank your Excellency for your participation in
the ceremonial act of taking the oath of office and
for the friendly words of praise and recognition of
the activity of my predecessor during his term of
office, as well as for the expression of hope placed
in me.

I can assure your Excellency that I will do
everything to justify the desires of the people whose
votes brought me to this high office, and that I, in
performing my duties, will be guided by the true love
of that city that I proudly call my native city and
to which all the memories of my life, in particular
those of my unforgettable parents, are forever and
indivisibly bound.

I thank all whose presence here today makes this
such a glorious occasion and such a powerful expression of that will that was demonstrated by all citizens of Vienna without exception, to maintain vigorously and to guard resolutely the great treasure of
a free mayoralty election, which his Majesty has so
graciously granted.

Your Excellency was right in pointing out that
the office that I assume today is not only important,
but also responsible, and it imposes on the holder
very serious duties.

I fully recognize this, and with all the strength
at my disposal, I am willing to meet the challenges.

Recognizing human shortcomings I pray for the
help of God, and during a time when belief in God and

[+]Governor Eric Graf Kielmansegg

public acknowledgment of this faith are often ridiculed, I consider it my duty to declare that the oath
I took today is not just an <u>empty legal phrase</u> for me
but an <u>appeal to God</u>, to whom all men are subject.

Your Excellency had the kindness to touch on
individual questions in your speech, whose satisfac-
tory solutions are very important to you.

I too applaud it, your Excellency, as a welcome
sign of the Christian spirit of the population of
Vienna that the existing <u>houses of God</u> are becoming
too crowded to meet the <u>religious needs</u> of the people.
I do not think I err in expressing the hope that the
Municipal Council of the City of Vienna will contribute its part to enable the construction of new
churches. After all, we have always contributed our
part, indeed <u>more than our part</u>, to such needs and
calmly tolerated the scorn and ridicule of our
opponents. Your Excellency will surely forgive me if
I take this opportunity to recall the <u>duties</u> for those
whom God has blessed with wealth, and <u>if I</u> hope that
the state, recognizing the significance of religion
for the <u>monarchy</u>, will contribute its part, especially
since in confiscating the property of the Church, it
also assumed its moral duties.

Your Excellency is correct in considering the
<u>present</u> condition of our city's <u>transportation system
inadequate</u>. Recognizing this as well, the City of
Vienna has approved the painful sacrifices for construction of the so-called transportation network.
But even when this will have been completed, <u>local</u>
needs will not have been entirely met. Your
Excellency knows as well as I where the problem lies.
For years I have led the struggle against a company
that in monopolistic fashion has exploited public
transportation needs and that practically grew into a
state within a state; unfortunately, I lost. The
contract between this company and the municipality
represents a kind of impregnable fortress, and the
person who drafted the agreement did so in such a way
that not even his opponents once in power could change
it. If I hope nevertheless that public interests will
eventually win out, I do so in the belief that people
will eventually realize that the purpose of public
authorities is not to fight one another, but to
cooperate to fulfill the legitimate demands of the
people. Electric power will be our main weapon in
this battle, and I count on the support of your

Excellency and all state authorities in this highly important issue to Vienna. Before I leave this topic allow me, your Excellency, to express the thanks of the population for your recent measures in alleviating the overcrowding of tramway cars and improvement of transportation.

The creation of a new building code to satisfy present requirements will occupy our constant attention for some time. We must prevent merciless exploitation of real property to the last inch, we must prevent zoning and subdivisions that will impose all burdens on the municipality, while private interests reap all the benefits; room must be left for light and air. Defacing of our beautiful city through gross violations in taste must be prevented; reasonable zoning corresponding to the historical character of the city must be made possible through a pertinent expropriation law. Because all of this is possible only through legislation, it is necessary for all public interests to work harmoniously, and I will certainly do my part.

A long-standing complaint is the deficient food provisioning system. The most diverse interest groups in this area bitterly oppose one another. I have always been of the opinion that the problem is with the unauthorized middle man who enriches himself at the expense of the producers and consumers and who represents an apparently invincible power who once before defeated the city. May the state authorities find enough courage firmly to oppose these exploiters of the public welfare. By organizing the farmers, may they create channels for enabling direct trade with the producers. The state authorities may count on my willing support and the community will gladly create all institutions and take all measures necessary to establish order once and for all in this area.

But there is much more to be done, and it will require the devotion of all who are called on to serve.

The operation of street sanitation leaves much to be desired. It must be reorganized in order to eliminate justified complaints.

Much to the dismay of all Viennese, a large part of the public gardens has been callously destroyed because of the construction of transportation lines.

It had to be this way, they say. Wisely recognizing the needs of a large city, we had set aside a section of the Guertelstrasse for gardens, which section now largely will be transformed into a heap of stone and brick called the Guertelbahn; where the worker after a hard day's work was to be able to breathe fresh air, smoking locomotives will poison the air. It had to be this way, they say. Assuming that this is correct, it follows that we are obligated to create more parks.

The question of supplementing the mountain spring water supply through new reservoirs is becoming more and more urgent.

Welfare services require reorganization, not in slavish imitation of foreign examples, but in such a way that the truly poor are treated humanely, and that it is recognized that the miserly amounts distributed as doles do not hinder begging, but rather encourage it; one must see to it that the bold, able-bodied beggar can no longer count on public charity.

The wages of many workers in the service of the city are insufficient and should be raised.

The civil service of the City of Vienna requires new regulations. The number of higher positions must be proportionally aligned with that of the lower ones so that the civil servants' future does not look bleak. We must stop the so-called trainee and Diurnisten business.[9]

The employment service must be taken over by the city.

The public health service must be expanded if it is to fulfill the great needs of a large city.

But all this requires money--much money. Considering the reduction in revenues resulting from the new tax laws, plus the tremendous burden the city will

---

[9]Temporarily employed office personnel who could not obtain civil service status.

have to bear as a result of the new Home Law,[10] and considering further the _expenditures_ resulting from the city's subsidy of the transportation system, one must realize that new and significant revenue sources must be made available to the city if it is to meet its obligations.

I certainly hope that the municipal gasworks, once in operation, will provide considerable revenues. I believe that the municipalization of the insurance and loan businesses can also create new revenues, or at least alleviate some of the financial burden on the population.

I expect that the state will realize how inappropriate it is for private enterprise to reap the unfortunately abundant income from that saddest of all businesses, the pawn business, instead of allocating these monies to the care of the poor.

But all of these are dreams of the future and not enough at that.

The _state_ must help _here_. It alone can and has the duty to do so.

If it can increase the burdens on the municipality through practically every new law, it must finally start thinking about methods to strengthen the municipality financially.

---

[10]Lueger was probably referring to an amendment to the so-called "Heimat Gesetz" of December 3, 1863, based on the Reichsgemeinde Gesetz of March 5, 1862, which states that anyone born or married into a particular community (or otherwise authorized by the appropriate authorities) was entitled to poor relief, among other things. The amendment to this law was passed December 5, 1896, and made it easier to obtain benefits. With the coming of industrialization, many flocked to industrial centers, and if they could not work could not claim poor relief at their new residences. Their home communities had to bear the cost of poor relief, but grew increasingly poor because they received no tax revenue from those who had left. See Adam Wandruszka and Peter Urbanitsch, Eds., _Die Habsburgermonarchie, 1848-1918_. Vienna, 1975, 2, pp. 222, 283, 300, 642.

We demand and shall continue to demand the
assumption of the food consumption tax by the municipality until our justified demands are met.

If your Excellency will study this question
carefully and benevolently appraise the situation, I
am certain that you will reach the same conclusions
and will join us in a common effort to realize our
demands.

And now a few words about the organization of the
municipality.

The statute has proved to be deficient in many
ways. The new institution of the City Council for
the City of Vienna has not met the test. It is beset
with trivialities and places inordinate demands on
those who are elected to it, while paralyzing the
efficiency of the remaining Municipal Councilors. I
will consider the elimination of this institution one
of my major tasks. It will be replaced by departments
whose heads will be responsible for the smooth execution of their assignments.

The district committees must be educated for
their tasks through appropriate directives.

The magistrate must again become an executive
organ that deals with the daily matters within the
framework of regulations.

Your Excellency was kind enough to maintain the
position of the magistrate as a high political
authority.

In the name of the civil servants, I express
thanks for the recognition that your Excellency has
bestowed on them, which they thoroughly deserve.

I add the promise that in the future, the demands
of the services will continue to be met in every
respect.

On this occasion, I would also like to touch on
commercial issues. I have always believed that commerce is one of the main pillars of the state, and
that it is therefore one of the first responsibilities
of the authorities to protect it. I will proceed
along these lines. I will always incline my ear to

the wishes of trade association leaders and I will
certainly help whenever I can.

In view of the seriousness of the situation, I
am obliged to say a few words about <u>politics</u>. I am a
German and will remain loyal to my people. National
thoughts and feelings are the duty of everyone.
Together with this duty must also go our thoughts and
feelings for our fatherland Austria.

The national struggle should never be used to
suppress social reform as has unfortunately so often
been the case. Protection of the working classes is
also the protection of the German people. The people
imperiously demand profitable work. Never should the
national struggle be exploited for the one-sided
advantage of a single political party, particularly
one whose activities heretofore have not served, but
rather injured the German people.

And now I ask all of you to support me, your
Excellency, my friend Deputy Mayor Dr. Neumayer, my
honorable colleagues in the City and Municipal Coun-
cils, the district superintendents and their deputies,
all district committees, welfare, district and local
school officials, trade association leaders, you, the
Director of the Magistrate, you, the Director of
Public Works, all officials of the magistrate, of the
Office of Public Works and auxilliary officers, you,
the comptroller, and all your officials. May we be
allowed to work together for the good of our beloved
City Vienna.

Loyalty to the Emperor and Empire is born in us,
and we will maintain this as long as we live.

It is our duty to work for the glory of our
fatherland Austria and to strengthen it even under
adverse circumstances.

We will oppose foreign influences with propriety
but with determination. We want to be, and remain,
free Austrians. United in the deepest love for our
imperial dynasty, we share its joys and sorrows.

We offer our thanks to the Emperor for his eter-
nal care for his Imperial and Residential City of
Vienna.

May God bless and protect our Emperor and his family.

I close with the words: Long live His Majesty, our most gracious ruler and Emperor Franz Joseph the First!

The effects of Lueger's advanced illness are evident in the handwriting of this, his last known speech draft, probably written about 1907. While this draft is one of the most fragmentary examples in the entire Lueger Nachlass, it hints at certain issues that were to contribute to the final crises of the pre-war years, and is therefore not without a certain significance.

Draft speech

Nachlass Karl Lueger
St. Slg. Zl. 1257/12
Box II
Mappe: Redekonzepte

Before I broach the subject of my talk today, I must _regrettably_ deal with a few remarks made by the previous speaker. In my capacity as mayor of Vienna, I am _obligated_ to protect the magistrate against untrue allegations.

Voter Lists

Why?

Is it relevant?
        no
On the 10th election.

The Socialists need a scandal.
Rebuffed by Gautsch
Pernerstorfer didn't fare too well.
Republ. emperor
But not the right Animo
Therefore against the Christian Socials.
Pan Germans   Viennese
Liberals
a)   Page 316 96

b) Jerabek
    Act 1

c) Ballot
    Theft. Act 2

I doubt whether this is possible in a strictly legal
way.
By the way, we already find ourselves in a situation
that is unconstitutional.
No one knows how the mutual expenditures should be
covered.
Hungary pays no taxes. . .
                        Hungary pays.

        Then there is I, of course. Dissolve every-
thing. . . here and over there. Now elections based
on the universal franchise.

Data about the activity of the election registry
offices.

Act 3

Are the Socialists even justified in making accusations?
No. (They) block elections, etc.

Act 4

Now to the point.
Emperor in Austria.
Republic in France.

Camarilla

Well, what did it do?
It shook Gautsch's hand. It spoke through him.
Is Gautsch so dangerous?

Jesuits

Silken undergarments
Old nursery tale
Dime novels

        "Deliver" archduke as next generation (or)
"eliminate" archduke . . . (meaning unclear, Ed.)
"Erzherzog als Nachwuchs 'liefern'"
        (Would) forbid anybody to talk about his wife,
sisters, mother in such a fashion.

But who will be the archduchesses decency and morality remain.

This unjustified crudeness ellicits <u>only</u> "amusement"

Now, to the Hungarian question:

. . . true 31692

If one wants to make a <u>clear judgment</u>, one must ask himself if <u>a compromise with Hungary is even thinkable</u>.

No

All Hungarian politicians, whether Tisza, Kossuth, Banffy, Andrassy, have only one goal, <u>the</u> suppression of Austria.

A) <u>Army</u>

and we are supposed to pay

B) mutual task
Minister of Finance
Hungary
Foreign Ministry
<u>Berlin</u>

and we are supposed to pay
Bosnia and Herzegovina
and we are supposed to pay

C) Industrial and
Agrarian interests
And we are supposed to pay
Answer:
We will <u>not</u> pay.

3) Personnel Union
. . . first, if everything . . . is.

King . . . Hungary

4) Hungary itself the <u>nationalities.</u>

Beginning of universal, equitable, direct, and secret franchise also for Austria in both cases, protection of the residents from the temporary inhabitants, and protection of the national minorities.

(Marginal note: ingratitude toward the different nationalities.)

THE PARTY PRAGMATIST:

LUEGER AND KARL FREIHERR VON VOGELSANG

THE PARTY PRAGMATIST

LUEGER and KARL FREIHERR VON VOGELSANG

The elegant pragmatism of Lueger's friendships is
many times borne out (perhaps even overborne out) by
the documents in this and other chapters. Karl
Freiherr von Vogelsang was a different kind of man,
simpler in his purposes and relationships. A convert
to Catholicism and "by birth and inclination a conservative,"[1] the force and simplicity of his beliefs
obviated the compromises and intricate expediency of
Lueger's style of politics. Yet at the same time,
Vogelsang was "one of those 'new conservatives'. . .
who realized that a true conservative movement must
have strong popular support."[2] This stance may
account for the attraction between him and the younger
Lueger, who also, if for different reasons, recognized
the necessity for "strong popular support." It seems
likely, however, although the alliance between the two
men was a productive one, that it may have lacked that
deeper coincidence of values and purposes that would
have enabled it to endure. But Vogelsang's accidental
death in 1890 leaves an open question whether or not
Lueger's situational behavior would sooner or later
have clashed with Vogelsang's more single-minded
Christian goals.

Nevertheless, the relation between Lueger and
Karl Freiherr von Vogelsang turned out to be a compatible one, and led to the formation of the
Christian Social Party. For up to 1887, factionalism
had remained a serious problem among the "Demokraten,"
the party with which Lueger maintained a nominal
membership; and about this time he must have seen that
this contentious coalition could not hold together
much longer. What he needed was a coherent political
base commanding a viable body of ideas through which
he could direct his nationalism, municipal socialization, and anti-Semitism toward his long-range goals.
He found, or thought he found, this center in the
coalition of conservatives, Democrats, and anti-
Semites who called themselves the United Christians,
and in the theories of Karl Freiherr von Vogelsang.

Vogelsang had absorbed much from the romantic
ideas of the German Catholic reform movement during
the 1850s and 1860s and by the 1880s was a seasoned
politician approaching the end of a long but
unfulfilled career. He saw that he had not achieved

the broad base the implementation of his theories required, and desperately sought someone who could, as an effective figure, engage the masses and "publicize the right ideas far, wide, and quickly,"[3] as he himself put it. It seemed almost inevitable that Vogelsang's power and ideas would find their needed political instrument in Lueger's talents. And it seems even more so, when we consider Wiard Klopp's appraisal of Vogelsang's public image. According to Klopp, Vogelsang:

> . . . was no public speaker. As fluent and stimulating as his conversation was from his chair in his study, he belonged among those who felt self-conscious when he stood and spoke to a larger circle.[4]

But Vogelsang knew his limitations. In a letter to Lueger on this very topic, he specifically praises him for having "publicized the right ideas far and wide," when he himself was limited to his own "comfortable study."[5] Vogelsang and Lueger not only needed one another; they seem to have been made for each other.

Vogelsang was a minor nobleman from Mecklinburg when he settled in Vienna in 1875. His Christian conservatism had grown out of his personal experiences. His youthful complacency had, in particular, been shattered by the events and the implications of the revolution of 1848, which became in his mind a threat to society and civilization itself. The sole guarantee, he came to believe, lay in the stability of the Catholic Church. Accordingly, at the age of thirty-two, in 1850, he renounced his protestantism and became a Catholic. Thus Vogelsang came to his Christian Social theories over a long period of time and grounded them on a deliberate analysis of the "social phenomenon of the proletariat"--a connection that the practical Lueger may have hit on directly without the elaborate assistance of historical analysis.[6] Lueger's generally direct apprehension of political realities, such as the role of the proletariat, made him something of an exception among his more theoretical contemporaries, and hints that he more than they was that rare phenomenon, the natural leader. At the very least, Lueger seems never to have felt obliged to articulate his behavior in any systematic way.

Lueger's first contact with the man he instinctively agreed with about the role of the masses appears to have occurred in 1883.[7] But he and Vogelsang did not formally join forces until six years later. The chief obstacle to any effective cooperation earlier than this may have been Lueger's conspicuous indifference to religion.[8] But his public avowal of Catholicism at the Katholikentag of April, 1889 quieted the misgivings of certain clergymen who thought Lueger "'didn't want to have anything to do with church and religion.'"[9] From then on, growing numbers of lower clergy especially swelled the ranks of his supporters.

The following documents reveal the close tactical cooperation between Lueger and Vogelsang. The three surviving letters from Vogelsang to Lueger have also been included for the light they shed on this alliance. A much more extensive correspondence between Lueger and Vogelsang must have existed, but only nineteen of Lueger's letters and only three of Vogelsang's apparently survive. Lueger's letters date from 1888 to 1890, and all of Vogelsang's from December, 1888, the month Lueger's mother died. The first letter in Vogelsang's Bismarckian script was written four days after her death on the customary black-edged stationery:

I N 40959

Vienna, December 10, 1888

Dear Doctor,

Permit me to express my most sincere thanks for the lines with which you honored me. If I value anyone's recognition, it is the recognition of him whose truly great, self-sacrificing work in the interest of the Christian people deserves the highest admiration.

I sincerely regret that you, dear Doctor, cannot attend today's festive evening of the "Vereinigten Christen," and I am especially sorry about the sad cause for your absence. May God console you for the most painful loss a man experiences only once in a lifetime.

Dr. Gessmann was surely kind enough to express my deep condolences and convey to you the urgent reasons that prevented my attendance at the funeral of your departed mother.

With my great respect I remain,

Most faithfully yours,

Vogelsang

The second letter was written the following day:

I N 40960

Vienna, December 11, 1888

Dear Doctor,

Yesterday's successful festive evening inspires me to express my sincere gratitude to you who has led his kindred souls from victory to victory with admirable courage and incomparable self-sacrifice and who quickly publicized the right ideas far and wide. It was easy and simple for me to publicize these ideas from my comfortable study; but he who faces the enemy so valiantly is the true hero.

May God protect you for the great cause of the Christian mission!

With my great respect,

Most faithfully yours,

Vogelsang

And the third two weeks later:

I N 40930

Vienna, December 25, 1888

Dear Doctor,

In remembrance of December 10th,[+] permit me to send my enclosed <u>Gesammelten Aufsaetze</u> to the courageous and untiring <u>leader of the "Vereinigte Christen"</u> as a humble sign of my gratitude.

With my great respect,
Most faithfully yours,

Vogelsang

[+]See Lueger's letter of December 27, 1888.

FOOTNOTES FOR

THE PARTY PRAGMATIST

LUEGER AND KARL FREIHERR VON VOGELSANG

1. Dirk van Arkel, Antisemitism in Austria. Leiden, 1966, p. 50.

2. Ibid.

3. See letter of December 11, 1888, below.

4. Klopp, Leben und Wirken, p. 349.

5. See letter of December 11, 1888, below.

6. Knoll, Zur Tradition, p. 105. Vogelsang's ideas are summarized between 105 and 110.

7. Johann Christoph Allmayer-Beck states: "In 1883, Vogelsang met Dr. Albert Gessmann for the first time and Dr. Karl Lueger a little later." Johann Christoph Allmayer-Beck, Vogelsang. Vom Feudalismus zur Volksbewegung. Vienna, 1952, p. 105.

8. Kurt Skalnik was the first Lueger biographer to challenge the myth of Lueger's piety. See Dr. Karl Lueger, p. 19.

9. Heinrich Abel, quoted in Klopp, Leben und Wirken, p. 346.

Four months before Lueger wrote this letter, Georg
Ritter von Schoenerer had led a foray on the editorial
offices of the Neues Wiener Tageblatt. Schoenerer
claimed that this liberal paper had published a prema-
ture report of Emperor William I's death in order to
sell more papers and manipulate the stock exchange.
Lueger, who had defended Schoenerer in the ensuing
furor, which involved violent mass demonstrations, the
stripping of Schoenerer's patent of nobility, and his
imprisonment, may have had some of this in mind when
he referred to "Schoenerer's blundering supporters."
For further details, see Dirk van Arkel, Antisemitism
in Austria. Leyden, 1966, pp. 189, 190.

To: Karl Freiherr von Vogelsang   Nachlass Vogelsang
                                     Mappe: XXII/268

Dr. Karl Lueger
Attorney to the Royal and Legal Courts
Vienna
I, Braeunerstrasse no. 5   Vienna, July 26, 1888

Most Honorable Sir,

    First and foremost, I must thank you for
fulfilling my request concerning Mr. Blaschek.

    Your warning about Baden is, I think, only too
justified; but one is just a slave of the party.
Thank God the outing went without problems and I was
only somewhat annoyed about Schoenerer's supporters,
who just can't act without blundering.

    But the actual reason for my writing is as
follows: I won't get around to transcribing my speech
on trade matters from shorthand into German script
until next week. Can it wait until then?

    With the expression of my highest esteem I
remain,

                         Yours most faithfully,
                         Dr. Lueger

Most Honorable
Mr. Karl Freiherr von Vogelsang   August 30, 1888

Dear Baron,

Enclosed is a brief article, if you can use it.
I don't think that the "Vaterland"[1] needs to fear the
"Deutsche Volkszeitung;" indeed, it might be well to
observe a friendly attitude right from the beginning.
This can only be useful, whether the paper appears or
not.

I had quite a lot to do recently, and thus the
paper on trade matters had to wait. I apologize; I
myself feel that it isn't quite right, but--ultra
posse, etc.

What's happening with the "Katholikentag?" Will
the certain monsignor really play the political first
violin? Are the anti-Semites really going to be
attacked? I am afraid so: yes, when I read Dr.
Kathrein's speech, for instance. If this happens,
then damage will be done that can't be repaired. But
then, I won't have anything to do with it. A little
appeasement wouldn't hurt.

You wished that I took a few weeks' vacation to
relax my nerves. What a nice idea and what good it
would do me! But I don't have the time. I literally
feel the weight of the work sometimes but I have to
stay in the harness nevertheless. Perhaps the
situation will improve sometime if only it isn't too
late then.

I was really very glad to read in your letters
that you're doing so well. If the "grand old man" of
our movement remains healthy, everything is saved and
we can look to the future with confidence.

---

[1]Vogelsang took over the Vaterland in 1875, and it
became the leading Catholic paper in the empire.

Therefore, have good weather for the remainder of the vacation.

    With the highest respect and esteem,

                        Yours most faithfully,

                            Dr. Lueger

In his attempts to uncover instances of corruption, Lueger concentrated his attacks on government abatements to privately-owned public transporation companies. His investigations are described in the following letter. His efforts in this area culminated in the attack on the Danube Steamship Company. See the introduction to "The Anti-Capitalist," and pp. 284-287.

                        Nachlass Vogelsang
                        Mappe: XXII/270

To: Karl Freiherr von Vogelsang

Dr. Karl Lueger
Braeunerstrasse Address   Vienna, September 5, 1888

Most Honorable and Esteemed Baron,

    Today I was at the Ministry of Commerce and inquired from Ministerial-Rathe <u>Wrba</u> and Sections-Chef <u>Wittek</u> about the question of abatements.

    <u>The report in the "Neue Freie Presse" is entirely</u> correct.[2] The abatements for the Galician provenances

---

[2]The <u>Neue Freie Presse</u> reported on the tariff concessions published in the commercial register of the Ministry of Commerce, which the Karl Ludwig Bahn granted as compensation for the recent approval of abatements for the Russian grain trade.

were published on August 30 in the commercial register
of the kk. Ministry of Commerce. The abatements for
Russian provenances are kept confidential in
accordance with the wishes of the Karl Ludwig Bahn,
which is unprecedented. They were supposedly granted
first in 1879 and then renewed annually. This year,
the Ministry of Commerce didn't want to renew it and
only after an alleged flood of petitions and after the
Bahn had granted the same abatements to the Galician
provenances was it decided to yield.

How odd the confidentiality is, can be seen from
the fact that the Karl Ludwig Bahn informs its con-
signees about that by means of circulars. In Russia,
these circulars have become under the counter items.
Apparently, the Karl Ludwig Bahn grants abatements
only to those who possess these circulars. I can't
imagine anything else.

This whole transaction is incomprehensible. It
is defended with the argument that if the abatements
are not granted, the Russians would seek other means of
transportation; thus the competition would remain;
moreover, financial harm would result if the Karl
Ludwig Bahn possibly used a state guarantee. The
transparency of this defense needs no further
elaboration.

I will try to get hold of a circular of the Karl
Ludwig Bahn and send it as soon as I have one.

With great respect and esteem,

Most faithfully yours,

Dr. Lueger

P.S. Because I am going away for a few days, I ask
that you don't write until Tuesday.

To: Karl Freiherr von Vogelsang

Dr. Karl Lueger
Braeunerstrasse Address   Vienna, December 12, 1888

Most Respected and Esteemed Baron,

Referring to our conversation of yesterday, I
take the liberty of drawing attention to an article in
today's morning edition of the "Deutsche Zeitung." It
really looks as though they intend to proceed against
Schneider because of the letter.[3] It would therefore
be advisable to undertake the necessary steps without
delay in order to forestall possible attack by our
opponents. Schneider's position must be maintained at
any price, if only in the interest of the united movement. The storm will now undoubtedly begin in the
other liberal papers, too, and therefore caution is
necessary. In particular, Schneider himself must
under all circumstances lie low, and only you,
esteemed baron, are able to make him understand this,
because he admires you greatly and trusts you
implicitly.

I thank you very much for your kind letter, which
I will keep as a memento, and which will always remind
me of my responsibilities.

Please convey my respectful handkiss to Baroness
Marie; I remain with the expression of my greatest
esteem,

Yours most faithfully,

Dr. Karl Lueger

---

[3]The Deutsche Zeitung reported on page 4 about a
letter that the mechanic and agitator Ernst Schneider
had sent to the Secretariat of the Allgemeine deutsche
Handwerkerbund on October 3, 1888. In all
seriousness, Schneider had demanded that the
Handwerkerbund testify falsely and illegally against
the Jewish-owned Moedling Shoe Factory because they
had cheated him.

To: Karl Freiherr von Vogelsang

Dr. Karl Lueger
Braeunerstrasse Address   Vienna, December 27, 1888

Most Respected and Esteemed Baron,

    I thank you very much for the keepsake you sent
me,[4] to which I will certainly assign a place of
honor.

    With the highest respect and admiration, I remain
as always,

Most respectfully yours,

Dr. Karl Lueger

To: Karl Freiherr von Vogelsang

Dr. Karl Lueger
Braeunerstrasse Address   Vienna, January 19, 1889

Most Respected and Esteemed Baron,

    Today was the hearing concerning the charge
brought by A.(lexander) Sch(arf), who, together with
Dr. Edu.(ard) Singer, appeared <u>personally</u>.[5] I objected

---

[4]Vogelsang sent Lueger his collected essays on
December 25, 1888. See Vogelsang's letter of December
25, 1888, in the introduction to this chapter.

[5]This letter refers to one of the numerous clashes
between the Vereinigte Christen and their opponents,
in this case the <u>Sonn-und-Montag-Zeitung</u>, whose
publisher and editor were Alexander Scharf and Eduard
Singer respectively. Apparently, <u>Das Vaterland</u> had
accused the two of having instigated a scurrilous campaign against Ernst Schneider.

to the last sentence.

Singer and Scharf gave in immediately and declared that they would withdraw the charge if the correction were made without this sentence.

Because under these circumstances a trial would have been pointless, I compromised and pledged to print the correction without the last sentence in either Sunday's or Tuesday's edition.

I ask therefore that you publish the enclosed correction in Tuesday's edition. The underlined words do not need to be italicized.

It is also permissable to include remarks. I suggest the following:

"A new creation
Mr. Alexander Scharf sent us the following correction:

(Correction)

This is the third version Mr. Scharf has submitted to us, after having withdrawn the previous two. All we have to say is that we can prove the truth of all our assertions, even those that Scharf has declared false, and leave it up to our readers whom they want to believe, us or Scharf."[6]

I want to note here that the misspelling of "Officiossus" should be printed. Perhaps it will lend itself to a good joke some day.

With the expression of my highest respect and esteem,

Most faithfully yours,

Dr. Karl Lueger

---

[6]The correction signed by Scharf and dated January 15, 1889, appeared on the front page of the Tuesday edition (January 22, 1889) of Das Vaterland, together with the almost verbatim remark suggested by Lueger. ⁻is influence on Vogelsang in these respects was undoubtedly considerable.

To: Gessman?   January 21, 1889

Dear Friend,

It appears that the matter in the 3rd District is
collapsing. <u>Hollomay</u>, etc., are acting like madmen.
On the other <u>hand</u>, Dr. Mandl is almost certain of
being elected. It is therefore sheer madness to
oppose him, because then both the 3rd and 2nd curiae
would be lost.

The liberals are busy as bees. For example, the
"Landstrasser Buerger-Zeitung" is being published
again. Therefore, the wretches must have money.

In spite of all this, there wouldn't be any
danger if there were unity among us.

Be so kind as to talk with Psenner. Perhaps he
knows a way.

Did you receive my letters concerning <u>Patruban</u>?

Do you have any time on Wednesday?

My hand-kiss to your wife and most cordial
greetings to you.

Your friend,

Dr. Lueger

To: Karl Freiherr von Vogelsang

Dr. Karl Lueger
Braeunerstrasse Address   Vienna, February 9, 1889

Most Esteemed Baron,

I consider the Mandl matter settled, because
Pattai also agrees with me. By the way, it appears

that our opponents are helping me out, because they are not offering any rival candidate to Dr. Mandl, thereby ending the struggle.

I thank you very much for your kind note and urge you to keep me informed of any such news.

With the expression of my highest respect and esteem,

Most faithfully yours,

Dr. Lueger

Three months intervened between these two letters, an interval that saw, in Gerhard Silberbauer's words, "the zenith of Vogelsang's influence on the Catholic social movement of Austria." See <u>Oesterreichs Katholiken und die Arbeiterfrage</u>. Graz: Verlag Styria, 1966, pp. 116-119.

Lueger was accused by his opponents of tampering with various stenographic reports and this letter suggests that the charges were not unfounded.

Nachlass Vogelsang
Mappe: XXII/276

To: Karl Freiherr von Vogelsang

Dr. Karl Lueger
Braeunerstrasse Address   Vienna, April 23, 1889

Most Respected and Esteemed Baron,

On Wednesday April 17, I went on a little trip to Dalmatia and I just returned today to Vienna.

These few words best explain my excuse for not writing until today.

My sisters read the card, but they don't know enough about politics to know what to do.

Now to its contents.

I am <u>not</u> in the possession of the second part, nor is it possible for me to get it. On Wednesday, the day of my departure, Dr. G. paid me a visit and said that correcting the stenographer's report was extraordinarily difficult. He told me about his trip to Iglau, and so I considered the matter settled.

As far as the district committee elections are concerned, they don't at all influence the announcement; on the contrary, I'd like to see it published <u>before</u> the elections.

If I should not happen to meet Dr. G. today, I will look him up tomorrow to take care of the matter.

Please convey my respectful handkiss to Baroness Marie, and I remain with my highest respect and esteem,

Most faithfully yours,

Dr. Lueger

Nachlass Vogelsang
Mappe: XXII/277

To: Karl Freiherr von Vogelsang

Dr. Karl Lueger
Braeunerstrasse Address   Vienna, July 24, 1889

Most Esteemed Baron,

The struggle between the "Vaterland" and the "Deutsche Volksblatt" compels me to trouble you with a few lines, my dear Baron.[7]

---

[7]Kuppe writes: "The two extreme wings of the anti-Semites, the Pan-German Nationalists and the Catholic Conservatives, presented formidable obstacles to Lueger's unification attempts because of their inter-necine journalistic struggles. The struggle between the 'Deutsche Volksblatt' and the 'Vaterland,' the latter of which had already outgrown Vogelsang's tutelage, lasted for over a year to the delight of the liberals. Schoenerer contributed by agitating against the 'Vereinigte Christen' and their leader in his 'Unverfaelschten deutschen Worten.' p. 196.

It goes without saying that these are dictated by my respect and admiration for you and by my interest in the common cause.

The developing ink war does not benefit any of the warring factions, but rather is detrimental to everyone, especially to the cause of the Christian people. Believe me, dear Baron, a lot has transpired recently that in particular has seriously discredited the Catholic Party in the eyes of the people. First, there was Father Hersan in the 8th district, then the often imprudent and liberalistic attitude of the clerical Municipal Councilor, Hosting, then the unfortunate utterance of Nuncio Galimberti, and finally, the famous Bishop of Tarnow. Laboriously, a small territory was conquered for the Catholic Party, and now the church dignitaries destroy the hard work of years in an outright frivolous and damnable way. The people - I am told candidly - feel that the shavelings aren't any better than the Jews.

On top of this, we now have the wrangle between the two papers the "Vaterland" and the "Deutsche Volksblatt."

Believe me, dear Baron, the chances of the "Vaterland" in this struggle are most unfavorable under the present circumstances, and I implore you to stop it.

You, most esteemed Baron, have served the people so well, that you can certainly ignore the attacks, which are not even directed against you personally.

With the expression of my highest respect and esteem, I remain,

Most faithfully yours,

Dr. Lueger

To: Karl Freiherr von Vogelsang

Dr. Karl Lueger
Braeunerstrasse Address   Vienna, July 26, 1889

Most Respected and Esteemed Baron,

First, let me say that I too preach peace to the gentlemen of the "Deutsche Volksblatt" whenever and wherever I can, even though I know it won't do much good. These men <u>want</u> to fight and I believe we shouldn't do them <u>the</u> favor.

Actually, we haven't accomplished anything in the Valeriestrasse.[8] He <u>didn't</u> say he would remain as chairman, but I think <u>that</u> he will if there isn't anything more powerful than his ambition. His mistake is that in politics he's too utopian. This is also why he doesn't have that flexibility in adapting to the changing political struggle that is so necessary for a relatively small party.

I don't identify at all with those who hang Hersan e tutti quanti on "V"'s coattails.[9] But I had to mention it to demonstrate the difficulty of the situation.

It almost hurt me when you, most esteemed Baron, spoke of retirement. No, that must not happen; even if things sometimes look bleak, you should never give up hope.

When I write I only want to draw your attention to dangers and to advise how these may be avoided.

With high respect and esteem,

Most faithfully yours,

Dr. Lueger

---

[8]"In 1876, named after the emperor's daughter Maria Valerie; renamed Boecklinstrasse" in 1920. Czeike, p. 821.

[9]"V" = Vergani?

To: Karl Freiherr von Vogelsang

Dr. Karl Lueger
Braeunerstrasse Address   Vienna, August 13, 1889

Most Respected and Esteemed Baron,

Today, I say today in the morning, the concierge
brought me your esteemed letter. I don't look at the
date, read the kind invitation, look forward to meeting Dr. Decurtins, put on my Sunday best, then re-read
the letter and--discover that the invitation is for
the 11th.

You can imagine, dear Baron, that I was somewhat
disconcerted by this discovery. You must certainly
consider me among the most impolite people who don't
come, don't excuse themselves, indeed, who totally
ignore the gesture.

The only good thing about this is that I am
really innocent, and therefore may expect your
forgiveness, for which I ask.

I'd like to take this opportunity to thank you
for the article about the Sunday outing that appeared
today.

These publicity wrangles are most unpleasant and
I can only hope that they are now ended. It may
interest you to know that the chief fighting cock Wolf
is supposed to go to Berlin as a correspondent. But
this is still a newspaper secret and I therefore
request that you not make use of this information for
a while. With the expression of my highest respect
and esteem,

Most faithfully yours,

Dr. Karl Lueger

Nachlass Vogelsang
Mappe: XXII/280

To: Karl Freiherr von Vogelsang

Dr. Karl Lueger
Braeunerstrasse Address   Vienna, September 9, 1889

Most Esteemed Baron,

Unfortunately, I didn't get back from a short trip, which I combined with a visit to the North Bohemian Katholikentag until <u>today</u>. I therefore couldn't honor your request nor inform you.

As far as I know, Dr. G.[10] is still in St. Veit a/d Goelsen.

With the expression of my highest respect and esteem,

Most faithfully yours,

Dr. Karl Lueger

Nachlass Vogelsang
Mappe: XXII/282

To: Karl Freiherr von Vogelsang   November 3, 1889

Most Respected and Esteemed Baron,

You certainly will allow one of your most loyal admirers to offer you, honorable Baron, his most sincere wishes on your name day tomorrow.

With highest respect and esteem,

Most faithfully yours,

Dr. Karl Lueger

---

[10]Gessmann?

To: Most Honorable
Karl Freiherr von Vogelsang

Dr. Karl Lueger
Braeunerstrasse Address   Vienna, November 26, 1889

Most Esteemed Baron,

Enclosed please find the revised "Open Inquiry" of Mr. Schneider.

I apologize, dear Baron, for its somewhat tardy arrival; but yesterday I didn't have a free minute, and the question is not too urgent at any rate.

With highest respect and esteem,

Most faithfully yours,

Dr. Lueger

To: Karl Freiherr von Vogelsang   (No date)

Most Respected and Esteemed Baron,

The facts mentioned in the enclosed article are completely true and verifiable. The article is therefore not dangerous and will not be protested in my opinion.[11]

The reference to the "Deutsche Volksblatt" is necessary here both factually and for the "Vaterland."

With my highest esteem,

Faithfully yours,

Dr. Lueger

239

11In the _Gewerbe Zeitung_, no. 1, December 1, 1889, whose motto was: "Labor should nourish and honor," the front page editorial, entitled "Our First Subscriber," read as follows:

We are not superstitious, but nevertheless consider it auspicious for the future of our paper that Dr. Lueger has become our first subscriber. For we believe that in a way we will share the same fate with this man who has selflessly and courageously assumed the leadership of the Christian Social reform movement and, ignoring the attacks by his enraged opponents, continues to penetrate enemy territory.

Education and ability no doubt would allow 'our Karl' to move in the higher circles of society, but he loves the people too much to separate himself from them. His place has always been at the side of the little man and neither the most tempting promises nor the most terrible threats persuaded him to become a traitor to 'his people' or a cowardly deserter. Dr. Karl Lueger should be our model. At his side we shall fight for economic order and commercial rights for the protection of the Christian people.

Like him, we shall faithfully support the peoples' labors, and won't be strayed from our path either by glittering promises or ignominious attacks.

But we expect that craft and tradesmen recognize and support our honest endeavors, for leaders without armies can never succeed. Knowing that the people are behind you strengthens and encourages.

Therefore, the banner of the 'Oesterreichische Gewerbe-Zeitung' should always wave in the vanguard of the battle to lead the commercial interest to victory. To unite all Christian craft and tradesmen in an impregnable phalanx against the Golden International should be our goal, and we dedicate this prospectus to Dr. Karl

Lueger, the first subscriber, mentor, and friend of our paper, the representative of the Christian people in parliament. Long live Dr. Karl Lueger!

The article frames a portrait of Lueger. Nachlass Vogelsang, Mappe: XXII/ 284.

Nachlass Vogelsang
Mappe: XXII/ 289

Postcard to: Karl Freiherr von Vogelsang

Most Esteemed Baron,

I have the honor cordially to invite you to a meeting of the Margarethen Voters' Association to be held at 8:00 this evening in the assembly room of "zu den 3 Engeln."[11]

It would be my very great pleasure to see you there.

With the highest respect,

Dr. Karl Lueger

Nachlass Vogelsang
Mappe: XXII/ 281

To: Karl Freiherr von Vogelsang

Dr. Karl Lueger
Braeunerstrasse Address   Vienna, December 5, 1889

Most Esteemed Baron,

My sincerest thanks for your friendly lines. There is such confusion and upheaval among the "Vereinigte Christen" that I have almost decided to weave a cocoon so that I can't hear or see anything of this snarl.

---

[11]Located in the 4th District, Grosse Neugasse 36. A folksingers' locale. See Czeike, 449.

You believe, esteemed Baron, it would be practical if I now emphasized very energetically the Austrian standpoint at any meeting. The situation is this: my Austrian sentiment is known to friend and foe. And because I'm certainly not a neophyte, I really don't need to demonstrate this. It would be a real tragedy, however, if I now proclaimed patriotism in the form of a declaration of war. That would mean destroying the party.

You see, dear Baron, today's edition of the "Vaterland" carries a positively malicious report about the Exner meeting. Because the "Vaterland," for reasons unknown to me, apparently did not send a reporter, the account of the "Deutsches Volksblatt" is being accepted as the basis of an appalling insinuation.

This meeting was a positive triumph for our party, and the "Vaterland" should be happy, should praise the men who made this possible.[12] Just because a few people may have shouted "Long live Schoenerer!" and the "Volksblatt" exploited the situation, the "Vaterland" furiously attacks some of our best men. It is not true that Hohenauer wanted to establish a Pan German Nationalist trade association. On the contrary, he prevented it. Hohenauer is chairman of one of the most active sections of the Christian Social Club, he is one of our best men, and to prove his attitude, I enclose the telegram that I received at home last night. And such a man, who is an Austrian and a Christian to the core is deprecated in the "Vaterland." That is tantamount to forcing

---

[12]At the meeting held in Hernals on December 4, the representative to parliament of the Viennese suburbs, Hofrat Wilhelm Exner, was supposed to have accounted for his activities, according to the Vaterland article. Because Exner's opponents were said to have made a racket even before the election of the chairman, the incumbent chairman Hohenauer, to whom "establishment of a Pan German Nationalist trade association was attributed," is reported to have waived the report, and with that the meeting came to an end. Furthermore, Vergani is held responsible for the disruption of the meeting. There is no mention of a triumph in the article.

people into the enemy camp. You, most esteemed Baron, can certainly imagine what kind of an effect this will have. So I say: in order to try to make up for what has been done at the very next opportunity, I will have the club offer a triple toast to Hohenauer and express its thanks.

I implore you, dear Baron, I beg you, to use the weight of your influence to bring this wretched struggle to an end. It will have just the opposite effect from our endeavors. We had almost reached the point where everyone's sympathy was on our side and now _____. If I were not such an incurable optimist, I would give up everything. But I don't want to give our enemies this satisfaction, and so, God willing, I continue to fight.

I have wanted to visit and discuss this with you for some time, but never had the time, and thus I took the opportunity your letter afforded to get things off my chest. You, Baron, are one of the few people I honor and love; therefore, please forgive me if I speak candidly. I want to protect the man of principles, the old man of the mountains, as I sometimes jokingly call him, from being unfairly judged.

With the expression of my highest esteem,

Most faithfully yours,

Dr. Karl Lueger

Nachlass Vogelsang
Mappe: XXII/ 285

To: Karl Freiherr von Vogelsang

Dr. Karl Lueger
Braeunerstrasse Address

Most Esteemed Baron,

First, my sincere thanks for your letter.

I would certainly be glad if Koller's confidence proved to be well-founded. I have become somewhat skeptical, because I noticed that Koller's imagination does not always jibe with reality.

The story about the telegram is not clear to me. Could it have been intercepted? Don't you, esteemed Baron, have the possibility to find out? How would it be if Mrs. Koller--because she seems to be the addressee--claimed the telegram at the head telegraph office? But then, Mrs. Koller is away on a trip. Perhaps someone else in her name?

With the expression of my highest respect and esteem,

Most faithfully yours,

Dr. Lueger

This is Lueger's last known letter to Vogelsang, who died in November, 1890 as a result of injuries sustained in a traffic accident. In view of his prior special pleading, Lueger's ostensible reluctance to involve himself here in the affairs of the Vaterland seem somewhat disingenuous.

Nachlass Vogelsang
Mappe: XII/ 286

To: Karl Freiherr von Vogelsang

Dr. Karl Lueger
Braeunerstrasse Address   Vienna, May 29, 1890

Most Esteemed Baron,

Dr. Gessmann was just here and, among other things, informed me that he had submitted a report to the editorial staff of the "Vaterland" on the meeting of the Christian Social Club in Gloggnitz, but that it was not published.

This is quite incomprehensible to me, and I am convinced that you, most esteemed Baron, have no knowledge of this action by the editorial staff. This encourages me to write to you, even though I have no right to involve myself in the question of what is printed in the "Vaterland" or not.

If the "Vaterland" doesn't sympathize with individual party groups, well and good. I don't consider it wise, perhaps, but I can understand it, and don't consider myself omniscient. It may very well be that the other way is the right one.

But to <u>cut off your nose to spite your face</u> just because A or B doesn't like the Christian Social Club any more--that is, as I've said, incomprehensible.

Out there in <u>Neunkirchen</u> and <u>Gloggnitz</u> are men such as Ritter von Troll and Dr. Trabert. I believe <u>nobody</u> doubts the patriotism of these men.

They are certainly no hypocritical Prussians, but true black-yellow, highly conservative men. The Christian Social Club tries hard for these men, holds meetings that are enormously successful and that conclude with a toast to his majesty, sends reports to the "Vaterland" and--the "Vaterland" <u>does not print them</u>. Why? Nobody knows.

I can report this all the more candidly because I wasn't at the meetings. Hence any personal bias is missing, and I speak only in the interest of the matter at hand.

And what do I ask for? A little hell from you, most esteemed Baron, to make good such oversights and, I hope, to avoid them in the future. You, dear Baron, are really the only one who can fix things. That's why I turn to you confidentially, and I know that everything will work out.

Forgive my frankness, most esteemed Baron, and permit the expression of my constant respect, with which I remain,

Most faithfully yours,

Dr. Karl Lueger

To: Marie Freiin von Vogelsang

Dr. Karl Lueger
Braeunerstrasse Address   Vienna, August 18, 1891

Most Esteemed, gnaediges Frauelein,

Dr. Brzobohaty is kind enough to deliver these lines to you, because I do not know your address.

I have written to Count Waldbott that I agree to being listed as a collaborator on the planned magazine, even though I won't have much time to justify this title.

Now, gnaediges Fraeulein, please excuse this question: would it be well to approach Dr. Gessmann as well? I believe so. When the magazine appears and his name isn't listed, he could feel hurt, and this should be avoided. I can't tell him about it because I respect its confidentiality, unless you, gnaedige Baroness, authorize me to do so. At any rate, I ask you to forgive my suggestions and kindly to consider it.

Kissing your hand, I remain with my highest esteem,

Your most humble servant,

Dr. Lueger

P.S. Won't the new magazine hurt the red pamphlets?[13]

---

[13]Lueger was probably referring to the <u>Monatschrift fuer Christliche Social-Reform</u>.

THE NATIONALIST

THE NATIONALIST

"If you cut me, you'll find black and yellow."[1] Lueger's allusion to the imperial colors should dispel any doubts about his Austrocentric monarchist loyalties, which mark his entire career. Were this not the case, much of his life and background would have been very different from what it appears to have been--his family background, his education, his relation to his times, all indicate that he was not highborn, excessively theoretical, or really an exception to the pervasive social and political currents of the late Habsburg Monarchy. Lueger's father always considered himself a "seasoned veteran" of the empire, even though his military service was routine and brief. His father's patriotism no doubt entered into young Karl's attitudes.[2] Lueger's first encounter with nationalism, although of another, larger variety, namely with that of the Pan Germans, influenced him as a university student, primarily by intensifying his own already monarchist sentiments, which were evident as early as 1870.[3]

A decade later, his national loyalties were fully acknowledged, and the documents in this section come from this period. Lueger would periodically reconfirm the legitimacy of his stance by pointing to the centrality of its origins and traditions. Yet in so doing, he would at the same time warn against the divisive, centrifugal dangers of lesser and more parochial nationalisms.

Notwithstanding the friction between Lueger and the emperor over the latter's initial--and repeated--refusal to confirm him as mayor, there was never any real doubt about Lueger's deep loyalty to the empire itself. His acceptance into the Belvedere Circle is a sound indication of the confidence he enjoyed with Franz Ferdinand.[4] Whether Lueger could have in fact saved the empire, as some of his apologists have claimed, is debatable, because the same hostility that soured his relationship with the Hungarians might well have caused him to fail in that and other areas. Yet he was totally imperial in his loyalties and identity. This genuine feeling was returned by Archduke Franz Ferdinand, who spoke of Lueger with "admiration and love."[5] Lueger was a politician, but his ability to make intelligent use of his nationalism and other attitudes often taken more seriously by others in other contexts should not be interpreted as proof of personal insincerity. He was also a subject, and a loyal one, as the following documents show.

FOOTNOTES FOR

THE NATIONALIST

1. Quoted in Friedrich Funder, <u>Vom Gestern ins Heute</u>. Vienna and Munich, 1952, p. 99.

2. Skalnik, <u>Dr. Karl Lueger</u>, p. 18.

3. Kuppe, pp. 17, 18.

4. Friedrich Funder, "Als er von uns ging," <u>Reichspost</u>, March 9, 1930, p. 4.

5. Johann Christoph Allmayer-Beck, <u>Minister-praesident Baron Beck Ein Staatsmann des alten Oesterreich</u>. Vienna, 1956, p. 207.

This document demonstrates Lueger's feeling for history, his sense of the dramatic, and an almost classical, Roman appreciation of the need to provide diversions for the masses. This resolution is also an oppositional tactic. It would have been easier for most to drift with the tide in the Municipal Council.

Draft   Nachlass Karl Lueger
                                   St. Slg. Zl. 1257/12
                                   Box III
                                   Mappe: Saekularfeier 1883

Resolution

WHEREAS, the glorious defense of the City of Vienna against the Turks and the final victory of the troops of Emperor Leopold I and his allies in 1683 saved not only Austria but all of Western Civilization from Asian barbarism;

WHEREAS, the German Emperor, his army and its courageous leaders, its loyal allies, (before: among those, most of all Pope Innocent XI and . . .) as well as the Viennese people share the glory of those days;

WHEREAS, it is the duty of the Municipality of Vienna as the Imperial and Residential Capital of Austria and as a German city to honor the bicentennial of the liberation of Vienna from the Turkish threat by a dignified and solemn celebration in which all the peoples of Vienna would be able to participate;

WHEREAS, the resolutions of the Municipal Council on the secular celebration are positively mean and show slight regard for the people, for whom fireworks in the Prater should suffice to remind them about the significance of this memorable day;

NOW THEREFORE, The political "Fortschrittsverein Eintracht" expresses its utter disapproval of the attitude of the majority of Vienna's Municipal Council in this question.

At the same time, it expresses its thanks and recognition to those twenty-five Municipal Councilors who had voted against the proposals of the commission.

251

Peter G. J. Pulzer has remarked that William Jennings Bryan as orator "would fit very easily into the sort of European (socio-political) movement" which began developing in Austria and Germany in the last two decades of the nineteenth century.[1] The following speech draft underlines Lueger's nationalism and also evinces Byranesque morality and populism. At this point in his career, Lueger would probably have agreed with Bryan that "social problems (were) essentially moral."[2]

Speech Draft   Nachlass Karl Lueger
                                     St. Slg. Zl. 1257/12
                                     Box V
                                     Mappe: Korrespondenzen,
                                     Notizen, Formblaetter e.c.,
                                     Wahlangelegenheiten be-
                                     treffend

In an unknown script: "After the parliamentary
election of 1885"

Honorable Assembly!

     In every constitutionally ruled empire, elections to the highest assembly generate powerful movements in the individual classes of the populace, particularly in those that have the right to influence the affairs of the empire through voting, movements that are all the more vital and formidable as more and more people can exercise their political rights.

     Each party makes great efforts to capture the majority of the electorate for its particular cause. Meeting follows meeting, campaign pamphlets follow one another and, unfortunately, instead of honorable fighting, only too often are unfair and reprehensible means employed in order to defeat the hated opponent.

---

[1]Peter G. J. Pulzer, The Rise of Political Anti-Semitism in Germany and Austria. New York: John Wiley & Sons, 1964, p. 48

[2]Richard Hofstadter, The American Political Tradition. New York: Vintage, 1948, p. 191.

If this applies to states where for many years the people or a part thereof have had a voice in government, and where solidly organized political groups struggle with one another for power, it applies even more so to our fatherland Austria, which is riven with party factions that are provincial, national, and confessional, etc., parties, some of which conceal their actual goals behind different slogans that are often changed according to the view of the electorate in one or another electoral district.

If an impartial observer were to view the squabbles of all these groups, if he were to see and hear how one talks of Deutschtum, the other only of the Crown of Bohemia, the third only of Galicia, then he would have to believe that he was in the Tower of Babel, and that the collapse of the empire was immanent, because the peoples don't understand one another.[3]

Nevertheless it is different.

Only a few individual classes of the population participate in all these movements that seem so fateful for the continuation of the empire--those that till now possessed power and who are inclined to mislead the people through conjuring up nightmares, so that their visual and mental perceptions are distracted from their true needs, and so that they may continue to consider the incumbent political leaders as their saviors.

This applies mainly to those two classes, one of which wields the power of international capital, and the other that seems to have a lease on so-called intelligence and considers the citizen and farmer merely a tool to realize its political aims.

But when one descends into the broad masses of the people, there is nothing to be found of all the squabble and strife that so powerfully agitate the

---

[3]Twelve years after Lueger was elected to parliament, "an impartial (American) observer" viewing the parliamentary squabbles, did in fact suggest that the days of the empire were numbered. See Mark Twain, Stirring Times in Austria, The Writings of Mark Twain. New York: P. F. Collier & Son, 1918, 24.

surface. The German doesn't hate the Czech, the Czech
doesn't hate the German, one confession lives peacefully with another, and all, whatever language they
speak, to whatever faith they belong, are united in
their loyalty to their fatherland Austria, are united
in the thought that their elected representatives will
finally provide them with the fruits of honest labor
instead of the chaff of political and national strife,
that they finally think about how we can all live
peacefully with one another and not always fight about
why we should not live with one another.

With these thoughts in mind, the voters of Vienna,
strengthened by the Five Gulden Men, went to the polls
and confirmed the description that our Austrian poet
Grillparzer sketched of his countrymen's character:

> It is quite possible that there are people
> in Saxony and on the Rhine who read more;
> but, what is needed and what pleases God,
> a clear and forward look, an open and just
> mind, there the Austrian is anyone's equal;
> he thinks his thoughts and lets the others
> talk.[4]

So the Viennese thought their thoughts, let the
others talk, and elected the Democrats.

They elected the Democrats, although they were
depicted as traitors to Deutschtum.

They elected them because they knew that they
did not want the rule of individual classes, but
rather that of the people; they elected them because
they hope they will have the welfare of the whole
fatherland in mind; they elected them because they
knew that they are good Germans as well as good
Austrians.

Thus the elections in Vienna demonstrate that the
future of our fatherland is to be found in the realization of the democratic ideas of the universal franchise and justice toward all, without regard to class
and standing, nation or confession.

---

[4]Ottokar von Hornek, in Grillparzer's Koenig Ottokars
Glueck und Ende, Act III.

Then all the ridiculous demonstrations with black-white-red flags,[5] with corn flowers,[6] and whatever you call it will disappear; no Czech will look toward Moscow, no Pole will think about his poor divided nation, no Slovene will think of the creation of a South Slav empire, and just as every Swiss is proud of his fatherland, whether he is German, French, or Italian, so will everyone, whether German or Slav, join us in the toast:

Long Live Our
Fatherland Austria!

The following two letters to unknown addressees may give the lie to the widely-held belief that Lueger was not a private anti-Semite.

I N 66.035

Dr. Karl Lueger
Attorney to the Royal and Legal Courts
Vienna
3rd District, Hauptstrasse no. 21

Vienna, December 18, 1893

Most Respected and Esteemed Colonel,

Let me first thank you for your kind letter of the 13th of this month.

Allow me to refer to my last speech in parliament. It is simply not true that I accused the Hungarians of cowardice. I know quite well that the Magyars are a brave people. My accusation concerns the Magyars'

---

[5]Flag of the Pan German Nationalists

[6]Flower of the Pan German Nationalists

cooperation with the foreign foe, and this is a historical fact that cannot be denied. Even before the war, the then-political leaders of the Magyars had cooperated with Bismarck, and the creation of the Klapka Legion[7] was the _last_ fruit of this alliance. The first was that the Magyars allowed themselves to be captured in droves, not out of cowardice, but because they opposed Austria. When Klapka died, he was celebrated as one of the greatest patriots, and his actions in 1866 were particularly emphasized. Is there any better proof for the truth of my above statement?

It is indeed sad that most Germans as well as Magyars let themselves be led politically by the Jews.

The honorable Mr. Schnabl[+] is certainly no hunter. Nonetheless, the farmers have complained to me as well that when there is no feed in the winter the rabbits gnaw the vines and thus cause great damage.[8]

In his speeches, Schnabl loves to use telling similes; sometimes they say too much.

I look forward to our cooperative efforts and hope that everything will proceed smoothly.

---

[7]Bismarck made use of the Hungarian General Georg Klapka in the Austro-Prussian War of 1866. The Klapka Legion, organized in Silesia, and comprised of prisoners of war and Hungarian exiles, penetrated Austrian territory, but on its further march toward upper Hungary, was resisted by the Slovaks.

[+]Josef Schnabl, Viennese curate and Christian Social Landtag representative.

[8]This type of veiled anti-Semitic gibe frequently appeared in the Christian Social press during this period. Lueger's remarks here anticipate Schneider's motion of 1898 in the Lower Austrian Diet that "bounties. . . be paid for the shooting of Jews as amendment to the law for the killings of birds of prey." Robert A. Kann, _A Study in Austrian Intellectual History_. New York: Frederick A. Praeger, 1960, p. 112 n.

Allow me to express my greatest respect,

Most faithfully yours,

Dr. Lueger

I.N. 66.033

October 1, 1895

Most Esteemed Friend,

Thank you very much for your successful activity on behalf of our party.

Will I be approved? I don't know, but Field Marshal Lieutenant Christianovic <u>doesn't know either</u>. But one thing is clear to me: not to confirm a man loyal to the emperor, whatever his name, would be the greatest mistake that could be made. It would mean: whoever wants to become something in Austria must never be a patriot (Schwarz Gelber) but must be a Kossuth supporter.

Field Marshal Lieutenant Schollai[+] is not a voter of the 7th District. That throws an interesting light on how voter lists are drawn up. The shabbiest Jew peddlar is included, sometimes even three times, but the Field Marshal Lieutenant--was forgotten.

With my great respect and high esteem, I remain,

Your grateful friend,
Dr. Karl Lueger

[+]Probably retired Feld Marschall Leutnant Otto Freiherr von Schollei, 7th District, Siebensterngasse 16.

Lueger here reveals his talent for blending religious, political, and economic symbolism.

Draft Speech

I N   41.515

Speech fragment for festive session of the Municipal Council on December 2, 1898.

A quorum is present.
The session is convened.

Introduction of the governor's two representatives and thanks for their appearance.

Honorable Gentlemen!

We inherited from our fathers the fine custom of blessing each important day in the life of a family by a prayer to God.

Thus, on this festive day we too have attended the service at St. Stephen's Cathedral, that much-loved church of all Viennese, in order to thank God that we with our emperor could experience this day.

And now we are festively gathered in this hall to express our feelings.

We are greeted here by the portraits of great men of times past.

They remind us of the heroic courage of our fore-fathers, of the rescue of Vienna and all of Western Civilization from the Turkish threat; they tell us that the German Emperors of the House of Habsburg were the champions of Christian culture and Vienna the bulwark of the German Empire; they tell us of the loyalty to the lawful ruler, which could not be broken even by death on the gallows.

The banners and flags of commercial associations and other corporations surround us. They tell us of the commercial dilligence of our city's citizens, of the love of singing of our people, of the practical participation in solving the social problems of the present.

Indeed, they are the silent witnesses of the millions of people who participate in spirit in today's celebration.

This celebration honors our emperor, whom God was kind enough to allow to complete the fiftieth anniversary of his reign, and whom we venerate as our father.

It is dedicated to our emperor, who always endeavored to show us only benevolence, who always had the welfare of his peoples at heart, and with whom we shared joy and pain.

Shortly after his reign began, the emperor was in the position to prove to the Viennese his sympathies for them.

(Here Lueger breaks off)

THE POLITICIAN AND THE PRESS

THE POLITICIAN and the PRESS

The press as a political power had come into its own in the last decades of the nineteenth century, and Vienna was a newspaper center. As a relatively new fact of public life, the press automatically became part of every politician's success or failure, and Lueger knew this. The liberal press was his most powerful and persistent enemy--a fact of which he was also not unaware. However, it was one enemy he never defeated.

Over a period of approximately thirty-five years, an undeclared if intermittent war raged between them, from 1875 until Lueger's death in 1910. Lueger precipitated the hostilities by criticizing Felder in 1875, and liberal journalists responded in kind. They saw in him a potential threat to the status quo they represented, and immediately recognized that Lueger was not an ordinary politician, and that he would not allow the way things were to stand in his way. In their role as champions of liberal political patronage, they sought to destroy him by undermining his increasing and thus dangerous popularity with the masses.

In contrast to his liberal rivals, at the beginning of his career Lueger did not command journalistic access to the public. For a time he could defend himself against his liberal enemies only by invoking Article 19 of the Press Law.[1] Among the first few papers regularly to publish Lueger's speeches was the <u>Oesterreichische Volksfreund</u>.[2] This relatively insignificant paper, however, could not compete with the powerful, liberal <u>Neue Freie Presse</u>.[3]

In 1888, Lueger finally found something of the coverage he needed in Ernst Vergani's <u>Deutsches Volksblatt</u>. But the publisher's involvement in political scandals was a source of frequent embarrassment. The chief editor of another Christian Social paper, the <u>Neuigkeits-Welt-Blatt</u>, once described the differences in temperament between Lueger, the Viennese, and Vergani, the Polish-Italian:

> Vergani's personality and his philosophy, so different from Lueger's, and even more so from the composition of his editorial staff, mainly the

political section, which was less than "pro-Viennese," prevented from the beginning any harmonious personal rapport. Lueger finally had his own press, which no doubt served the party unconditionally, yet Lueger's personal relationship to it was courteous rather than friendly over a very long period, and remained always somewhat cool and reserved, not only towards Vergani, but also toward his political associates, who could never quite make the transition to the Viennese mentality and who remained separate from Lueger's essence and sensitivity.[4]

The association of personalities so different could be only a nagging source of friction.

Besides deep differences in political philosophy between himself and the liberal journalists, Lueger appears to have resented the mere existence of an independent, apparently non-political power. It seemed invulnerable, and could not be defeated at the polls or neutralized with counter-propaganda. Lueger did somewhat ingenuously accuse the liberal press of corruption, in what could have been little more than a demagogic ploy; but the alleged corruption among his opponents could hardly have disquieted this cunning politician when the very same thing among his own supporters never seemed to trouble him.[5] This fundamentally philosophical incompatibility precluded any accommodation, let alone an armistice, right from the very beginning. Lueger's emotional rhetoric could not prevail over the critical analyses of his relentless opponents.

In the following letters, written between 1876 and 1892, Lueger repeatedly protested the liberal abuse of press freedom. However, as his own Christian Social press grew in the 1890s, Lueger's direct concern with the actual management of the press--both friendly and hostile--seems to have diminished. This now more and more became the duty of Christian Social journalists. His own increasingly busy political life and his publicist instinct led him to leave newspaper matters to the professionals.

FOOTNOTES FOR

THE POLITICIAN AND THE PRESS

1. Article 19 is quoted on p. 126.

2. Hans Arnold Schwer, "Persoenliche Erinnerungen an
   Dr. Karl Lueger," Reichspost, August 7, 1921, p.
   9. Mandl's paper Fortschritt published Lueger's
   speeches as early as 1878.

3. See Kurt Paupié, Handbuch der oesterreichischen
   Pressegeschichte. 2 vols., Stuttgart, 1960, 1,
   pp. 144-150, and the sources cited therein, and
   Adam Wandruszka, Geschichte einer Zeitung. Das
   Schicksal der "Presse" und der "Neuen Freien
   Presse" von 1848 zur 2. Republik. Vienna, 1958.

4. F. Micheu, "Lueger und die Zeitungsleute,"
   Neuigkeits-Welt-Blatt, September 19, 1926, p. 44.
   For information about Vergani, see Werner
   Adelmaier, "Ernst Vergani," Ph.D. dissertation,
   University of Vienna, 1969.

5. A catalog of Christian Social corruption may be
   found in Marie Goetz, Schmutzige Waesche der
   Christlich-Sozialen, Eingesammelt von einer
   Christlichen Waschfrau. Vienna, no date. Also,
   Eduard Pichl, Georg Ritter von Schoenerer. 5
   vols., Berlin, 1938, 5, pp. 392-396.

Letter draft   Nachlass Karl Lueger
                                      St. Slg. Zl. 1257/12
                                      Box V
                                      Mappe: Gemeinde Propria

Propria
Gemeinde
KK.
Public Prosecutor's Office
Vienna
Dr. Karl Lueger
Attorney to the Royal and Legal Courts in
Vienna

requests correction of the newspaper
report mentioned herein and confirmation
of facts presented.
Mandl   September 25, 1876

Most Honorable kk. Public Prosecutor's Office,

     In the morning editions of several Viennese
papers of September 23, 1876, it is asserted that on
the basis of my statements or, as the "Neue Freie
Presse" alleges, my denunciations of the former
Chairman of the Third District and Municipal
Councilor Matthaeus Mayer, a criminal investigation
of fraud has been undertaken. The inaccuracy of these
newspaper reports is well-known to the honorable kk.
Public Prosecutor's Office and having read them in the
"Neue Freie Presse," "Presse," and "Neues Wiener
Tagblatt," I humbly request:

          That the honorable kk. Public Prosecutor's
          Office deign to authorize an official
          retraction of the above-mentioned articles
          and to confirm to me that I, neither directly,
          nor indirectly, caused the kk. Public
          Prosecutor's Office to proceed against the
          Municipal Councilor and Chairman of the
          Third District Matthaeus Mayer.

                          265

Letter draft to an
unknown editor

Nachlass Karl Lueger
St. Slg. Zl. 1275/12
Box II
Mappe: Redekonzepte

Dear Editor,

In your editorial "The Honor of the City of
Vienna," in today's edition of your esteemed paper,
motives were attributed to the opposition party in the
Municipal Council because of its attitude in the legal
proceedings against the "Kreuzzeitung" and "Augsburger
Postzeitung," which are not true and may induce the
readers of your paper to believe that the opposition
has not fulfilled its duties in this question.

Even though I am unaccustomed to attaching great
importance to journalistic attacks, I feel obligated,
in spite of political differences, to correct the
views presented in your paper, in so far as they concern my party, because the same criticisms have
already been voiced by individual voters, especially
to me.

My attitude and those of my political friends in
this matter were neither influenced by any sort of
kindness nor consideration for individuals. Despite
various provocations, we have refrained from any
debate only because first, according to the Berlin
public prosecutor, not the Municipality of Vienna, per
se, but rather other individual persons appear slandered in the incriminating article, and second,
because we believe such questions should be handled at
home and not abroad.

I request that you, dear editor, print these
lines in your paper and remain,

Respectfully yours,

Dr. Lueger

Letter Draft

Nachlass Karl Lueger
St. Slg. Zl. 1257/12
Box II
Mappe: Duellfrage,
Politischer
Fortschrittsverein,
Affaere Mandl

The Honorable Mr. Eduard Huegel
Editor-in-Chief of the "Constitutionelle
Vorstadt-Zeiting," Vienna, 3
Hauptstrasse 9.   Vienna, June 26, 1883

Dear Editor,

Pursuant to Article 19 of the Press Law, please
print the following correction:

It is not true that I jumped up at the committee
meeting of the politische Fortschrittsverein Eintracht
held on the 22nd of this month because of a voter's
accusation of criminal assault against the new club
leadership and that I threatened this voter with an
unmistakable gesture. Furthermore, it is untrue that
I was asked by anyone whether I will side with the
right or left wing in parliament, and it is therefore
also untrue that I gave the response suggested by you.
Finally, it is also untrue that at the conclusion I
requested not to hold the next plenary session of the
club for at least two weeks, so that I could win time
to be able to study my political program.

                              Dr. Karl Lueger

Nachlass Karl Lueger
                                       St. Slg. Zl. 1257/12
                                       Box III
                                       Mappe: Affaere
                                       Wilhelm Pfister

Presumably to Josef Mittler
Editor-in-Chief of the
"Neue Freie Presse"
Vienna I
Fichtegasse 11   Vienna, July 3, 1886

Dear Editor,

        Pursuant to Article 19 of the Press Law, please
print the following correction:

        It is untrue that a member of our party had to
retire, not too long ago, because it was revealed that
he was involved in less than an unselfish way with the
support of candidates for the magistrate offices.

        Rather, the municipal councilor in question was
a member of the Club "Auesserste Linke," which belongs
to the Municipal Council majority.

                              (before: For the Club
                              "Linke," C. Reisinger
                              Deputy Chairman;
                              Dr. Karl Lueger
                              Secretary)

Letter draft

I N   41529

Mr. W. Czernotzky
1, Steyrerhof 3   Vienna, July 21, 1892

Dear Editor,

        With reference to the report "Christian Social or
Social Democratic," published on July 20, 1892, concerning a meeting on July 19th of this year of the
Social Democratic workers, I request that the
following correction be printed pursuant to Article 19
of the Press Law:

It is not true that I shook with excitement at this meeting, that when leaving the hall, I turned around again and shouted something at the speakers' platform.

It is untrue that Leihtner said the following to me: Why are you leaving? Because you can't take the truth. Because you are a scoundrel. It is untrue that I shrugged my shoulders.

It is untrue that I forced my way through the crowd.

It is untrue that I shouted: "Yes, long live Christian work!" It is untrue that I shouted: "Long live Jesus Christ!" It is untrue that I was pursued as I was leaving by the scornful laughter of the Social Democrats.

Tagblatt

My party colleagues who had not been admitted to the meeting cheered me when I was still in the entrance hall and even more on the street. In order to avoid a street scene, I got into a coach that had just happened to come along and drove off.

Letter draft

I N 41528

Ferdinand Klebinder
1, Wollzeile 16   Vienna, July 21, 1892

Dear Editor,

With reference to your report, "The Flight of Dr. Lueger," about the Social Democratic workers' meeting of July 19th of this year in your July 20th 1892 edition, please print the following correction pursuant to Article 19 of the Press Law:

It is untrue that I jumped up enraged at something Leihtner said, that I clenched my fists, that I turned towards the podium on which Leithner and the other leaders stood and let out an inarticulate scream. It is untrue that I suddenly dropped my hands and said as I was leaving: "I thank you." It is untrue that I withdrew from the platform towards the exit as quickly as I could. It is untrue that the insults of individual persons bothered me, that I turned toward the masses and yelled in a loud voice: "I'll repay you for this! Long live Jesus Christ!"

Rather, the following is true:

When I realized that the speaker Leihtner only intended to insult Dr. Gessmann and me, I calmly got up, took my overcoat, hat and umbrella and turning to the chairman said the following: "I did not come to be insulted, but rather to speak factually. My compliments, gentlemen; I'm leaving." Mr. Schuhmeyer wanted to talk me into staying. I told him: I'll stay, if Leihtner retracts the words "deliberate lie" and "political scoundrel." Meanwhile, the meeting was declared adjourned and I slowly left the hall, passing through the midst of my most angry opponents. To my opponents' shouts I responded with the words: "Long live the people!" and "Long live Christianity!" My opponents' threats I countered with the lines: "I wouldn't be afraid if thousands of you came!"

I N 66.034

(Addressee unknown)   September 1, 1893

Most Respected and Esteemed Colonel,

I'm using a little break, first, to thank you kindly for your attentions and second, to make a few comments about the "Volksblatt."

I have long since stopped trying to exercise any influence on the "Volksblatt," because first, it doesn't do any good, and second, I want to retain my complete independence. Everyone who writes articles for this paper fares the same as you did, most esteemed Colonel. Acceptance of an article is con-sidered a dispensation of Providence. I noticed this early enough and thus avoided being favored with such

"dispensations" myself. This will change with competition. It will be most advantageous and will convince all that you should have had some education in
order to become a newspaper writer. Hoepfully, you'll
receive this letter while still in Gmunden. I'm sure
you welcome the beautiful weather.

I'm leaving today for northern Bohemia to agitate. May I be successful!

With the expression of my greatest respect and
esteem, I remain,

Most faithfully yours,

Dr. Karl Lueger

THE ANTI-CAPITALIST

THE ANTI-CAPITALIST

Lueger played many political roles; the anti-capitalist was among them. The problem of how Lueger the man actually fit into these roles has never been too far in the background. In the "Party Pragmatist," Lueger's multivalent attitude toward mass power was implicitly contrasted to Vogelsang's apparently similar attitudes. Yet the simpler thought of Vogelsang stands out against the subtle flexibility of Lueger's use of "the same thing." This problem of how much of the man--and how permanently and to what ultimate end --was involved in any course of action, cause, party affiliation, or belief that Lueger appears to have embraced is nowhere more acute than in the Nordbahn Affair.

This political crisis turned on the renewal of the railway franchise for the Nordbahn in 1886. It was argued by the opposition that there were severe abuses in the operation of the company, and these charges galvanized what had ordinarily been a heterogeneous group of squabbling and locally opportunistic political parties into something of a unified political "sector"--the people, opposed as a unit to capitalism, as an alignment of money and old-style imperial power. There was a "general confusion" of party lines, and Schoenerer, the leader of the Pan German Nationalists, emerged as the leader of a "wide movement" and "'the first victory for the people'."[1]

In this crisis, Lueger supported Georg Ritter von Schoenerer in the latter's directly anti-capitalist position. Here as elsewhere, however, Lueger's anti-capitalism, in contrast to that of his contemporaries, was aimed at specific political goals--winning and maintaining the support of the ever-necessary masses. Lueger often accommodated his position on key issues to the prevailing circumstances. During the Fogerty Affair, he had also taken an anti-capitalist position as he did here, and his attitude became widely known. This posture evidently won him some support in the following years. But many of his consituents were also small property owners and shareholders, so by 1889, his original stance on capitalism had softened. At the Second General Austrian Katholikentag, for example, Lueger addressed the question of capitalism indirectly through the specific problem of usury, which had preoccupied Vogelsang and like-minded conservatives for many years. The issue was resolved among Vogelsang's group with Lueger's appeal to moderation before the Katholikentag participants, who were uncertain about whether or not to pass an anti-usury resolution. Here Lueger made something of a commonsense distinction between good and bad capitalism:

> Gentlemen! We Catholics are generally poor people, but each of us has a few annuity bonds and debentures. In my humble opinion, it would create considerable anxiety among our people if they were troubled about a few coupons by such a resolution. I therefore strongly suggest, gentlemen, that we refrain from drawing up such a resolution.[2]

In short, small business is all right, but big business is not in the best interests of the people. In this way, Lueger forestalled this particular anti-capitalist measure.

In the following years, however, he carried his tactical battle against capitalism into parliament. In 1891, he attacked stock market corruption, and a year later the financially troubled Danube Steamship Company. This operation, whose solvency was supposed to have been guaranteed by an annual government subsidy of 500,000 gulden, was nevertheless suffering from mismanagement. The documents presented here relate to Lueger's various positions toward this and other capitalistic enterprises, such as the Nordbahn. In a demagogic and strongly anti-Semitic speech in parliament on February 9, 1892, Lueger criticized the shipping company's corrupt practices, accused the liberal press of complicity in them, and suggested that the liberal members of parliament supported the subsidy only to enrich themselves. He concluded by calling for the nationalization of the company. His attacks became so vehement and even seditious that he had four times to be called to order.[3] And as a result, he was challenged to a duel by a company official, whose honor he was supposed to have impugned.[4] Lueger, however, declined the challenge, reminding his opponent at once of his parliamentary responsibilities to expose corruption as well as of the immunity they conferred. Instead, he proposed a course of legal action, which was never followed. The approval of a reduced subsidy of only 250,000 gulden concluded the

affair and made Lueger into a hero who had been able
to resist the capitalists. Recognition came from the
usual--and some unexpected--quarters.[5]

The effectiveness of Lueger's demagogy is
attested to by the following laudatory letter. It was
signed by ninety-eight people, and in it his own class
sentiments, nationalism, and hatred of the liberal
press find expression:

Kemnitz in Bohemia
February 27, 1892
Most Esteemed Dr. Carl Lueger
Member of Parliament
Vienna

With unswerving loyalty, with courage and
candor, you represented the interests of the
working tax payers during the debate over the
Danube Steamship Company; you again demonstrated,
most esteemed representative, that you tirelessly
continue to struggle against the corrupt capitalist hydra. Everywhere light industry is
definitely declining; the once so flourishing,
prosperous, and state-supporting middle class is
getting poorer and poorer; and that is exactly
why it is most regrettable that representatives
squander their votes for million gulden gifts to
rich stockholders, money that has been sucked
from the blood of the people.

In all regions of our fatherland, the
broader masses of the people enthusiastically
applaud your honest and courageous intervention;
and it is all the more gratifying for us to see
how the corrupt venal press is more and more
despised everywhere, and we see that honest popular newspapers promote more and more the germ of
the right kind of education in the interest of
the people. We who have directly subscribed for
some time to the stenographic minutes of
parliamentary proceedings would welcome it if
they were offered directly to the individual
trade associations for easier and wider dissemination. We know that you, by your honest and
dignified presence, contribute a great deal
towards establishing order in our confused
parliamentary situation.

277

> Allow us, the undersigned municipal councilors, guild wardens, citizens, and tradesmen, to express our heartfelt thanks for and trust in your actions in parliament.
>
> With Genuine German Greetings[6]
>
> (signatures)

Lueger's spectacular involvement in the Danube Steamship Affair and his investment in criticism of big business clearly paid political dividends.

But when, as mayor, he found himself managing the city's finances, the need of capital for construction projects compelled him once again to soft-pedal his anti-capitalism. The construction of the second mountain spring water line obliged him to turn to the Rothschild family, in order to acquire a right of way through their property. This, as well as other privileges, they granted unconditionally and free of charge. Lueger publicly expressed his appreciation of the Rothschilds' generous cooperation.[7] The rabidly anti-Semitic paper <u>Kikeriki</u> pilloried Lueger's "Canossa" and hinted that this constituted the beginning of the moral bankruptcy of the Christian Social Party.[8]

FOOTNOTES FOR

THE ANTI-CAPITALIST

1. Andrew G. Whiteside, The Socialism of Fools.
   Berkeley, Los Angeles, and London, 1975, pp. 110,
   111. See Lueger's draft letter of April 9, 1884,
   where he evinces awareness of this unit.

2. Quoted in Klopp, Leben und Wirken, p. 350.

3. Stenographische Protokolle ueber die Sitzungen
   des Hauses der Abgeordneten des oesterreichischen
   Reichsrathes im Jahre 1892, 11. Session, 112.
   Sitzung, February 9, 1892 (Vienna, 1892), pp.
   5090-5138.

4. This was Heinrich von Etienne, brother of the
   founder of the Neue Freie Presse.

5. Even the Socialist Arbeiter Zeitung had words of
   qualified praise:

   > It is very probable that Lueger, who lacks
   > any sense of truth, made a number of false
   > or at least unverifiable statements. But
   > even if only one-tenth of what he said was
   > true...Lueger was one hundred per cent right
   > in calling a spade a spade and it is cer-
   > tainly to his credit that he was prepared to
   > deliver a few blows to the ignominious
   > hypocrites and that he had the courage to
   > disturb the supposedly noble harmony by a
   > 'discordant sound,' in the commerce
   > minister's words.

   "Von Nah und Fern," Arbeiter Zeitung, February 12,
   1892, p. 1.

6. Nachlass Karl Lueger, St. Slg. Zl. 1257/12, Box
   II, Mappe: Korrespondenzen, Notizen,
   Zeitungsblaetter, und Dokumente, die
   Donaudampfschiffahrtsgesellschaft und die
   Valutaregulierung betreffend.

7. Kielmansegg, pp. 382, 383.

8. "Antisemitisches und Nicht Antisemitisches,"
   Kikeriki, February 2, 1902, p. 2.

The following three documents pertain to the Nordbahn Affair.

Draft   Nachlass Karl Lueger
                          St. Sg. Zl. 1257/12
                          Box III
                          Mappe: Tramway Gesellschaft

To the Voters of Vienna!
Fellow Citizens!

Shortly, the representatives you sent to parliament will be called on to cast their votes to solve the Nordbahn question.

If it was ever necessary for the voters to raise their voices loudly and clearly to protect the interests of the people, now is the time. After all, the Nordbahn issue decides whether your welfare, your business, your industry, your household should continue to depend on the dictates of a private business concern, or whether the acknowledged defender of the public good, the state, should replace it.

Therefore, we herewith summon all voters of the City of Vienna to a meeting

on_____

at_____

Fellow Citizens! Come one, come all! Let no one fail to come so that we may demonstrate our unity in guarding our rights.

25 Municipal Councilors

only 9 Municipal Councilors

Draft   Nachlass Karl Lueger
                               St. Slg. Zl. 1257/12
                               Box III
                               Mappe: Tramwaygesellschaft

Motion of Urgency
of the listed Municipal Councilors

On March 4, 1886, the exclusive concession
granted to the Banking House S. M. von Rothschild and
its stock company, respectively, for the construction
of a rail line between Vienna and Bochnia with branch
lines to Bruenn, Olmuetz and Troppau, and to the salt
mines in Dwory, Wieliczka, and near Bochnia will
expire.

In view of the stipulation in section 10 of the
relevant concession contract, it is extremely important that all those authorities and corporations in a
position to judge the effectiveness of the kk.
strictly private Kaiser Ferdinand Nordbahn, and especially the representatives of the communities most
affected by the subject train company, raise their
voices and undertake all necessary steps to effect a
solution in the general interest to the so-called
Nordbahn question.

Recognizing this duty, the Krakau Chamber of Commerce and the Lower Austrian Trade Association here in
Vienna have already taken a stand toward the Nordbahn
question that the independent classes of the population will gladly welcome.

But if it is anybody's task to address this
question and to express the sentiments of the people,
it is first and foremost the Municipal Council's of
the City of Vienna.

It is Vienna, the imperial and residential capital of Austria, that suffers most painfully from the
ruthless exploitation of the Nordbahn concession,
whose population was practically forced to pay tribute
to a private business, whose..., commerce and trade
suffers badly from the Nordbahn's tariff politics, in
fact, whose arteries, necessary for the growth and
prosperity of the city, were drained. It would go too
far to document the correctness of the above in all
respects. It should suffice to refer to economic

reports, to the constant and justified complaints about the transport of cattle and other vital goods, as well as to state that the transport and sale of coal has been monopolized through <u>cartels and abatement abuses</u>, thereby annually cheating the population of Vienna out of millions that profited only a few.

In view of these facts, and considering that state-operated railroads have proved advantageous and useful to the population, and considering further that it would appear necessary, both from the standpoints of strengthening state authority and protecting military and financial interests, to refrain from extending the concession or granting a new one, but instead, to have the state assume control of the rail lines in question, we therefore propose the following

<u>Motion of Urgency</u>:

That the Municipal Council of the City of Vienna resolve:
to address a petition to the kk. government, particularly to the prime minister and the ministers of commerce and finance, as well as to both houses of parliament, requesting that the Nordbahn lines, whose concession expires on March 4, 1886, be taken over by the state. (before, or in the unlikely event that the railroad remains in private hands the state has exclusive authority over tariffs.)

Because this subject falls within the purview of several different sections, the proposal is to be submitted to a commission of twelve members selected from the plenum of the Municipal Council for urgent attention.

Draft of a letter, probably written on April 9, 1884	Nachlass Karl Lueger St. Slg. Zl. 1257/12 Box III Mappe; Tramwaygesellschaft

Invitation, because I was elected to the commission

1.) <u>position in the Municipal Council</u>
   Motion of Dr. Mandl
   therefore consensus necessary

2.) <u>Agitation in the populace</u>
<u>Schoenerer</u>
<u>Parliamentarians do nothing</u>

Most Honorable Sir,

   As the Nordbahn concession will soon expire, its
future is one of the most important political and economic questions that require decisions by the representative bodies since the re-emergence of constitutional life in Austria.

   If, however, the newspapers with very few exceptions did not discuss this question at all, or in a
manner detrimental to the people's interests, the
reasons for this deplorable condition are known to
everyone familiar with journalism and therefore need
not be discussed here.

   Because, however, other more reputable parties
have not made an attempt to acquaint themselves with
the views of the electorate on this question, and
because, consequently, only a few clubs have been
active in this regard, the undersigned municipal
councilors consider it their duty to assemble delegates from all districts to discuss how best to
achieve such a solemn declaration of the people's
will.

   We are convinced that all honest thinking
patriots are of one opinion in solving the Nordbahn
question and that all will stand united for the good
of the people, regardless of other political and personal differences.

   We cordially invite you, honorable sir, to a
meeting that will be held tomorrow, Thursday, April
10, at 8:00 in the evening in the restaurant "Zum
roemischen Kaiser," I, Renngasse I, and hope you will
attend.

                                   Most respectfully yours,

The remaining documents in this chapter deal with Lueger's attack on the Danube Steamship Company.

Draft speech

Nachlass Karl Lueger
St. Slg. Zl. 1257/12
Box II
Mappe: Korrespondenzen, Notizen, Zeitungsblaetter u Dokumente, die Donaudampf- schiffahrtsgesellschaft und die Valutaregulierung- betreffend

Before I discuss the _proposal_ of the subsidy for the Danube Steamship Company,[+] allow me to make a few remarks about my position on the general question of waterways.

The defenders of the proposal say: those who support the continuation of shipping on the Danube _must be for the proposal_. Therefore, if someone is _against_ it, he must be for the stagnation of trade along and on the Danube and the disappearance of the Austrian trade flag from this river.

This is not so.

For instance, I have always been of the opinion that waterways are a _necessary_ component of any integral transporation system, and that it is there- fore the state's responsibility to maintain and to develop natural waterways and to link them, if possible, with man-made ways in such a way that any natural water route is not only a _means of transpor- tation_ for _the valley in question, that it not only has local significance_, but rather that it achieves _significance for the whole empire_, indeed _for inter- national transportation_.

As a Viennese and Austrian, it has always hurt me to hear about the increase in shipping on the Rhine and Elbe, etc., and to think about my poor old Danube, and to remember that whenever I had an opportunity during the last decade to travel in the Danube vallies, the feeling of isolation has crept over me; it always struck me as though I were traveling through a bygone world.

[+]Hereafter referred to as the DDSchG

I have always regretted that in Austria not enough attention has been paid to waterways, and therefore welcomed any advocate no matter who, on the premise that rich and poor, liberal and antiliberal, capital and labor, are equally interested in the flourishing of transporation. . . . We are now of the opinion that only state administration can help, that the shareholders must agree to this, that the shareholders have to wait until the state is nourished. Who are the shareholders?. . . . (Lueger seems to have intended this as a rhetorical question. Ed.)

The minister thinks the government had no reason to step in, heretofore, that is, before 1891. The DDSchG is supposed to have met its responsibility as public transportation; it is supposedly a private enterprise and only after it could not meet its public responsibilities was the question broached to the government whether it could help the company out. . . Government had to step in, as soon as such facts were known, which are either subsumed under the criminal law or which, if continued, had to bring

about the bankruptcy of the company. . .

I have no intention of telling what is already contained in the business reports for 1890. I can only say: if the administration were to report about the conduct of a creditor. . . any public prosecutor would bring charges of fraud and the person in question would be sentenced to a lengthy prison term.

But I am not so relentless; some of the commerce minister's good nature has rubbed off on me: I would let the directors and the administration retain their honored freedom if they were only kind enough to give back the millions they squandered away. Also, I will not repeat the arguments my esteemed colleagues have presented, but rather stress only one point: forwarding agencies.

Their names have already been mentioned: Kohn & Mittler, Pollak & Co., Karl Gluecklich in Galatz.

These agents are the actual cancer cells of the company; they are its parasites. They have become millionaires, multi-millionaires, while the DDSchG has gotten poorer and poorer.

They received simply enormous abatements up to

50 gulden, even 70 gulden, and it is therefore understandable that in spite of high freight charges, only a very moderate average profit was made.

They took the fat, then the meat and, if this situation continues, they'll even get the bones, but they will certainly get the 5 million subsidy which the state provides.

How tremendous the incomes of these people are can be seen by the fact that Kohn & Mittler concluded a compensation agreement with another shipping firm whereby the latter was paid an amount of 100,000 gulden for the sole purpose of preventing any competition with the DDSchG.

Therefore, direct business between the DDSchG and shippers has almost stopped. The officials of the DDSchG, on the orders of the management, had to take care of the business of the shipping agents, and if one or another refused, reprimands and fines resulted.

The forwarding agents were the all-powerful lords and enjoyed the support of the management.

Particularly interesting is the story of <u>Karl Gluecklich</u> in Galatz. From a lowly clerk in the DDSchG, he soon rose to its all powerful master on the Lower Danube.

In 1879, a transit forwarding agency was established in Galatz whose owner was <u>Karl Gluecklich.</u> Its purpose was to forward transit goods which arrived by ship via Braila in Galatz. This amounts to relatively little. Important are the local goods and Gluecklich concentrated on these. I will tell you later about his machinations in this regard. An official of the company, Franz <u>Chwoika</u>, who headed the agency in Galatz, was to prevent this, but ignored his direct supervisor's orders to the contrary and restrained Gluecklich instead. <u>Chwoika is transferred to Braila.</u> He continues his efforts. He describes how the Russians are gaining more and more ground; he receives a reprimand. In a word, Gluecklich monopolizes all the trade on the Lower Danube.

Throughout the Danube area, it is generally known that Gluecklich was intimately associated with some higher officials; it is generally known that the officials of the company immediately transferred all the orders for goods to Gluecklich's bills of lading; in a word, the scandal is so bad that it couldn't be any worse.

Then on October 25, 1890, under the new regime, the auditor Leopold Mayer visited Franz Chwoika with discretionary powers. . . . And now, with the president's kind permission, I'll turn the floor over to Mr. Franz Chwoika, i.e., I ask permission to read his testimony and submitted documents. . . .

Now, gentlemen, you would think that the new regime would initiate an investigation to correct all the irregularities. No, Chwoika, an official in the prime of life, is retired. . .

Perhaps something was done in other areas. Perhaps the shipping agencies were eliminated. No, gentlemen; they may have had it announced in the newspapers that this happened, but in reality the contracts for 1891 were renewed and Gluecklich is still the happy master of the unhappy steamship company on the Lower Danube. . . .

And after all this, the minister of commerce says that the new administration is better than the old one. No, it is just as bad as the previous one.

The savings that are made are at the expense of the pension fund. . .

Oh, there is something else: the lump sum allocation for writing materials was reduced from 3 to 2 gulden. Further, if I understand correctly, soap was disallowed for officials and servants.

Officials who serve an unwashed company, don't need to wash themselves, either. . . .

Draft Memorandum

Nachlass Karl Lueger
St. Slg. Zl. 1257/12
Box II
Mappe:
Korrespondenzen, Notizen
Zeitungsblaetter u
Dokumente, die
Donaudampfschif-
fahrtsgesellschaft
und die
Valutaregulierung
betreffend

1.) On the 10th of this month, a staff member of one of the papers published in Vienna came to my apartment and told my sisters, because I wasn't there, that he had learned that two officials of the Steamship Company who are officers would visit me in order to challenge me in the name of Mr. von Etienne. Since that time, newspaper reports have been published that Etienne had challenged me.

2.) On the 11th of this month, at 8:00 a.m., Suppan and Krieghammer appeared in my apartment. They told me that they had come about a matter of honor and in the name of von Etienne requested me to retract the accusations made against the latter in parliament and in newspapers. I told them: "As soon as Herr von Etienne returns to me or Mr. Franz Chwoika the files that Franz Chwoika had given to the auditor Mayer, and as soon as I can ascertain therefrom that Franz Chwoika had deceived me, I am prepared to offer satisfaction."

3.) On February 12th of this year, the challenge to a duel did not take place; instead, Messrs. Suppan and Krieghammer demanded only the name of confidants. I expressly asked them whether they were here to relay a challenge to a duel, a question that was <u>not</u> answered.

4.) Decisive for judging this whole question of honor is the fact, uncontested by Etienne, <u>that he knew about the accusations of Franz Chwoika even before February 9th of this year, and nevertheless took no action against him</u>.

5.) For statements made in the performance of one's official responsibilities, a person cannot be held responsible in the manner proposed by von Etienne.

This is an uncontested principle even in those states where duelling is all the rage.

It is the duty of any member of parliament to address anything that is relevant and was transmitted by credible and honorable parties in the deliberation of any subject. I have fulfilled this responsibility in the DDSchG matter and will continue to do so in the future.

Draft Memorandum

Nachlass Karl Lueger
St. Slg. Zl. 1257/12
Box II
Mappe: Korrespondenzen,
Notizen,
Zeitungsblaetter und
Dokumente, die
Donaudampfschiffahrts-
gellschaft
und die Valutaregulierung
betreffend

Considering that Herr von Etienne definitely knew about Franz Chwoika's accusations against him and did not take any legal action, and further, that Dr. Lueger only brought the above matters to the attention of parliament referring to his sources and in compliance with his official duties, and lastly, because someone not associated with Lueger requested an official legal inquiry into the affair, Dr. Lueger does not consider a duel an appropriate way to handle the matter and therefore refuses to accept the challenge.

THE PRIVATE MAN

THE PRIVATE MAN

In addition to those documents dealing with
Lueger's public life, there are a number of others
difficult to classify, mostly letters to friends and
business colleagues, which deal with his private life
and personal tastes. These have been gathered here.
Some critics might say, of course, that Lueger was
simply not a private person, that, as the consummate
politician, he was never an entirely private person in
anything he did. His well-known willingness to
intercede and assist those in difficulty may be attributed to covert politicizing, ego-gratification, or
less well-disguised self-seeking. But Lueger was certainly not without a capacity for genuine sympathy,
nor incapable of sincere charity for those of his
acquaintances less fortunate than he. And there was a
relation between the public man and the private man;
he was, after all, a man among men, and no degree of
political acumen could have rendered him entirely
immune to the ordinary emotions of everyday life.

That he was not immune, but fully capable of
ordinary jealousy, is readily apparent in a surviving
draft of a letter to Fuerst Rudolf Liechtenstein in
1903. This rare document from the post-1897 period
shows that Lueger was indeed jealous of his
prerogatives as mayor. Lueger had been invited to
attend a memorial service in the Hofburgpfarr Kirche.
When he arrived, however, through some misunderstanding he was denied admission. He was doubly
humiliated, because he had to turn around and leave
in front of others who were arriving. In this letter,
Lueger falls back on his legal right to attend this
function, stressing that as Buergermeister it was his
duty to participate. This affront may well have
evoked bitter memories of the emperor's repeated
refusals to sanction his election to mayor in the
first place. The vehemence of Lueger's pencilled
corrections suggests that this affair touched a
sensitive spot. He was, in any case, often a
legalistic and willful person, who, once his mind
was made up, could not be deterred from what he
thought was correct and his due without the greatest
difficulty.

Another, quite different document, dating from
Lueger's political youth, is a poem written by an
anonymous voter and included in a ballot, in May, 1878.
Lueger thought enough of this poem to have it mounted.

At the time, he had just been reelected to the Municipal Council, only two months before, after more than a year's absence; and he must have applied this poem and its sentiments to his own situation and the arduous campaign he had just been through.

Yet another aspect of Lueger's character, which perhaps bridged the difference between strictly private and public spheres, was his rather conventional taste in art. The supposed cultural philistinism and general aesthetic obtuseness on the part of Christian Social leaders, particularly Karl Lueger, were a perennial topic for derision by friend and foe alike. Lueger's gaffes were a public target; one of his most relentless critics, the Socialist satirist Habakuk (Emil Kralik), made fun of Lueger's ostensible inability to communicate in any but the dialect of the Viennese petit bourgeoisie. In one of Habakuk's sallies, a comedy of errors and misunderstandings, Lueger is depicted as struggling in vain to speak French to the wife of the Belgian Prime Minister Beernaert, at a festive banquet in the Rathaus. Exhausted by his efforts, Lueger is made to conclude:

> I surely would prefer to go somewhere else where
> I can speak Viennese. I'm soaked in sweat from
> the mental strain.[1]

Even sixteen years after his death, Lueger's reputed insensitivity to culture was still the butt of jokes. In 1926, at the time of the unveiling of the monument in his honor on the Karl Lueger Platz, the Christian Social Neuigkeits-Welt-Blatt published an anecdote in which Lueger identified a baritone as a tenor. When corrected, Lueger shook his head and responded: "As mayor I'm not obliged to know that."[2]

Although his cultural tastes could not be described as elegant, let alone esoteric, Marianne Beskiba maintained that he understood nothing at all about art:

> You know, Mariannscherl, I do like beautiful
> things, but The Secession, good grief! That's a
> misconception, you have to admit![3]

Lueger's dislike of Secessionist art was shared by many of his fellow Christian Socials and Christian Social journalists. They were particularly put off by its writhing, serpentine profusion, its "creeping vines," as they were called, and "polyp-like excrescences." Lueger had a good eye for sculpture,[4] though he mostly preferred the classical school. He did attend the theater more or less regularly and was an indefagitable promotor of singing groups.[5] At the time of his death, his sisters received condolences from organizations as far away and diverse as the Nuernberger Liederkranz, the Liechtenthaler Maenner-Gesangverein (whose motto was: "Vom Donaustrand aus voller Brust, Ein deutsches Lied mit Herzenslust"), the Bukarester Deutsche Liedertafel, the Schubertbund, the Akademie der Bildenden Kuenste, and the Oesterreichischer Buehnenverein, of which he had been an honorary member.[6]

Lueger had been enthusiastic about a municipal theater, where his followers could enjoy "wholesome" and inexpensive entertainment long before he became mayor. After he was elected, he supported the Kaiserjubilaeums-Stadttheater, until Adam Mueller-Guttenbrunn's inept artistic and financial management cooled his interest. After the opening night performance, in 1898, Lueger attended a banquet and made a speech in which he designated the premier play, Kleist's Hermannsschlacht, "a disgrace." This afforded his enemies the opportunity to criticize Christian Social cultural pretentions, although some liberal critics conceded that this particular play was not Kleist's best effort. What many of the papers did not quote, however, was another section of Lueger's remarks, where he advised Mueller-Guttenbrunn to put on the kind of quintessentially Viennese works that could more reasonably be expected to guarantee success. This advice serves as an additional comment on Lueger's own tastes:

> The true Viennese always mixes seriousness and levity, laughter and tears. Every Strauss and Lanner waltz laughs and cries at the same time, as do Schubert's dances. Even the greatest Viennese vernacular poet, Ferdinand Raimund, could laugh and cry at the same time, as well as perhaps the greatest poet of all times, Shakespeare. We have to try to produce the right mélange. At this we Viennese are past masters.[7]

In such directional criticism as this, Lueger made his private taste into something of a public force.

Lueger's taste and views on art became something of a political issue for the additional and subtler reason that they commanded a symbolic significance. An idea current in German thought at this time was to see in art a remedy to cultural disunity. The power of folk art in particular, which so attracted Mueller-Guttenbrunn, and may in part account for much of Lueger's indulgence of his inefficient theater manager, was regarded as a solution to many of the social ills attributed to the "private" forces inherent in "Christian" society. Such views on art could easily align themselves with more obvious issues. In any case, Lueger's views on art own a significance, both biographical and political, that justifies the inclusion of the following documents.

FOOTNOTES FOR

THE PRIVATE MAN

1. Habakuk, "Vom Friedensbankett im Rathause," Arbeiter Zeitung, September 13, 1907, p. 7.

2. Michael Epstein, "Dr. Karl Lueger und die Kuenstler," Neuigkeits-Welt-Blatt, September 19, 1926, p. 46.

3. Beskiba, Erinnerungen. p. 22.

4. Ibid.

5. In the Maennergesangsverein Archiv in Vienna are approximately forty congratulatory documents addressed to the Verein, bearing Lueger's signature or a facsimile.

6. Nachlass Karl Lueger, St. Slg. Zl. 1257/12, Karton II, Mappe: Beileids-Schreiben an Hildegard und Rosa Lueger.

7. "Das Festbankett des Jubilaeums-Stadttheaters," Deutsches Volksblatt, December 16, 1898, pp. 8, 9.

In Lueger's handwriting:

Poem enclosed in a ballot of the opposition party at
the district committee election of May 24, 1878, in
the Third District.

In unknown handwriting:

Let them grumble, let them rage;
Let them quarrel about nothing;
We, we fight to live.

With much sound and little substance,
Only caring for their own well-being,
That's all they do and want.

When will peace come back again?
Will justice ever be prized again?
Can one still harbor such wishes?

Yes, when passions are defeated,
When everyone is always given his due.
Then happiness and prosperity will return.

Letter copy

Honorable
Dr. Prix
Attorney to the Royal and Legal Courts
Vienna
4, Schleifmuehlgasse 8   Vienna, December 1, 1878

Honorable Colleague,

    I confirm receipt of 150 Gulden with your letter
of November 28, 1878 and hereby declare paid the
expenses in the case of Mr. von Trexler./ Klemm.

I took this opportunity to compare the amount you charged in this matter with my bill and I admit that it would very much interest me to find out how you, dear colleague, arrived at the figure of 150 gulden. If you value your work just as much as I do mine, then I can only congratulate your clients that they have such an outstanding and at the same time inexpensive attorney. Please accept these remarks in the way I mean them, dear colleague; I had hoped that a colleague would charge an amount commensurate with his abilities and a case. Never a friend of haggling and based on this supposition, I have agreed to the amount of 150 gulden you mentioned in the Municipal Council without knowing the amount of my claim. I now must suffer the consequences of my error; it is not because of the money but because it might appear as if I had made an improper demand.

I remain with the expression of great esteem,

Faithfully yours,

I N   151.956

To an unknown friend

Dr. Carl Lueger
Attorney to the Royal and Legal Courts
Vienna
1, Weihburggasse no. 8   March 20, 1879

Dear Friend,

Enclosed you will find the certificate of good conduct issued by the kk. police headquarters, Vienna.

Don't be alarmed by the negative wording of this document. This is now being used in Austria in order to avoid misunderstandings.

Now you can take off your Austrian garments and put on Prussian clothes. In this metamorphosis, the good wishes of an old colleague accompany you, especially the one that this new garment will not become too tight for you either physically or spiritually.

I got the impression from your letter that you
are completely satisfied in your new domestic happiness. I am very happy about this, and I sincerely
hope that it will always remain so. This appears to
be all the better for you as it will certainly
encourage you to avoid the dangers of your position,
which are probably quite substantial out there. I
don't know which party you call your own in Germany,
but if you are as oppositional in Prussia as you once
were here, things could become unpleasant for you.

You wished me similar happiness! I thank you,
but that will only remain a wish. I entered the
hostile arena a little too early. Business and politics occupy me completely and won't let go. If I
someday tire of politics and could have time for
marriage, I'm afraid it would be too late.

I don't want to disturb your congress with your
wife with my scribbling. I'll close, therefore, and
send my best greetings to you and your wife and remain
as an old Austrian vis-a-vis a newly-born Prussian,

Your loyal friend,

Dr. Karl Lueger

The next three letters reveal Lueger's tact and diplo-
macy but also his reluctance directly to involve himself in the appeals of others.

Nachlass Karl Lueger
St. Slg. Zl. 1257/12
Box 1
Mappe: Eigenhaendige
Konzepte in
Prozessangelegenheiten und
Studienexzerpte

Letter draft, probably
to Mayor Eduard Uhl

Wilhelm Gruensfeld
Disciplinary investigation
directed against <u>Bayer</u>

Honorable Mayor,

I should have spoken with you last night,
honorable mayor, about a matter that concerns a favor
requested of me by a friend who is also your friend,
which I could not refuse. To be honest, I lacked the
courage, and after contemplating the matter further, I
found that it would be better anyway to set down this
matter in writing because only this way will you,
honorable sir, have the opportunity, quietly and
impartially, to arrive at a decision that you consider
correct. And now to the point.

Our mutual friend, Mr. Karl L. Lustig, unfortunately is not in the kind of financial situation
that is necessary for a tranquil and orderly conduct
of business. For some time he has owed the firm
Bissinger & Co., in Pforzheim near Baden, approximately 12,000 gulden (Austrian currency). This
company admittedly had made an (arrangement, Ed.) with
Lustig not unfavorable to him, but after it too found
itself in straightened circumstances, it used its
earlier concession to induce Lustig to sign accommodation drafts whose face value matched the amounts
owed; in fact, they exceeded them. Shocked by the
large amount of the drafts in circulation, Lustig in
the first months of this year declared his inability
to go on in this manner and that he could not provide
any more drafts. At the time, Lustig was terribly
depressed and confided in me. Shortly thereafter, he
told me that he had now been relieved of his
anxieties. Bissinger would honor the drafts and make
an arrangement with him that would finally remove him
from under the Sword of Damocles. I was, of course,
happy that things had worked out and didn't say
anything more about it. Yesterday Lustig again paid
me a visit and, with tears in his eyes, told me the
following: on Saturday he had received a letter from
the Bissinger Company in which they again demanded
acceptance of the drafts in the amounts of 2980
gulden, 40 kronen, and 1119 gulden, 60 kronen. He
could not meet this demand because the following two
drafts issued and endorsed by him, and accepted by
Bissinger, were in circulation, i.e., due June 29,
1882, for 2,175 Reichsmarks, and due July 14, 1882,
for 2,095 Reichsmarks, plus one draft for 2,490 gulden
due September 5, 1882, issued and endorsed by
Bissinger & Co., and accepted by Lustig. He feared
the worst as the company did not keep its promise not
to demand any more accommodation drafts from him. He

301

said he could no longer endure this situation as the constant worry paralyzes his capacity to work. He asked me to speak with you, honorable mayor, to describe his situation to you, and to ask you to help him. He didn't dare speak to you directly about this; I could do it more easily. Mr. Lustig now believes that the Bissinger Company would be satisfied with regard to their demand for 12,000 gulden if he, Lustig, would honor the above-mentioned drafts for which he would need an amount of 5009 gulden, 80 kronen. He now asks you, honorable mayor, whether it would not be possible for you to render him this good office as a friend. You would save him and his entire family, and he would certainly be in a position to repay this loan gradually, and in order to secure this amount in the event of his death, he would mortgage his policy for 10,000 gulden.

This is what I wanted to tell you yesterday and is probably also the reason why Lustig didn't come.

Lustig already paid me a visit this morning to learn the result of my efforts; I told him that your brother had been here and therefore I couldn't say anything to you.

Honorable mayor! You can imagine how embarrassing it is for me to write this. I know which sacrifices you've made and how many have already appealed to you. But you will forgive me if I was not able to refuse our friend's request, which he made with tears in his eyes.

Since I know how kind you are, I have no intention of wasting any words, either for or against. Whether your response is affirmative or negative, my admiration and friendship for you remains the same, because I know that a denial will only mean that it is impossible. I also hope that your friendship for me will remain the same in spite of the unpleasant hour I must again have caused you.

With great respect,

Your Honor's most humble,

N B   455/14-2

Probably to Eduard Uhl

Dr. Karl Lueger
Attorney to the Royal and Legal Courts
1, Kaernthnerstrasse no. 8
1, Seilergasse no. 5   Vienna, September 25, 1886

Honorable Mayor,

     You know from the newspapers that I am still
alive; but because I haven't visited you for such a
long time you could almost believe, and rightly so:
"He, too, is ungrateful and has forgotten me."

     However, this is not so. That I didn't come can
be ascribed either to my having been too busy or in
such a bad mood because of events that I wouldn't
have been very pleasant company.

     Last Wednesday, Dr. von Mauthner turned to me
with the following request:

     The painter Felix, who had been commissioned by
the Municipal Council to paint your portrait, said
he had met you in Gmunden and spoken with you about
the matter. You had been very polite, but had
declined the invitation to sit for the portrait in
Gmunden; nevertheless, you had promised to let him
know your decision. Felix had not yet heard from
you and finds himself in a very embarrassing situation,
all the more as he considers it importunate to visit
you again uninvited. Felix now had turned to Dr. v.
Mauthner to ask him to intervene. Mauthner then asked
me to inquire about your disposition. I told him that
to my knowledge you were sticking to your decision
that your portrait had no place in the town hall and
that you, therefore, would not sit for any painter for
this purpose. Dr. von Mauthner now believed that you
should be dissuaded and that especially he and his
friends, even though they had been your opponents,
recognized your merits and would welcome your indulgence in this matter. I agreed to bring this to your
attention but added that I had no influence on your
decisions.

     I would have preferred to relate this in person,
but I didn't have one free evening this week. I
therefore must resort to the pen in order to fulfill

my promise. Perhaps I'll find some time Monday
evening to visit you with your permission. If not,
I ask you to inform me of your decision, which I know
anyway, either in writing or through one of your sons.

Please extend my respectful handkiss to your
wife. I remain, with greetings and my great respect,

Most faithfully yours,

Dr. Lueger

I N 29252

To an unknown friend:[+]

Dr. Karl Lueger
Attorney to the Royal and Legal Courts
Vienna
1, Braeunerstrasse no. 5   Vienna, July 26, 1886

Dear Friend:

Mr. Ballon was here to complain bitterly. You
are supposed to have promised him to arrange for a
collection for him during the trip. Because this did
not happen, he is in a desperate situation. He needs
50 gulden to pay his rent and he now appeals to me.
I personally cannot help and I don't know whether a
part of the net proceeds, if such are available, can
be used for that purpose. Ballon is actually a victim
of the Schoenerer Party, which probably includes some
wealthy people who could help this really poor man. I
received a negative response from another source to
which I turned, and it is difficult to tell Ballon
this.

[+]Leopold Gundlach contributed this letter to the
Handschriftensammlung. Although the friend is not
identified, he is probably Leopold Hollomay, one of
Lueger's supporters in the late 1880s. In Lehmanns
Adressenbuch of 1886, the name Gundlach is mentioned
only once, i.e., Anna Gundlach. She worked for the
lithographer L. Hollomay.

Enclosed is 1 gulden, which Krautmann sent as a contribution to defray the costs. Is the account settled yet?

                              Cordial greetings,
                              Your faithful friend,

                         Dr. Lueger

The following letter is addressed to Lueger.

Dr. Carl Lueger   Nachlass Karl Lueger
Attorney to the Royal   St. Slg. Zl. 1257/12
and Legal Courts   Box II
Vienna   Mappe: Politische
1, Seilergasse 5   Korrespondenzen

              Neubauer Creditverein
         registrirte Genossenschaft mit
             unbeschraenkter   Haftung

                    Vienna, November 11, 1886

Honorable Sir,

     We were informed that you had said the following in a speech at the recently-held Trade Association Day: "The Austrian-Hungarian Bank had previously not extended any credit to loan associations, except to the Neubauer Creditverein, which had received such because of the patronage of the former member of parliament Wiesenburg and had been treated by the bank as its pet. Only after the Czech loan associations had taken the matter in hand, had other Viennese loan associations received credit from the bank."

     We now ask you whether you actually made the above remarks about our association and, if applicable, whether they were worded any differently.

We would appreciate your response by the 15th of this month.

Truly yours,

Neubauer Creditverein
Zweig Preis Vogler

This draft seems to have been Lueger's response to the preceding letter.

Nachlass Karl Lueger
St. Slg. Zl. 1257/12
Box II
Mappe: Politische Korrespon-
denzen

With regard to your letter of the 11th of this month, you better please tell me first who gives you the right to ask such a question...and...in such a tone.

I expect a prompt response and remain,

Respectfully yours,

This is the Neubauer Creditverein's second letter to Lueger.

Dr. Carl Lueger	Nachlass Karl Lueger
Attorney to the Royal and	St. Slg. Zl. 1257/12
Legal Courts	Box II
Vienna	Mappe: Politische
1, Seilergasse 5	Korrespondenzen

Neubauer Creditverein
registrirte Genossenschaft mit
unbeschraenkter   Haftung

Vienna, November 15, 1886

Honorable Sir,

You answered our inquiry of the 11th of this
month with the question, who gives us the right to ask
you such a question.

If you mean that there is no applicable law that
would expressly give us the right to pose such a
question, you are correct. The laws of everyday
social intercourse have not yet been codified. After
we had learned of your publicly pronounced untrue
assertions about our Verein, and assuming that we were
dealing with a gentleman who would not be opposed to
repeating to us what he had said publicly, we turned
directly to you as the source for the most reliable
information about what had been said. Incidentally,
we also believed we should afford you through our
inquiry the opportunity to correct yourself, as we
assumed that especially you would not make such
remarks about our Verein, because you, as the former
representative of our institute, had to know from
drafts that we turned over to you that our Verein had
already received direct credit from the former
national bank, with which Mr. Wiesenburg, as is known,
had no position whatsoever.

Since your answer does not contain any clarifica-
tion, we must assume that we have been correctly
informed.

The tone of our letter was within the rules of
social decorum and courtesy. We won't talk about the

tone of your letter.

Respectfully yours,

The Management of the
Neubauer Creditverein

registrirte Genossenschaft mit

unbeschraenkter   Haftung

Zweig   Vogler   Preis

This is Lueger's last reply to the Neubauer Creditverein.

Draft letter

Nachlass Karl Lueger
St. Slg. Zl. 1257/12
Box II
Mappe: Politische
Korrespondenzen

Dr. Karl Lueger
Attorney to the Royal and Legal Courts
Vienna
1, Kaernthnerstrasse no. 8
1, Seilergasse no. 5   November 16, 1886

Messrs. Zweig, Dr. Vogler, Preis,
Directors of the Neubauer Credit-Verein, registrirte
Genossenschaft mit unbeschraenkter Haftung, Vienna

As you appealed to the laws of social intercourse
in your letter of the 15th of this month, I must
unfortunately point out to you that you have forfeited
this right through your two letters to me. For this
reason, I have no intention at all to discuss the contents of your letter any further. Your procedure is
simply unqualified and condemns itself in the eyes of
every decent person. (before: I only add as a
warning, that I will carefully keep your two letters
so that if untrue remarks are published on any occasion or in any newspaper, the written proof of the

contrary is in my hands.)

(before: Most)   Respectfully yours,

Dr. Lueger

I N   33164

To: Franz Stauracz[+]

Dr. Karl Lueger
Attorney to the Royal and Legal Courts
Vienna
1, Braeunerstrasse Address   Vienna, May 1, 1888

Reverend Sir,

On Sunday, as I wanted to keep my promise and attend the end of the celebration, I found the church and yard so crowded that it was impossible for me to force my way through, or at least it would have caused such a scandal and such a stir that trouble would have resulted.

Of course I didn't arrive until 3:15 p.m. and the festivities were well under way. I was delayed because I didn't arrive home to eat until 2:00, and despite my hurrying on foot--I couldn't get a coach-- could not be in Matzleinsdorf at 3:00 o'clock.

I cannot come to the Catholic Political Casino today, because I need to prepare for my talk on "school supervision."

With cordial greetings, I remain in gratitude,

Faithfully yours,

Dr. Karl Lueger

[+]Stauracz was one of Lueger's earliest biographers.

I N   33159

To: Franz Stauracz
written on black-
edged stationery

December 10, 1888

My Dear Friend,

My sisters and I most cordially and sincerely
thank you for the sympathy you have shown us in a most
difficult and bitter hour of our lives, particularly
for the <u>manner</u> of your sympathy, which touched us most
deeply and which will always be remembered.

May I ask you for a favor? I don't know the
names of two reverends. There were the Reverends
Latschka, Doerfler, Moser, you, and two more whom I
know by sight but whose names I do not remember.
Would you kindly let me have them?

I entrust the soul of my dear mother to your
prayers, thank you again, and remain, with most cordial greetings,

Your loyal and devoted friend,

Dr. Karl Lueger

Memorandum

Nachlass Karl Lueger
St. Slg. Zl. 1257/12
Box II
Mappe: Wiener Presse,
Affaere Wrabetz,
Marktordnung, u.s.w.

In the first place, I am astonished to be queried
about matters that transpired between members of
parliament and that have an exclusively political
background.

On the day after Wrabetz's abusive language
towards me, I went to my friend and colleague,
Representative Dr. Pattai, and asked him to intervene.
He regretted not to be able to render this service
because, as far as he was concerned, Wrabetz no longer
existed in matters of honor. With the same request I

then turned to my friend and colleague, Representative Professor Fiegl. He did indicate his willingness to intervene, but he could not transmit a challenge to a duel. I thankfully accepted with the remark that the present state of affairs did not entail such a challenge and that I might choose another friend in his, Professor Fiegl's, stead.

Major von Dobner and Professor Fiegl went to Wrabetz and related to me the results of their efforts as follows: Wrabetz refused to retract his abuse by saying he would account for it only in court. Major von Dobner then asked Wrabetz on his own initiative whether he would thereby refuse any other chivalrous satisfaction, to which Wrabetz responded in the affirmative.

On the basis of this information, the necessity of any further action on my part was eliminated, all the more so as Wrabetz's reputation is well known among honorable men.

Therefore, there can be no talk of a challenge to a duel with pistols in this case.

Draft letter   Nachlass Karl Lueger
                                      St. Slg. Zl. 1257/12
Addressee unknown   Box II
                                      Mappe: Wiener Presse,
                                      Affaere
                                      Wrabetz, Marktordnung,
                                      u.s.w.

Honorable Sir,

As I learned from the newspapers, only Wrabetz and his assistant were called as witnesses in the matter concerning my friend and colleague, Representative Professor Fiegl, and the records are now supposed to be submitted to the Mittel Schule deputation and to the kk. governorship, respectively.

Because personally I couldn't care less about my opponent's opinion of me, I wouldn't care at all about the procedure used. But because it concerns the fate

of my friend Fiegl, a man of honor, and because I consider myself obligated to do everything possible to
prevent him from becoming the victim of a cowardly,
untruthful denunciation, I ask that you subpoena Karl
von Dobner, Major in the Royal Hungarian Honved
Hussars in Vienna, 7, Heumarkt 7 in this matter.

In none of his other writings is Lueger's injured ego
more apparent than in this typewritten draft. Only
the corrections in parentheses and underlining are in
Lueger's hand.

Draft letter   Nachlass Karl Lueger
                                      St. Slg. Zl. 1257/12
                                      Box II
                                      Mappe: Aktenstuecke,
                                      Dokumente, Audienzen-
                                      angelegenheiten

                                      Vienna, February 19, 1903

To: His Serene Highness, Prince Rudolf von und zu
Liechtenstein, First Obersthofmeister to his K.K.
Apostolic Majesty.

                    Your Serene Highness!

      I was sent the following Court announcement to
the memorial service in the Hofburgpfarrkirche for her
deceased K. & K Highness, the Most Serene Archduchess
Elisabeth, for Thursday, February 19, 1903:

                  Court Announcement

      On Thursday the 19th of February
      1903 at 11:00 o'clock in the fore-
      noon, a memorial service will be
      held at His Majesty's Order for her
      Imperial and Royal Highness the
      Most Serene Archduchess Elisabeth.

                        312

The K. and K. courtiers will appear
in black attire with damascened
swords, the military officers will
appear in dress uniforms, without
service insignia, with crepe arm-
band on the left arm.

The ribbons of the grand crosses
will not be worn.

Approach will be in the
Schweizerhof at the
Botschafterstiege.

There will be no attendance for the
vigils (the previous evening at
5:00).

Because this court announcement represents an
invitation to this service, I considered it my duty
as Mayor of the Imperial and Residential City of
Vienna to attend. As I (fulfilled my duty), I was
told (by Loebenstein) that I was not authorized to
attend the memorial service. (I) had to turn around
(and pass all the rows of people, etc., which must
have appeared as if I had wanted to force my way
unauthorized into the funeral service. Because such
behavior is alien to me, the described) incident was
exceedingly embarrassing to me, (and I) take the
liberty of asking your Serene Highness for clarifica-
tion of this extremely unpleasant incident, and
further, to request that in the future you refrain
from sending to me any court announcements or invitations I may not use.

Allow me, your Serene Highness, the expression
of, etc.

Mayor

Appel (signature)

Although the following speech reveals Lueger's customary nationalism and rhetoric, its main purpose was to
honor an artistic event. As such, it is unique among
Lueger's writings.

Draft of a speech probably held on July 9, 1885, in
Kerling's Gasthaus-Garten "zum Wilden Mann," 5,
Hundsthurmerstrasse no. 27.

It is a venerable custom to pause and reflect
from time to time in one's life. On such solemn occasions, we inwardly review the past and remember all
those we have met, recall the joys we have
experienced, the pains we have suffered, and shed a
tear for our departed loved ones. We thereby also
look to the future, and, uplifted by the remembrance
of things past, purified by trials we have endured and
enriched by experiences along the way, we continue
toward our goals.

Just as this applies to each of us individually,
it applies to any group that has set aside days of
remembrance providing the occasion to review past
achievements and to determine whether and how the common goal has been achieved, to praise the cooperation
of the group, and to strengthen unifying bonds.

Today we are celebrating exactly such a day.

It has been twenty-five years since a few citizens of Vienna got together to sponsor a Christmas
tree celebration for the benefit of poor children.
Its success led to the formation of a Maennergesangsverein for the preservation of the German Lied.

Initially, this organization had many obstacles
to overcome, but thanks to the members' unity, they
were happily resolved.

Thanks to the board's vigor and to its honorary
directory Johann Umlauft, as well as the deserving
choir director Kristinus, the Verein has achieved its
present position, commands the respect that is its
due, and is in a position to foster further
development.

And so today, we can rightfully say: it was a
happy inspiration to create this Verein and to dedicate it to the purpose that it has never lost sight

314

of: the preservation of the German Lied. Among all
peoples, at all times, singing has been praised.

After all, singing is the noblest and most enthusiastic of all human expressions.

Singing gives expression to the love of mother
for her child and the child for her mother; the love
of a young man for a young woman; pain and sorrow;
enthusiasm and love for the fatherland and for the
nation are expressed in song; song accompanies the
warrior in battle, greets the singer, and comforts
those who have suffered misfortune.

The richer the feelings of a people, the richer
the treasury of songs that give it expression, the
more immediate and deeper is the effect that the Lied
produces in the people.

The infinite richness that the German people, and
especially the German-Austrians, manifest in this
cultural area attests the depth of feeling that per-
meates the soul of our people.

Therefore, preservation of the German Lied is one
of the most justified and noble expressions of
national sentiments, and we can safely say: "As long
as a people remembers its songs, it cannot perish."

Therefore, I warmly greet the members of the
Wiener Liedertafel[1] on their festive occasion today,
and greet all their friends who help us celebrate.
They seem like mighty trees in the forest, each
unselfishly wishing and promoting the thriving of the
other, no one overshadowing the other, united in their
purpose that one's prosperity is the pride of the
other.

I greet the women who are here today; their presence attests their sincere interest in the efforts of
our youth and the respect of our men, and that they
are always the first ones to advance the good and the
noble. May they find rich rewards in the enthusiasm

---

[1]Wiener Liedertafel (1859-1938), German-Nationalistic
singing group; Lueger became an honorary member in
1885. See Albert Benedikt, Anton Erjantz, Wiener
Liedertafel. Jahresbericht ueber die Taetigkeit des
Vereines im 76. Vereinsjahr 1934-35, Vienna, 1935.

the German people always accord their women:
And so I conclude with the wish:

May the Wiener Liedertafel continue to celebrate
such days.

May the flag that is presented today accompany
them to victory in friendly competition.

May it always blossom, grow, and prosper.

And may everybody remember its slogan:

"Happy must the singer be
and he must always be free!"

Long before illness necessitated extended stays in
health spas, Lueger loved to travel. His trips took
him to such places as Monte Carlo, Fiume, Dubrovnik,
Amsterdam, Cracow, Trieste, Milan, Berlin and
Bucharest. Lueger probably sent the following
instructions to Franz Josef Mayer, the head of his
secretariat in the town hall.

I N   40955

December 13, 1904

Dear Director,

We shall leave tomorrow, Wednesday, at 5:35 p.m.,
from Abbazia. The train will arrive in St. Peter at
7:10 p.m. From there, the express train will leave
for Vienna at 8:21 p.m., arriving on Thursday at 6:45
a.m.

Please arrange with the Suedbahn for the reservation of a coupé, first class, for me and Wimberger,
and a coupé, second class, for Mr. and Mrs. Hallmann.
I assume that the Mattuglie-Abbazia train to St. Peter
has no direct car to Vienna and that therefore the
reservation for the coupés will have to be made from
Trieste.

As to the weather, the first day was splendid. On the second day we had scirocco, magnificent surf, and finally rain. On the third day it rained. On the fourth, it was so-so. Today it is raining again. But it looks as though it might clear up. Most cordial greetings to you, dear director, and to all friends from me and all.

Faithfully yours,

Dr. Karl Lueger

Please <u>do not</u> forget the coach.

THE ANTI-SEMITE

The documents presented in this final chapter
contain empirical evidence of anti-Semitic judgments
and statements on Lueger's part. A problem always
remains, however, of deciding if he meant what he said
as political expediency or belief. This psychological
conundrum requires the greatest precision. For
example, Dirk van Arkel faults Kurt Skalnik for
defending Lueger with a false analogy:

> ...Skalnik...solves the problem by saying that
> Lueger did indeed play with antisemitism but
> should not be condemned for that reason because,
> in an age of security, he could morally afford to
> do so. This is, of course, the same thing as
> arguing that it is moral for a man to go out and
> steal as long as there is a sufficiently strong
> police force to prevent him from being successful
> at it.[1]

But Arkel's analogy is also at fault, because the
counterpart would be to assume that stealing is
equivalent to murdering. The logical error resides in
the meaning of anti-Semitism: Arkel suggests that it
was always the systematic, violent thing it became in
the twentieth century, particularly after World War I;
whereas Skalnik distinguishes the anti-Semitism of the
nineteenth century from that of the twentieth. Such
academic altercations prompt a return to primary
sources.

Too much of the discussion of Lueger's
anti-Semitism has been conducted on the basis of
secondary sources and the traditions of interpretation
these have given rise to and tend to sustain. It is
proverbial that Lueger used anti-Semitism for his own
political purposes. The full import of his statements,
however, may have escaped notice. Documents often
prompt reconsiderations of old conclusions. Count
Kielmansegg, for example, reported that Lueger's "own
anti-Semitism reached only as far as the Fichtegasse,
the location of the editorial offices of the Neue
Freie Presse."[2] Alexander Spitzmueller claimed that
Lueger's anti-Semitism was only "the sport of the
rabble" once it had fulfilled its purpose.[3] There is

a question, however, whether or not these two observers said more than they realized. For Lueger's concern with "editorial offices" may have indicated his insight into the importance of propaganda and mind control; and "the rabble" may similarly point again to his instinctive use of the masses. The documents presented here suggest that this is in fact the case.

There is no source for the only words for which Lueger is today remembered: "I decide who is a Jew." This statement may well be a misunderstanding and distortion of a recorded anecdote. The liberal Dr. Oskar Hein, at the time when Lueger's monument on the Wollzeile was unveiled in 1926, related the following anecdote, which later appeared in the Neue Freie Presse:

> Once a deputation from the teacher's association in the Second District had asked me to intervene with the mayor concerning the advancement of a Jewish temporary assistant teacher who had been there a decade. Dr. Lueger, to whom I had mentioned the matter, told me: 'You are also a politician. You know that we must accommodate the party to which we owe everything.' I responded that the party owed more to Dr. Lueger than he to the party. Dr. Lueger explained that he realized that these poor teachers were being unfairly treated, but that he could not prevail on the party in this matter. When I doubted this, he responded with a genuine Lueger witicism: 'In those things in which I am smarter than the others, I always succeed, but what a Jew is, everyone knows as well as I.' After repeated urgings, I finally received the promise that the City Council would successively appoint the assistant teachers. This promise was loyally kept.[4]

Lueger's recorded statement, "...but what a Jew is, everyone knows as well as I," may be the original of "I decide who is a Jew." Both statements are open to a variety of similar interpretations, yet the attested statement, in its finality, seems the more ominous of the two. In parliament, Lueger once remarked that certain Jewish sects practiced ritual murder, and that "it would be in the interest of all, if the truth about this were finally made known."[5] And at an electoral meeting in 1895, he said that the Dreyfus

322

"Affair opened the eyes of the French, and even they will one day realize that the Jew has no Fatherland and therefore knows no Fatherland."[6]

Regardless of how such statements are interpreted, the important thing is that Lueger made them, and in making them legitimized anti-Semitism. He early appreciated its political worth, as did Georg Ritter von Schoenerer, the leader of the numerically insignificant Pan German Nationalist Party. But Schoenerer was considered a crank in imperial Austria, and his pronouncements were accordingly ignored by all but a few die-hard supporters. However, Lueger, as the leader of a party of imperial stature, presents a different picture. He was, at least in the eyes of his numerous followers, a respectable politician, so that what he said inevitably became a legitimate basis for action. Therefore, he bears the greater responsibility.

It should be observed that considering the bulk of Lueger's surviving papers, anti-Semitic statements are relatively rare. But because much appears to have been lost, there is no way to determine how much of his writing was devoted to anti-Semitic topics. The documents presented here therefore, require interpretive discretion.

FOOTNOTES FOR

THE ANTI-SEMITE

1. Van Arkel, <u>Antisemitism in Austria</u>, p. 69.

2. Kielmansegg, p. 382.

3. Alexander Spitzmueller, <u>'...Und hat auch Ursach
    es zu lieben.'</u> Vienna, Munich, Stuttgart, and
    Zuerich, 1955, p. 74.

4. "Persoenliche Erinnerungen an Dr. Lueger von Dr.
    Oskar Hein," <u>Neue Freie Presse</u>, September 19,
    1926, p. 4.

5. <u>Stenographische Protokolle ueber die Sitzungen
    des Hauses der Abgeordneten des oesterreich-
    ischen Reichsrathes im Jahre 1899</u>, 16 Session, 14
    Sitzung, November 16, 1899 (Vienna, 1900), p. 895.

6. "Waehlerverein des 5. Bezirkes," <u>Deutsches
    Volksblatt</u>, January 15, 1895, p. 4.

Fragmentary draft of a speech presented in Moravia about 1891.

Gentlemen!

<u>Citizens</u> of this city have asked me time and again to deliver a talk in Iglau about the principles of the Christian Social Party, and when I heeded this appeal, I considered this the fulfillment of a duty everyone has who represents the interests of the people.

Before I address the topic at hand, I want briefly to discuss two matters:

1.) I did not come to set citizen against citizen.

The Christian Social Program does not aim to <u>incite</u>, but rather to <u>reconcile</u>; it is not a <u>fight</u> of <u>all</u> against <u>all</u>, but rather <u>a harmonious formation of different</u> <u>interest</u> groups against the <u>stratification</u> of <u>human society</u> by <u>professions and occupations</u>.

2.) <u>Press</u>: here, too, as always in the liberal press, <u>abuses</u>, invectives and the <u>most insolent lies</u>. After 15 years of fighting with the liberal press, I have developed a rather <u>thick skin</u>, thank goodness. Therefore, I shall limit my comments and simply say that the liberal press, sometimes also called Jewish liberal, or Jewish Press, is the most impudent press on this earth, that it was and is the ally and accomplice of all robberies and thefts that have been committed against the Christian people. In Vienna, only fools and those on the same moral level support it; all decent and intelligent people reject it with disdain. Whether or not what the "Maehrische Grenzbote" has said about me is true, you will be able to decide for yourselves by attentively listening to my talk. You will be able to judge whether I speak the truth or not--therefore, whether I belong to the instructors or the corrupters of the people.

When the ideas of freedom swept victoriously from France throughout Europe all people embraced them joyously. A new time of happiness had dawned; the road was paved for mankind to achieve its highest ideal of perfection. Barriers erected through the wisdom of our forebears for the purpose of upholding order were impetuously torn down. Old and established institutions that constrained the titanic powers of mankind were ridiculed. People yearned for the splendid dawn of a new day rising from the ruins.

In Austria, too, Enlightenment...People waited and waited for the happiness that was to come.

But happiness did not come. On the contrary, one felt ever more uncomfortable.

Even more freedom; perhaps this will help.

More freedom came, but happiness did not.

Shares were printed, banks were founded, wildest speculations were carried on at the stock market; then came the crash and lo and behold: the people were left with printed paper while others prospered with money.

Of course, in Austria, the so-called freedom turned into an incredible fraud. . . .

Representatives of the people became representatives of capital and oppressors. The representatives were the ones who participated in all the fraudulent activities, and when salvation was necessary, they proceeded on the premise of manus manum lavat. You bow to me, I'll bow to you. . . .

Tremendous amount of justified embitterment among the people.

When particularly in Bohemia and Moravia there wasn't a breakthrough, this was because of the nationalities' problem.

The embitterment is the reason for new parties.

A long period of strife.

Finally, Vereinigte Christen; now, strife again, but people will know how to put the agitators in their proper place. Therefore, together: the <u>Christian Social Program</u>.

Protection of honest work, i.e., both physical and mental, against the oppression by international capital.

a) <u>Farmers</u>

1) suspension of land division

2) land tax relief and determination of a debt ceiling

3) protective tariffs. Promotion of farmer's district cooperatives.

b) Craftsmen
Development of a cooperative system, etc.

c) Workers
international protection, etc.

d) Suspension of work on Sundays and holidays-- also for officials

e) Improvement of civil servants' skills

f) Private Officials
against abuses of temporary office worker system
Protection against arbitrary termination

Nationalization
re state
monarchists
re politics
for support and development of peoples' freedoms
re education
Christian school and therefore <u>separation</u>
according to university (and) confessions. . . .
State revenues for the benefit of citizens
<u>Criticisms</u>: extra homework, military supplies

a) Clericalism
hatred for priests.
loss of countless German positions
Jews to cherish their religion

b) Nationalism
Bruenn, Germans in the Czech camp.

c) Anti-Semitism
Jews, the leaders of the liberals
Capital
usurers. Exploiters of property. . .
incite the classes
incite the nations. . . .

Jewish press against clergy and religion, there-fore, we believe: the Jews have no right to become judges, political officials and officers, and must be pushed back.

Christians again have upper hand
indigenous property
indigenous labor

then peace and quiet will return. . . .

Fragmentary speech draft

Nachlass Karl Lueger
St. Slg. Zl. 1275/12
Box II
Mappe: Redekonzepte

Gentlemen!

Each of you will admit that my political struggle is a <u>difficult</u> one.

Belonging to a small party lacking financial resources, relying solely on my intelligence, my knowledge, and the power of my speeches, I lead an implacable war against the now all-powerful Golden International which possesses all the necessary ammunition: money, press, a large party, etc.

I feel like a mountain climber who is surrounded by the dangers of ice and rock. A single false step will result in death.

I know that they literally lurk, waiting to destroy me and, if possible, to inflict the same fate on me as on another leader of the Christian Peoples.[+]

Caution is therefore necessary and advisable.

I believe to have done the right thing in the case at hand.

This is affirmed not only by the expressions of approval from all parts of Austria-Hungary, but also by my opponents' fits of rage, particularly the practically unheard of abuses of the Jewish papers.

A trap was prepared for me, and all had hoped and expected that I would fall in. I did not fall in; hence, the rage of my opponents. They would gladly have heard the verdict: Dr. Lueger is guilty, etc...

One more word to characterize my opponents and my situation:

Corstans-Laur

Challenge of the "Wiener Tagblatt," the "Neue Freie Presse," etc., to beat me, to slap me, to censure me.

Indeed, even Etienne says: he doesn't consider it worthy of the lawful state in which we live to censure me.

That even Etienne says who had challenged me to commit a crime. This same Etienne talks of the "lawful state in which we live" and that he Etienne respects this state.

One is astonished over this confusion in concept and I say:

I consider it unworthy of the lawful state in which we live that it should be possible to challenge people to acts of violence without punishment or retribution.

Misuse of Immunity. . . .

[+]The reference is probably to Georg Ritter von Schoenerer.

But when the machinations of the Golden
International are attacked, then misuse of immunity is
charged.

Oh, no! It is...in the latter case of the
greatest significance.

But my opponents may rage and shout, may abuse
and calumniate me, they may beat me whenever they want
and can.

Nothing will dissuade or hinder me. I will continue the fight as long as the voice of the people,
the voice of God, summons me.

Yes, I appeal to the people. . . .

Here in the circle of my friends, I thank <u>all
from afar</u>, thank all <u>like-minded comrades</u>...thank my
loyal friends, and this wreath is to remind us forever
of the times of bitter struggle, but also of the
unswerving loyalty you always demonstrated, of the
loyalty that shall forever unite us until death.

Speech draft   Nachlass Karl Lueger
                                St. Slg. Zl. 1257/12
Ca. 1886   Box II
                                Mappe: Redekonzepte

<u>Gentlemen!</u>

Since I last spoke to your club on <u>September
23rd, a new element</u> has emerged in the party affairs
of our city, viz., the realization of <u>solidarity</u> among
all parties that have proclaimed on their banners an
<u>honest</u> and <u>legal</u> struggle in economic matters against
the supremacy of big business, and that are
endeavoring for the last time to free Christian
society in a peaceful way from the tentacle embraces
of the monster suffocating it.

While some of our party comrades, led astray by
the old slogans <u>liberalism, clericalism, feudalism</u>,
could not decide to serve the <u>new alliance</u> unconditionally and joyfully; while some participate only

reluctantly, forced only by the overwhelming demonstration of the people's will, and every now and then cast longing looks at the fleshpots of liberalism; thus, while the power of unity was not recognized by all in the Christian camp, the liberal party has immediately appreciated the magnitude of the danger of having to fight against a united army rather than against individual divisions that often enough fought one another; a united army whose only goal, even if their weapons are different, is: "liberation of the Christian People and states from the discreditable rule of the power that we Democrats call big business and the anti-Semites call Jewry."

The liberal party, headed by the liberal press, immediately mobilized its fighting forces. For some time, the liberal party thought the opposing movement could be silenced. When this failed, they wanted to eliminate it by ignoring it, and especially the anti-Semitic movement didn't exist for the liberal party for quite some time. They confined their efforts to hurling the basest, most mendacious, and dastardly attacks in their weekly and bi-weekly papers. And because this didn't bear any fruit, because the anti-Semitic party in particular grew more and more, and because the mutual cooperation of the three congruent parties in economic matters scored successes at the trade meetings at Linz, St. Poelten, and in the elections at St. Poelten, the liberal press was ordered to begin the fight.

In the two "Tagblaetter," in the "Consititutionelle Vorstadt Zeitung," in the "Neue Freie Presse," in the "Deutsche Zeitung,"...etc., the press campaigns began, and it is unbelievable to what a brazen extent lies, defamations, and denunciations were disseminated.

The anti-liberal league was pilloried as a pack of crude scandal mongers, even accusations were insolently invented, and on the basis of this lie, they wrote about the stone age primitivism of the anti-liberal league. On the basis of this lie, the police was loudly requested to incarcerate a few, as the others, it was hoped, would then run off anyway. This lie was spread to all corners of Austria; even the official papers printed the lie without correcting themselves after the truth was later officially revealed.

(Here, Lueger breaks off)

331

Lueger's criticism of the liberal press here anticipates Karl Kraus.

Speech draft   Nachlass Karl Lueger
                                      St. Slg. Zl. 1257/12
Ca. 1886   Box II
                                      Mappe: Redekonzepte

    <u>Margarethen</u> Meeting of the trade association.
Thousands of posters. <u>All voters.</u> When they came
they were rudely insulted and depicted as disturbers
of the peace and scandal mongers in the liberal
papers, and the papers lied about a <u>reign of terror</u> of
the <u>anti-liberal league</u>.

    <u>Friday</u> a meeting of the Democratic Club in the
7th District was held.

    <u>Kronawetter</u>, Dr. <u>Lueger with his staff?</u> Dr.
<u>Lueger</u> did not rise. <u>Opponents and followers of</u>
<u>Kronawetter</u>. Naturally, you don't hear a whisper
about those meetings attended by many thousands that
proceed quietly, at which even our opponents can speak
undisturbed--these meetings are simply ignored.

    Whether these tactics will be useful? I doubt
it. For a while, the one or the other who gets his
wisdom only from the daily press may let himself be
deceived; those, however, who know the truth only hate
and resent this brood of liars all the more; each one
of them becomes an enthusiastic apostle of our
teachings who will conquer for us more and more new
territory among the people and who will undermine the
ground on which the liberal press carries on its
doings.

    But if you ask yourself: why has the liberal
press sunk to such depths? There is only one answer:
it sunk to this depth because the party it serves had
long since disappeared, and was replaced by lies and
hypocrisy, corruption and thirst for power.

    That is how it is with the "<u>Presse</u>." In addi-
tion, it mostly belongs to Jews, and all events,
therefore, are treated solely on the basis of whether
they are useful or damaging to the Jew.

    I said: <u>lies</u> and <u>hypocrisy</u>; <u>corruption</u> and <u>thirst</u>
for power.

That the liberal press is full of lies needs no further proof.

It lies in editorials, reports, in local news, in municipal reports, in telegrams in the economic section; it lies between the lines in the feuilletons, it lies in novels, it lies in advertisements.

It lies directly by inventing untruths, deliberate untruths.

It lies indirectly by ignoring important facts and thereby inducing readers to draw incorrect conclusions.

It is hypocritical. It flatters the powerful as long as it believes they are serving its interests. It does so in order to deceive the powerful and the dangerous enemies who constantly work towards undermining the last vestiges of power...

It feigns reverence for the pope, because it believes it to be momentarily advantageous to throw sand into the eyes of the people. But it continues to ridicule Christianity, to undermine faith among people, solely so that the masses are robbed of any moral footing, that they become easy prey for big business and sink into slavery.

It feigns love for Vienna, lauds the golden Viennese heart, the good nature of the Viennese, and their cheerfulness, but it is the liberal press that drove us Viennese out of the theaters, that made us suspicious and robbed us of our cheerfulness. It feigns love for the German nation; but not the true national sentiment, rather only agitation against other nations. Any attempt to solve the national question is cunningly defeated; anybody who views a Czech or a Slav as a human being is branded a traitor and encouraged to keep fighting; all that just so the sharks among the people can complete their destruction undisturbed.

It preaches love for property, but only insofar as it concerns its own property and that of its clients. It praises the great robbers who seize millions, even billions, in property of others, as the masters of mankind; and if one of these robbers has the misfortune of being accused by the public prosecutor, then he is treated as kindly as if he had perished on the field of honor.

It is the great and overt opponent of the <u>little lottery</u> because its profit does not fill their pockets or those of certain bankers. On the other hand, it lauds certain minor lottery tickets and does everything possible to induce people to play the stock market.

Now and then, they even oppose corruption, but only when they believe they can conceal their own corruption. They act like a thief who is being pursued and while trying to escape shouts with the rest "stop him!"...

The liberal press is corrupt; it is corrupt because it exclusively serves high finance. . . .

Internal and external entanglements are created in order to carry out stock market maneuvers; telegrams are forged; men with great influence on world affairs are left to become sicker and sicker and then they are made well again in a piquant way, however the press wishes. Pronunciamentos of monarchs are misquoted because the press knows very well that retractions are not requested pursuant to Article 19. But if an official paper prints a correction, then the matter is twisted in such a clever way that the impression remains that the original article was true.

The way wages are paid is also corrupt. . . . The exploited are being paid according to their cooperation. . . .

It doesn't matter whether a company is solid and respectable or not. If the people are cheated, what does the press care so long as it profits? The people are stupid, forget quickly, and are gladly taken in again by the sharks.

The liberal press is immoral. <u>Only piquant</u> --that's the slogan. Whether family happiness is destroyed or people are sent to their death doesn't matter. . . .

The liberal press doesn't spare the <u>family</u>. It isolates the most intimate affairs in order to publicize them, and if there is nothing, it simply fabricates stories. King Ludwig of Bavaria, and Crown Prince.

Reports about court trials are corrupt, and the public literally has become a curse for the administration of justice.

The <u>advertisement business</u> is corrupt. Secret <u>illnesses, fraudulent transactions, matchmaking ads</u>...

Prying and merciless persecution mania.

Prying everywhere: Municipal Council, parliament, at all levels. If misfortune happens, janitor, Greissler. If he is thrown out, or he can't find out anything, then he lies. If he is corrected, he says: the correction is wrong. . . .

<u>Conclusion</u>: The Viennese liberal press is the most corrupt and disgraceful press in the whole world... "Neues Wiener Tagblatt"--we do nothing; we only shout, don't improve things. It is true; we always want to fight these bandits on legal grounds, and we keep on believing that our call for help will be heard. We hope the state authorities not only will continue to enforce the present measures against the press, which we applaud, but also will vigorously proceed against the excesses of the liberal press.

But I warn the liberal press: it should not ridicule and scorn those whom it deceived, lied to, and exploited.

Farmer	cries for vengeance
Tradesman	cries for vengeance
Official	cries for vengeance
Widows and Orphans	cry for vengeance

Religion and fatherland cry out for liberation, and the day will come when these cries will be heard by the proper authority. The day of liberation for the Christian people from servitude in which we now languish will come and the day of vengeance for the disgrace tolerated and suffered.

EPILOGUE

Karl Lueger's career contributed to the rise of popular mass movements, out of which his own political existence sprang. Until the last two or three years of his life, he never separated himself from the masses. Only after the complications of diabetes and its deleterious effects on his eyesight would no longer allow him to continue did he gradually withdraw from his long and active political life. Yet the power he drew from the people fed a political millenialism that in the end came to distort his objectivity, ultimately crippled his ability to compromise, and thus robbed him of those two requisites of successful statesmanship. He and his closest advisors paid too much attention to the immediate feelings, prejudices, and violent hatreds of their political supporters and, thus failed to attend to their own genuine needs and long-term interests. His Christian Socials failed to foresee the consequences of their internal disputes. They underestimated, for example, the need for low income housing for Vienna's working class, a need that the rival Social Democrats had clearly seen and adroitly exploited. The Social Democrats were therefore able to take advantage of such tactical mistakes. Omissions like this explain in part the accelerating erosion of Christian Social popularity after Lueger's death in 1910.

Yet at the same time, an effective and inclusive consistency can be found at the heart of Lueger's political technique. Perhaps better than any other Austrian politician of his time, he intuitively understood the need for a strong community in a time of uncertainty and confused values. As a consequence, he sought to centralize his party and supported state intervention in the private sphere, according to poli cies in fact begun by his liberal predecessors and sustained by later Social Democrat mayors. He also valued the role of the arts, especially in Vienna, the cultural capital of central Europe. Along with Kaiser Wilhelm II, he fully appreciated the power of art to disseminate politically-slanted cultural messages, and was himself honored as an earnest leader of the arts as early as 1896. All told, he became a symbol of the frustrated ambitions and disappointed hopes of his followers. Emperor Franz Joseph rejected Lueger as a demagogue, a Magyarophobe, and an anti-Semite; but when the emperor finally confirmed Lueger's fifth election to mayor, in 1897, the man became in the eyes of the people "the savior of Vienna."

In this light, it is easier to understand how Lueger offered himself to the masses as something of an idol. Elaborate mass pageants of Christian Socials, where Lueger was the star attraction, were worked out and staged to dramatic effect, and, by 1910, had become an unexceptional feature of public life in the city. To what extent these mass demonstrations served to satisfy Lueger's personal needs is not at issue; they doubtless answered to something in his nature. Even today, however, the apparent need of a political figure to identify with the masses and, on the other hand, the complementary need of the masses to identify with a leader who elicits trust, such as Lueger did, has become one of the marks of twentieth-century charismatic politics.

While the Christian Social Party clearly lacked the cohesiveness of modern totalitarian parties-- Lueger's regional politics aroused distrust and resistance among his own party in western Austria-- Lueger himself was more than just another colorful politician of the transitional fin de siècle. The experience of his innovations reaches into the tech- niques and events of the twentieth century. Aspects of his political personality--its dictatorial ten- dencies, emotional compulsions, and nationalistic propensities--more closely resemble those of a modern totalitarian than of a political moderate of his own generation.

GLOSSARY OF NAMES

Able, Heinrich S.J. (1843-1926), Christian Social
publicist.
Andrassy, Julius (1860-1929), Hungarian statesman.
Appel, Karl (1862?-1919), Obermagistratsrat, head of
the Praesidialbureau and the Secretariat of the
Municipal Council, City Council and magistrate.
Arndts, Karl Ludwig Ritter v. (1803-1878), Dr. jur.,
Upper House of Parliament, University Professor.
Bachmayr, Emanuel (1842-1911), produce dealer,
Municipal Councilor.
Bacquehem, Olivier, Marquis (1847-1917), Minister of
Commerce, Upper House of Parliament.
Badeni, Kasimir (1846-1909), Prime Minister.
Ballon, Theodor, Merchant.
Banhans, Anton (1825-1902), Dr., Minister of Commerce,
President of the Danube Steamship Company,
Sektionschef.
Baertl, Josef (1827-1913), glove manufacturer,
Municipal Councilor, City Councilor.
Bayer, Georg (? -1887), police superintendant.
Beernaert, Auguste (1829-1912), Belgian Prime
Minister, Nobel Peace Prize, 1909.
Berg, Leopold (1840-1909), Dr. jur., lawyer, Municipal
Councilor.
Beskiba, Marianne (1869-1934), artist.
Bismarck-Schoenhausen, Otto, Eduard, Leopold, Prince
von (1815-1898), Prussian statesman, Chancellor of the
Second German Empire.
Blaschek, Josef Karl (1851-1920), commercial and
socio-political writer, newspaper publisher.
Bloch, Josef Samuel (1850-1923), Rabbi, Dr., writer
and newspaper editor, Lower House.
Bode, Rudolf, builder deputy of Viennese public works.
Braun, Karl (1822-1893), Dr. jur.
Brzobohaty, Josef (1841- ?), Dr. jur., lawyer.
Buchwald, Alois Theodor (1846?-1896), plumber.
Castel Marino, Radislav Merzik Ritter von, legal
assistant.
Christianovic, Julius (1833-1907), Feldmarschall-
Leutnant, Infantry Regiment No. 6.
Decurtins, Caspar (1855-1916), Dr. jur., Swiss
sociologist and social politician, co-founder of the
Catholic University of Freiburg, Swiss Nationalrat.
Deutsch, Friedrich (1840- ?), university friend of
Lueger.

Deutsch, Julius (1884-1968), Dr., Secretary of the
Austrian Socialist Party, writer, Member of
Parliament.
Dobner, Ritter von Rantenhof, Dettendorf and
Gimajlebaren, Karl. Royal Hungarian Honved Hussar
Major.
Dotzauer, Karl Ludwig (1848-1895), master baker,
Municipal Councilor.
d'Urfé, Honoré (1568-1625), French author.
Dreyfus, Alfred (1859-1935), French officer falsely
accused of espionage for Germany.
Drumont, Edouard (1844-1917), publicist, editor of the
anti-Semitic paper la libre Parole.
Dworzak, Joseph Franz (1822-1866), Dr. phil. und der
Rechte, University Professor of Roman Law and Civil
Common Law.
Ebenhoch, Alfred (1855-1912), Dr. jur., lawyer, Lower
House of Parliament, Minister of Agriculture,
Landeshauptmann of Ober Oesterreich.
Elisabeth, Marie Henriette Stephanie Gisela,
Archduchess (1883-1963).
Epstein, Moritz (1844-1915), journalist.
Etienne, Heinrich von (? -1894), naval officer and
official of the Danube Steamship Company.
Etienne, Michael von (1827-1879), brother of Heinrich,
co-founder and publisher of the Neue Freie Presse.
Exner, Wilhelm Franz (1840-1931), Dr. phil., Upper and
Lower Houses of Parliament, professor at the
Hochschule fuer Bodenkultur.
Fajkmajer, J.A., licensed agent in iron and metal
goods.
Felder, Cajetan von (1814-1894), Dr. der Rechte, Mayor
of Vienna, Municipal Councilor, Upper House of
Parliament.
Felix, Eugen (1837-1906), painter.
Fenauer, Adolf, brush manufacturer, Chairman of the
Verein "Gewerbebund."
Feucht, Karl (1822-1895), confectioner, Municipal
Councilor.
Fiegl, Josef (1845-1900), Gymnasialprofessor in
Vienna, Lower House, Municipal Councilor.
Flucher, Jakob (1841-1892), Municipal Councilor.
Franz Ferdinand, Erzherzog von Oesterreich-Este
(1863-1914), Successor to the Throne.
Franz Joseph I. (1830-1916), Emperor of Austria, King
of Hungary, etc.
Friedmann, Alexander (1838-1882), Municipal
Councilor, Lower House.
Fronz, Jakob (1828-1902), legal court physician,

Municipal Councilor.
Funder, Friedrich (1872-1959), Dr. jur., Christian Social publicist, editor of the Reichspost, City Councilor.
Fuerst, Hermann (1849- ?), editor of the Neues Wiener Tagblatt, journalist.
Galimberti, Luigi (1836-1896), Cardinal. Papal Nuncio in Vienna.
Gallmeyer, Josefine (1838-1884), popular actress.
Gautsch von Frankenthurn, Paul Freiherr von (1851-1918), Dr. jur., Upper House, Prime Minister.
Gessmann, Albert (1852-1920), Dr. phil., librarian, Lower House, publicist, minister.
Glaser, Heinrich, Dr. jur., lawyer.
Glossy, Karl (1848-1937), Dr. jur.
Gluecklich, Karl, agent of the Danube Steamship Company in Galatz.
Goldschmidt, Theodor Ritter von (1837-1909), public works official, civil engineer, Municipal Councilor, City Councilor, speaker for the Guertelbahn Commission.
Gradt, Julius (1843?-1907), Dr. theol.
Granitsch, Georg (1833-1903), Dr. jur., lawyer, Municipal Councilor, Lower House.
Grassl, Ignaz (1795-1889), Dr. der Rechte, University Professor of Austrian Civil Law, Dean of the University of Vienna.
Gréy, Valerie, nee Caroline Valerie Loewey (1845?-1934), actress, theater founder, rhetoric teacher, author.
Gruebl, Raimund (1847-1898), Dr. jur., lawyer, Municipal Councilor, City Councilor, Vice Mayor, Mayor.
Gugler, Josef (1839-1917), Gymnasialprofessor, Director of the Teacher College in Vienna, Municipal Councilor.
Gunesch, Rudolf Ritter von (1837-1911), engineer, Municipal Councilor.
Gunesch, Wilhelm (1830-1895), Dr. jur., lawyer, Municipal Councilor, member of the Guertelbahn Commission.
Guenter, Wenzel (1820-1897), priest.
"Habakuk," see Kralik, Emil.
Haimerl, Franz Xavier Ritter von (1806-1867), Dr. jur., University Professor, Member of the Provincial Diet, President of the Education Council
Hallmann, Karl (1842-1923), Municipal Councilor, City Councilor.
Hasenauer, Karl (1833-1894), architect, Municipal Councilor.

Hersan, Michael (1842-1923), Dean of the Piaristen
Collegium in the Josefstadt and Provinzialassistent.
Hertzka, Theodor (1845-1924), editor, economist.
Hess, Heinrich (1827-1880), merchant, Municipal
Councilor.
Heyssler, Moriz (1814-1882). Dr. der Rechte, University
Professor of Legal Philosophy, Chairman of the Law
Faculty of the University of Vienna.
Hintermayer, Franz, merchant.
Hitler, Adolf (1889-1945), politician, Fuehrer of the
Third Reich.
Hohenwart, Karl Sigmund von (1824-1899), Prime
Minister, leader of the Hohenwart-Klub in Parliament.
Hollomay, Leopold, lithographer.
Hostnig, Florian (1836-1910), Municipal Councilor,
administrator of the church sekretariat St. Stephen.
Huber, Josef (1814-1896), barkeeper, Municipal
Councilor.
Hybler, Wenzel, municipal garden inspector.
Innocenz XI, Odescalchi Benedetto (1611-1689), Pope
1676-1689).
Jerábek, Franz (1836-1893), Dr., Lower House.
Kaftan, Johann (1841-1909), Dr. techn., civil engineer,
Lower House.
Kagerbauer, Peter (1808-1873), public prosecutor.
Karny, Theodor, hairdresser, member of the Democratic
Party and chairman of the Verein "Die Biene
Weihnachtsbaum."
Kathrein, Theodor (1842-1916), Dr. jur., Lower House,
President of the Lower House, Landeshauptmann from
Tirol.
Kelsen, Hans (1883-1973), Dr. jur., jurist, creator of
the new Austrian constitution, legal theorist.
Khunn, Franz Ritter von (1802-1892), Chairman of the
Bakers' Guild, Municipal Councilor.
Kielmansegg, Eric (1847-1923), Governor of Lower
Austria, short-term Prime Minister.
Kienboeck, Karl (1839-1931?), Dr. jur., lawyer, father
of Dr. Viktor Kienboeck, Finance Minister of the First
Republic, Municipal Councilor and City Councilor.
Klapka, Georg (1820-1892), Hungarian general and
politician.
Klebinder, Ferdinand (1847- ?), journalist, newspaper
publisher.
Kleebinder, Josef, hairdresser.
Klimt, Gustav (1862-1918), important fin de siècle
Austrian painter.
Klopp, Wiard (1860-1948), writer and historian. Karl
Freiherr von Vogelsang's son-in-law.

Knab, Josef (1846-1899), priest of the Archdiocese of Munich and Freising, publicist, member of the provincial diet.

Kohler, Karl Felix (1838- ?), journalist.

Kohn, Emanuel, agent for the Danube Steamship Company in Vienna.

Koller, Alexander Freiherr von (1813-1890), Upper House, cavalry general.

Kopitschek, Josef, plumber.

Kopp, Hermann (1830-1891), Dr. jur., lawyer.

Kossuth, Lajos (1802-1894), Hungarian statesman, revolutionary leader, Hungarian Prime Minister.

Kralik, Emil, pseudonym "Habakuk," (1864-1906), publicist, politician, satirist, regular contributor to the Arbeiter Zeitung.

Krammer, Karl (? -1877), Attorney to the Royal and Legal Courts.

Krautmann, Ferdinand, teacher.

Kreuzig, Anton (1828?-1905), taylor, Municipal Councilor, Lower House.

Krieghammer, Julius, Office Chief of the Danube Steamship Company.

Kristinus, Karl Raimund (1843-1904), church choir director.

Kronawetter, Ferdinand (1833-1913), Dr. jur., Lower House, leader of the Democratic Party, later prominent Socialist.

Kruegermaier, Wilhelm, watchmaker.

Kulisch, Theodor (1839-1888), Municipal Councilor, druggist.

Kupka, Augustin (1844-1897), Dr. jur., Municipal Councilor, City Councilor.

Kuppe, Rudolf (1883-1950), teacher, Christian Social historian.

Laur, Theodor, accountant.

Lenz, Alfred (1832-1907), engineer, Municipal Councilor administrative council member of the Elisabeth-Westbahn, Lower House.

Leopold I (1640-1705), Holy Roman Emperor, King of Hungary, etc.

Loebenstein von Aigenhorst, Heinrich Ritter von (1847-1923), Hof Rat and Hof Ceremoniel Director im Obersthofmeister-Amte.

Lobos, Ignaci (1827-1900), Bishop of Tarnow (1880-1892).

Loquai, Ferdinand (1838-1899), venetian blind manufacturer, Municipal Councilor.

Ludwig II von Bayern (1864-1886), King of Bavaria.

Lott, Ludwig (1820-1891), printing press owner, Municipal Councilor.

Lueger, Hildegard (1847-1938), Karl Lueger's older sister.
Lueger, Juliana, nee Schuhmayer (1811-1888), Karl Lueger's mother.
Lueger, Leopold (1806-1866), Karl Lueger's father; janitor of the Polytechnic Institute.
Lueger, Rosa (1849-1920), Karl Lueger's younger sister.
Lustig, Carl (1834-1899), jeweler, Municipal Councilor.
Mandl, Ignaz (1833-1907), Dr. med., Municipal Councilor, publicist, newspaper editor.
Matznetter, Karl (? - ?), florist, Municipal Councilor.
Mauch, Richard (1832-1899), civil engineer, owner of metal works and engineering factory.
Mauthner, Hermann, Dr. jur.
Mayer, Ferdinand (1835-1893), dealer in feather ornaments, Municipal Councilor.
Mayer, Franz Josef (1861-1922), director of Lueger's secretariat.
Mayer, Matthaeus (? - ?), bathhouse owner, house owner, Municipal Councilor.
Meisl, Salomon, conductor of the Vienna Tramwaygesellschaft.
Menčik, Ferdinand, teacher, Hof librarian.
Mittler, Josef, editor of the Neue Freie Presse.
Mueller, Karl Johann (1837-1901), Municipal Councilor.
Mueller-Guttenbrunn, Adam (1852-1923), author, publicist, theater founder and director.
Neuhaueser, Theodor, linen manufacturer.
Napoleon I (1769-1821), French Emperor.
Neumann, Leopold Freiherr von (1811-1888), Dr. jur., University Professor, Upper House.
Neumayer, Josef (1844-1923), Dr. jur., lawyer, Lower House.
Newald, Julius (1824-1897), Dr., Deputy Mayor, Mayor, Municipal Councilor.
Niese, Hansi (1875-1934), actress.
Oberzeller, Anton (1815?-1882), farrier and coach builder, treasurer.
Oberzeller, Anton, engineer.
Pachmann, Theodor (1801-1881), Dr. der Rechte, University Professor of Church Law.
Pappenheim, Gustav, owner and editor of various newspapers, vice-president of the Austrian Mill Association.
Patruban, Franz (1849-1897), Dr., notary and Ortsschulrat.

Pattai, Robert (1846-1920), Dr. jur., lawyer, Upper House, President of the Lower House.
Payer, Julius Ritter von (1842-1915), polar explorer.
Penn, Heinrich (1845- ?), Dr., editor and author.
Pernerstorfer, Engelbert (1850-1918), writer and editor, Lower House, Democrat, later Socialist.
Pfister, Wilhelm (1834-1897), Municipal Councilor.
Philippovich, Eugen von (1858-1917), Dr. jur., economist, social politician.
Pinó Friedenthal, Felix Freiherr von (1826-1906), Governor of Triest, Lower House.
Pollak, Leopold (1839-1900?), Lower House.
Porzer, Josef (1847-1914), Dr. jur., Municipal Councilor, Vice Mayor.
Possinger, Ludwig Freiherr von Choborski (1823-1905), Governor of Lower Austria.
Prix, Johann (1836-1894), Dr. jur., lawyer, Municipal Councilor, Deputy Mayor, Mayor.
Proskowitz von Proskow und Marstorff, Emanuel Ritter (1818-1909), industrialist, Upper House, Lower House.
Psenner, Ludwig (1834-1917), publicist and leader of the Christian Social Verein in Vienna.
Puchwein, Benedict, inn keeper.
Pumera, Anton (1861-1936), Lueger's bodyguard.
Rau, Karl Heinrich (1792-1870), University Professor.
Redl, Moritz (1832-1890), food store owner, Municipal Councilor.
Reisinger, Karl (1825-1893), wine dealer, Municipal Councilor.
Renner, Karl (1870-1950), Dr. jur., Chancellor and President of the Second Austrian Republic, leading Socialist.
Riby, Moritz (1820-1888), Municipal Councilor.
Riss, Alexander (1830-1896), professor, director of the Handels-Schule in Rudolfheim, Municipal Councilor.
Rohatschek, Josef (1814-1896), bar keeper, Municipal Councilor.
Rothschild, Albert Salomon Anselm (1844-1911), financier and industrialist.
Ruthner, Anton Edler von (1817- ?), Dr. jur., lawyer.
Salten, Felix (1869-1945), theater critic and author.
Schallaboeck, Franz (1844-1911), dairy farmer, Municipal Councilor.
Scharf, Alexander (1834- ?), newspaper editor and journalist.
Scheffer, Franz Josef (1821 - ?), women's dressmaker and house owner, Municipal Councilor.

Schembera, V.K. (1841-1891), newspaper editor, President of the journalists' and writers' association "Concordia."

Scherer, Franz (1824-1895), straw hat manufacturer, Municipal Councilor.

Schmolek, Antonie, President of the Ortsgruppe Margareten of the Viennese Christian Women's League.

Schnabl, Josef (1859-1923), Clergyman.

Schneider, Ernst (1845-1913), mechanic, publicist, Lower House.

Schollei, Otto Freiherr von (1823-1907), Feldmarschall-Leutnant.

Schoenerer, Georg Ritter von (1842-1921), Lower House, leader of the Pan German Nationalist Party.

Schrank, Johann Ferdinand (1830-1881), Dr., commercial school teacher, professor, Municipal Councilor, Deputy Mayor.

Schuhmeier, Franz (1864-1913), editor, Municipal Councilor, Lower House.

Schwer, Hans Arnold (1865-1931), journalist, Municipal Councilor, City Councilor.

Seitz, Jakob Ludwig, customs officer.

Siegel, Heinrich (1830-1899), Dr. jur., Upper House, University Professor.

Simon, Gustav (1819-1897), metal fancy goods dealer, Municipal Councilor.

Singer, Eduard (1844- ?), Dr., newspaper publisher.

Singer, Franz Ignaz Ritter von (1828-1886), newspaper publisher, Municipal Councilor.

Sommaruga, Guido (1842-1895), Dr. jur., lawyer, Lower House.

Spitzmueller, Alexander von (1862-1953), K. u K. Commerce and Finance Minister.

Stauracz, Franz (1855-1918), publicist, Spiritualdirektor der Klosterfrauen vom Guten Hirten.

Stein, Lorenz von (1815-1890), Dr. phil., University Professor of Economics, economist and leading Hegelian.

Steudel, Johann Heinrich (1825-1891), innkeeper, Municipal Councilor, Vice Mayor, Lower House.

Stipek, Eduard Franz (1851-1918?), Dr. jur., lawyer, Valerie Gréy's second husband.

Suess, Eduard (1831-1914), Dr., University Professor, Municipal Councilor, Lower House, President of the Akademie der Wissenschaften.

Sturm, Eduard (1830-1909), Dr. jur., lawyer, Lower House.

Suppan, Karl Victor, boat inspector for the Danube Steamship Company.

Suppantschitsch, Leo (1847- ?), university friend of Lueger.

Taaffe, Eduard Franz Joseph (1833-1895), Lower House, Prime Minister.

Tisza, István von (1861-1918), Hungarian statesman, Prime Minister, President of the Hungarian Lower House.

Tisza, Kálmán von (1830-1902), Hungarian statesman, Prime Minister, father of István.

Trabert, Adam (1882-1914), Dr., writer, co-founder with Richard von Kralik of the Catholic conservative Gralbund.

Trexler, Eduard Edl. von Lindenau, newspaper publisher and editor.

Troll, Walther Ritter von (1856-1937), Upper House, Member of Provincial Diet.

Tugendhat, Victor, Dr. jur., lawyer.

Uhl, Eduard (1813-1892), Municipal Councilor, Deputy Mayor, Mayor.

Umlauft, Johann (1806-1889), Municipal Councilor.

Unger, Josef (1828-1913), Dr. jur., University Professor, Upper House, Lower House, Minister of Justice.

Vaeth, Jakob (1828-1901), Municipal Councilor.

Vaugoin, Carl (1822-1904), Municipal Councilor, City Councilor, father of the later Defense Minister.

Vergani, Ernst (1848-1915), newspaper founder and publisher, Lower House.

Vetter, Cornelius (1850-1919), Municipal Councilor.

Vogelsang, Karl Freiherr von (1818-1890), journalist, social theoretician and politician.

Vogelsang, Marie Freiin von (1853-1925), publicist and daughter of Karl Freiherr von Vogelsang.

Vogler, Ludwig (1849-1922)., Dr. jur., Municipal Councilor, City Councilor, Lower House.

Wahlberg, Wilhelm Emil (1824-1901), Dr. der Rechte, University Professor of Criminal Law.

Waldbott und Basssenheim, Friedrich Lothar Felix Jacob Freiherr von (1845-1923), landowner, treasurer and secretary in the chief treasury office.

Weil, Robert, pseudonym "Homunculus" (1882-1960), Dr. der Rechte, author.

Wengraf, Hermann, Dr. jur.

Weyprecht, Karl (1838-1881), North Pole explorer.

Wittek, Heinrich Johann Ritter von (1844-1930), Prime Minister, Railroad Minister.

Wolf, Karl Hermann (1862-1941), Lower House, newspaper publisher.

Wolf-Eppinger, Sigmund, Dr. jur., lawyer.

Wrba, Ludwig (1843? - 1927), Railroad Minister.

Wrabetz, Karl (1846-1924), photographer, lawyer, Municipal Councilor, Lower House.

Zelinka, Andreas (1802-1868), Dr. jur., lawyer, Municipal Councilor, Deputy Mayor, Mayor.

Zerboni di Sposetti, Karl von (1803-1892), newspaper publisher.

Zimmermann, Karl (1834-1915), Dr. jur., lawyer, Municipal Councilor.

Paternal Ancestors

grandparents (paternal)	great grandparents (paternal)	great-great grandparents (paternal)
Josef Lueger b. 1759 d. 1812	Johann Lueger b. 1729 d. 1812	Michael Lueger b. ? d. 1755
Maria Anna b. 1778 d. 1832	Maria Schauberger b. 1725 d. 1802	Katherina Star (Sar?) b. 1690 d. 1775
		Josef Schauberger b. ? d. before 1758

great grandparents (maternal)	
	Magdalena Mayrhofer b. ? d. ?
Jakob Picker b. 1726 d. 1782	
Katherina Dorn b. 1732 d. 1787	great-great grandparents (maternal)
	Christopher Picker b. ? d. ?
	Affengrueber Maria b. 1692 d. 1752
	Johann Dorn b. 1709 d. 1759
	Maria b. ? d. ?

Appendix I

Karl Lueger's Family Tree

Maternal Ancestors

grandparents (paternal)	great grandparents (paternal)	great-great grandparents (maternal, only)
Franz Schuhmayer b. 1780 d. 18 ?	Josef Schuhmayer died before 1808	Simon Haidinger Magdalena
Josefa b. 1773 d. 18 ?	Theresia Meidinger died after 1808	Josef Werner Maria

great grandparents
(maternal)

Johann Georg Haidinger
b. 1716
d. 1806

Eva Maria Werner
b. 1737
d. 1791

Appendix II

Lueger's School Notebooks in the Nachlass Lueger, St.
Slg. Zl. 1252/12, Box I. Professors' names have been
included wherever possible.

1. Anfangsgruende der Astronomie
2. Auessere Geschike (sic) des roemischen Rechts von
   Dr. Dvoorzak (sic).
3. Buergerliches Recht nach Vorlesungen von Dr.
   Grassl.
4. Civilprocess--Dr. Dworzak
5. Deutsche Reichs u. Rechtsgeschichte vorgetragen
   von Dr. Siegel.
6. Eherecht Erklaerungen von Pachmann.
7. Encyclopaedie der Rechtswissenschaft.
8. Erb-und Familienrecht--Dr. Dworzak.
9. Finanzwissenschaft--Dr. Stein.
10. Die Geschichte des Altertums--von der Suendfluth
    bis zum Sturze des erstroemischen Reiches von 2328
    v. Ch. bis 476 n. Ch.
11. Geschichte der Quellen des roemischen Rechts--Dr.
    Arndts.
12. Gleichungen.
13. Griechische Schulaufgaben--1858.
14. Grundsaetze der Volkswirthschafts Politik von Rau.
15. Handels und Wechsel--Recht--vorgetragen von Dr.
    Haimerl.
16. Institutionen des roemischen Rechtes von Dr.
    Arndts.
17. Von den Logarithmen.
18. Obligationen, roemische--Dr. Arndts.
19. Oesterreichisches buergerliches Recht--erklaert
    von Dr. Grassl.
20. Oesterreichisches Erbrecht--Nach Dr. Unger.
21. Pandecten Auszug--Dr. Arndts.
22. Physik.
23. Physikaufgaben--VII Klasse.
24. Planimetrie.
25. Rechentheke 1858.
26. Rechentheke (1859 u 1860).
27. Rechentheke--VII Klasse I. Kurs 1860.
28. Rechentheke--1860/61.
29. Rechentheke--1861.
30. Rechentheke--1862.
31. Rechnungen.
32. Rechts Wissenschaft--nach Vortragen von Dr.
    Lorenz Stein.

33. Roemischer Civilprocess.
34. Roemisches Erbrecht--Dr. Arndts.
35. Strafprocess--Dr. Wahlberg.
36. Ueber Vermaechtnisse--Dr. Unger.
37. Uebungen in italienischer Sprache.
38. Verwaltungslehre--innere Verwaltung--nach
    Vorlesungen von Prof. Dr. Stein.
39. Verwaltungslehre I Theil. Vollziehung. Nach
    Vorlesungen (von) Prof. Stein.
40. Voelkerrecht in Friedens-u Kriegszeiten von Dr.
    Neumann.

Select Bibliography

Unpublished Sources

Nachlass Karl Lueger, Handschriftensammlung der Stadt
und Landesbibliothek der Stadt Wien.

Nachlass Ferdinand Menčik, Handschriftensammlung der
oesterreichischen Nationalbibliothek.

Nachlass Vogelsang, Theologisches Dekanat,
Universitaet Wien.

Secondary Sources

Adelmaier, Werner. "Ernst Vergani." Ph.D. dissertation, University of Vienna, 1969.

Allmayer-Beck, Johann Christoph. Vogelsang, Vom
Feudalismus zur Volksbewegung. Vienna and
Munich, 1951.

_____. Ministerpraesident Baron Beck.
Ein Staatsmann des alten Oesterreich.
Vienna, 1956.

Beskiba, Marianne. Aus meinen Erinnerungen an Dr.
Karl Lueger. Vienna, 1911.

Boyer, John W. "Church, economy and Society in Fin de
Siècle Austria. The Origins of the
Christian Social Movement, 1875-1897." Ph.D.
dissertation, University of Chicago, 1975.

_____. Political Radicalism in Late
Imperial Vienna: Origins of the Christian
Social Movement 1848-1897. Chicago, 1981.

Bruegel, Ludwig. Geschichte der oesterreichischen
Sozialdemokratie. 5 vols., Vienna, 1922.

Castle, Eduard (Ed.). Deutsch-Oesterreichische Literaturgeschichte. 4 vols., Vienna, 1937.

355

Czeike, Felix. Liberale, Christlich soziale und Sozialdemokratische Kommunalpolitik (1861-1934). Vienna, 1962.

Czelechowski, Maria. "Hansi Niese." Ph.D. dissertation, University of Vienna, 1947.

Deutsch, Julius. Ein weiter Weg. Lebenserinnerungen. Zuerich, Leipzig and Vienna, 1960.

Felder, Cajetan. Erinnerungen eines Wiener Buergermeisters. Vienna, Hannover, and Bern, 1964.

Friedlaender, Otto. Letzter Glanz der Maerchenstadt. Das war Wien um 1900. Vienna and Munich, 1976.

Funder, Friedrich. Vom Gestern ins Heute. Vienna and Munich, 1952.

Geehr, Richard S. Adam Mueller-Guttenbrunn and the Aryan Theater of Vienna, 1898-1903. Goeppingen, 1974.

Goetz, Marie. Die Frauen und der Antisemitismus. Vienna, no date.

_____. Schmutzige Waesche der Christlich-Sozialen eingesammelt von einer Christlichen Waschfrau. Vienna, no date.

Gréy-Stipek, Valerie, Paula. Leipzig, 1894.

Groner, Richard and Czeike, Felix. Wien Lexikon. Vienna and Munich, 1974.

Guglia, Eugen. Das Theresianum in Wien. Vergangenheit und Gegenwart. Vienna, 1912.

Hausner, Eduard. "Die Taetigkeit des Wiener Gemeinderates in den Jahren 1884-1888." Ph.D. dissertation, University of Vienna, 1974.

Heer, Friedrich. Der Glaube des Adolf Hitler. Anatomie einer politischen Religiositaet. Munich and Esslingen, 1968.

Hitler, Adolf. Mein Kampf. Boston, 1943.

_____. _Hitler's Secret Conversations_. New York, 1972.

Holeis, Eva. _Die Sozialpolitische Partei_. Vienna, 1978.

Inama-Sternegg, Karl Theodor von. _Vertreter des modernen Verwaltungsstaats. Staatswissenschaftliche Abhandlungen_. Leipzig, 1903.

Jenks, William A. _Austria Under the Iron Ring, 1879-1893_. Charlottesville, 1965.

Johnston, William. _The Austrian Mind_. Berkeley, Los Angeles, and London, 1972.

Kann, Robert A. _A History of the Habsburg Empire, 1526-1918_. Berkeley, Los Angeles, and London, 1974.

_____. _A Study in Austrian Intellectual History_. New York, 1960.

Kielmansegg, Erich Graf. _Kaiserhaus, Staatsmaenner und Politiker_. Vienna and Munich, 1966.

Klopp, Wiard. _Leben und Wirken des Sozialpolitikers Karl Freiherr von Vogelsang_. Vienna, 1930.

Knauer, Oswald. _Das oesterreichische Parlament von 1848-1966_. Vienna, 1969.

_____. _Der Wiener Gemeinderat, 1861-1962_. Vienna, 1963.

Knoll, Reinhold. _Zur Tradition der christlichsozialen Partei_. Vienna, Cologne, and Graz, 1973.

Kosch, Wilhelm. _Deutsches Theater Lexikon_. Klagenfurt and Vienna, 1960.

Kralik, Richard von. _Karl Lueger und der christliche Sozialismus_. Vienna, 1923.

Kuppe, Rudolf. _Dr. Karl Lueger, Persoenlichkeit und Wirken_. Vienna, 1947.

_____. _Karl Lueger und seine Zeit_. Vienna, 1933.

Lewis, Gavin. Kirche und Partei im politischen Katholizismus. Vienna and Salzburg, 1977.

Macartney, C. A. The Habsburg Empire, 1790-1918. London, 1971.

May, Arthur J. The Habsburg Monarchy, 1867-1914. New York, 1968.

Mueller-Guttenbrunn, Adam. Erinnerungen eines Theaterdirektors. Leipzig, 1924.

_____. Der Roman meines Lebens. Leipzig, 1927.

Neuwirth, Irene. "Dr. Cajetan Felder, Buergermeister von Wien." Ph.D. dissertation, University of Vienna, 1942.

Paupié, Kurt. Handbuch der oesterreichischen Pressegeschichte. Vienna and Stuttgart, 1960.

Petermann, Reinhard E. Wien im Zeitalter Kaiser Franz Josephs I. Vienna, 1913.

Pichl, Eduard. Georg Ritter von Schoenerer. 5 vols., Berlin, 1938.

Planer, Franz (Ed.). Das Jahrbuch der Wiener Gesellschaft. Vienna, 1929.

Pulzer, Peter G. J. The Rise of Political Anti-Semitism in Austria and Germany. New York, 1964.

Renner, Karl. An der Wende zweier Zeiten. Vienna, 1946.

Santifaller, Leo, et al. Oesterreichisches Biographisches Lexikon 1815-1950. Vienna, 1959.

Schorske, Carl E. Fin De Siècle Vienna: Politics and Culture. New York, 1980.

Silberbauer, Gerhard. Oesterreichs Katholiken und die Arbeiterfrage. Graz, Vienna, and Cologne, 1966.

Sitte, Camillo. City Planning According to Artistic Principles. London, 1965.

Skalnik, Kurt. Karl Lueger. Der Mann zwischen den Zeiten. Vienna and Munich, 1954.

Soukup, Richard. Dr. Karl Lueger. Ein Volksbuch um den grossen Buergermeister Wiens. Vienna, 1953.

Spitzmueller, Alexander. '. . .Und hat auch Ursach es zu lieben.' Vienna, Munich, Stuttgart, and Zuerich, 1955.

Stauracz, Franz. Dr. Karl Lueger, Zehn Jahre Buergermeister. Vienna, 1907.

Stoeger, Gertrud. "Die politischen Anfaenge Luegers." Ph.D. dissertation, University of Vienna, 1941.

Van Arkel, Dirk. Antisemitism in Austria. Leiden, 1966.

Wagner-Rieger, Renate. Die Wiener Ringstrasse, Bild einer Epoche. 5 vols., Wiesbaden, 1975.

Wandruszka, Adam. Geschichte einer Zeitung. Das Schicksal der "Presse" und der "Neuen Freien Presse" von 1848 bis zur 2. Republik. Vienna, 1958.

_____ and Peter Urbanitsch (Eds.) Die Habsburgermonarchie. 2 vols., Vienna, 1973, 1975.

Weil, Robert. Rueck naeher, Bruder! Der Roman meines Lebens. Vienna and Berlin, 1920.

Whiteside, Andrew. The Socialism of Fools. Berkeley, Los Angeles, and London, 1975.

Williams, C. E. The Broken Eagle. The Politics of Austrian Literature from Empire to Anschluss. London, 1974.

Ziegenfuss, Werner. Handbuch der Soziologie. Stuttgart, 1956.

Articles and Periodicals

Czeike, Felix, "Buergermeister Cajetan Felder und seine Zeit," in _Oesterreich in Geschichte und Literatur_.

_____ "Die Reisen des Wiener Buergermeisters Dr. Cajetan Felder," in _Jahrbuch des Vereines fuer Geschichte der Stadt Wien_. Vienna, 1967/1969.

Schorske, Carl E. "Politics and the Psyche in fin de siècle Vienna: Schnitzler and Hofmannsthal," _American Historical Review_, 66, (1961), pp. 930-946.

_____. "Politics in a New Key: An Austrian Triptych," _The Journal of Modern History_, 89, (1967), pp. 343-386.

Wandruszka, Adam, "Das Christlichsozial-Konservative Lager," in _Geschichte der Republik Oesterreich_. Vienna, 1954.

Newspaper collections of the oesterreichische Nationalbibliothek and Wiener Stadtbibliothek.